亚洲文明对话大会

Conference on Dialogue of Asian Civilizations

大美亚细亚

亚洲文明展

The Splendor of Asia
An Exhibition of Asian Civilizations

国家文物局　编

National Cultural Heritage Administration

文物出版社

Cultural Relics Press

图书在版编目（CIP）数据

大美亚细亚：亚洲文明展 / 国家文物局编. -- 北京：文物出版社, 2020.7

ISBN 978-7-5010-6469-4

Ⅰ.①大… Ⅱ.①国… Ⅲ.①文物—亚洲—图录

Ⅳ.①K883.002

中国版本图书馆CIP数据核字(2019)第286889号

大美亚细亚：亚洲文明展

编　　者：国家文物局

封面设计：鲁　人

摄　　影：宋　朝　王　伟　张　冰

版式设计：孙木槿

责任编辑：孙　霞

责任印制：张道奇

出版发行：文物出版社

社　　址：北京市东直门内北小街 2 号楼

邮　　编：100007

网　　址：http://www.wenwu.com

邮　　箱：web@wenwu.com

经　　销：新华书店

印　　刷：北京荣宝艺品印刷有限公司

开　　本：889mm×1194mm 1/16

印　　张：25

版　　次：2020 年 7 月第 1 版

印　　次：2020 年 7 月第 1 次印刷

书　　号：ISBN 978-7-5010-6469-4

定　　价：480.00

序 言

　　亚洲是世界上面积最广袤、人口与民族最多的大洲，是人类文明的重要发祥地。亚洲的黄河和长江流域、印度河和恒河流域、幼发拉底河和底格里斯河流域，以及中亚、东南亚地区孕育了众多古老文明。这些文明交相辉映，在世界文明史上写下浓墨重彩的一笔，成为人类文明进程中璀璨辉煌的篇章。回顾中华文明的历史变迁，张骞出使西域，丝绸之路驼铃声声；客商熙来攘往，海上丝绸之路帆影幢幢。玄奘西行取经，鉴真东渡日本，郑和七下西洋，和平交流的文明佳话至今传续，向世界展现了文明互学互鉴、繁荣多彩的美丽画卷。

　　为了追溯亚洲文明的起源与发展历程，描绘亚洲各国文明对话交流的历史轨迹，展现当代中国与亚洲各国的友好交往和文化遗产合作成果，我们积极践行习近平主席关于举办亚洲文明对话大会的重大倡议，联合起亚洲大家庭全部47国与希腊、埃及等文明古国伙伴，共同举办"大美亚细亚——亚洲文明展"，打造亚洲国家的一次文明大联欢。

　　"等闲识得东风面，万紫千红总是春。"每个国家所创造的文明各有千秋、各具姿容。正因如此，人类文明的百花园才会姹紫嫣红、生机盎然。我们愿与亚洲各国，乃至世界各国一道，进一步密切文化遗产合作关系，拓展亚洲文明对话的多样化渠道，继承和发展和而不同、和谐共生的亚洲文化，为构建亚洲命运共同体和人类命运共同体贡献历史智慧和文化力量。

　　我相信，"大美亚细亚——亚洲文明展"一定会给中外观众留下美好的记忆，也一定会对增进亚洲各国友谊、促进民心相通、弘扬亚洲文明成果、增强亚洲文化自信作出重要贡献！

雒树刚
中华人民共和国文化和旅游部部长

PREFACE

Asia is a continent with the widest area, largest population and greatest number of ethnic groups in the world, and it is an important birthplace of human civilizations. Many ancient civilizations have taken shape and flourished near the Yellow and Yangtze river basins, the Indus and Ganges river basins, the Tigris and Euphrates river basins, and other regions of Central Asia and Southeast Asia. Each civilization shines in its own way yet complements the others, and has made important contribution to the development and progress of human civilization. The long course of Chinese history has witnessed a myriad of peaceful exchanges with different civilizations. Camel bells rang melodiously along the ancient Silk Road as Zhang Qian set off on his way to exploring the Western Regions. Numerous ships lined up along the coasts as an endless stream of merchants traveled along the Maritime Silk Road. Xuanzang traversed a long path to India for Buddhist scriptures. Jianzhen sailed to Japan six times. Zheng He ventured out onto the western seas seven times. Such great stories of cultural communication have continued through to today, composing a splendid chapter of mutual benefits and mutual understanding among different countries.

"The Splendor of Asia – An Exhibition of Asian Civilizations" has been held in order to trace the origin and development of Asian civilizations, depict the history of cultural communication among various Asian countries and display the friendly interchanges and cooperation between China and other Asian countries in preserving cultural heritages in modern times. Following the initiative on holding the Conference on Dialogue of Asian Civilizations by President Xi, this grand event celebrating Asian civilizations brings together all 47 Asian countries, as well as two other countries rich in the history of ancient civilizations – Greece and Egypt.

"It can be spring only when all the flowers are in bloom". Each civilization has its own splendor. Together they form a marvelous garden of human civilization ablaze with color. We would like to join hands with all countries from Asia and other parts of the world to further expand the scale of cooperation in preserving cultural heritages, to develop diverse channels of dialogue among Asian civilizations, to inherit and develop the tradition of embracing diversity and advocating coexistence, and to contribute our wisdom and cultural influence to building a community of shared future for Asia and all mankind.

I believe this exhibition will surely provide a wonderful cultural experience for Chinese and foreign visitors alike. It will also play an important role in promoting friendship and mutual understanding among various Asian countries, in promoting Asian civilizations, and in boosting cultural confidence in Asia !

Luo Shugang
Minister of Culture and Tourism
People's Republic of China

目 录
CONTENTS

第二部分　美在通途　行久致远

VOYAGE OF DISCOVERY BRIDGE OF COMMUNICATION

第三部分　美美与共　天下大同

EMBRACE DIFFERENCES STRENGTHEN COOPERATION

第四部分　美人之美　礼尚往来
RESPECT DIVERSITY ENHANCE FRIENDSHIP

结束语
CONCLUSION

鸣谢
ACKNOWLEDGEMENT

前　言

　　在漫长历史长河中，亚洲的黄河和长江流域、印度河和恒河流域、幼发拉底河和底格里斯河流域，以及东南亚等地区孕育了众多古老文明，彼此交相辉映、相得益彰，为人类文明发展和进步作出了重要贡献。今天的亚洲，多样性的特点仍十分突出，不同文明、不同民族、不同宗教汇聚交融，共同组成多彩多姿的亚洲大家庭。

PREFACE

　　History, over the past millennia, has witnessed ancient civilizations appear and thrive along the Yellow and Yangtze Rivers, the Indus, the Ganges, the Euphrates, and the Tigris River as well as in Southeast Asia, each adding its own splendour to the progress of human civilization. Today, Asia has proudly maintained its distinct diversity and still nurtures all the civilizations, ethnic groups and religions in this big Asian family.

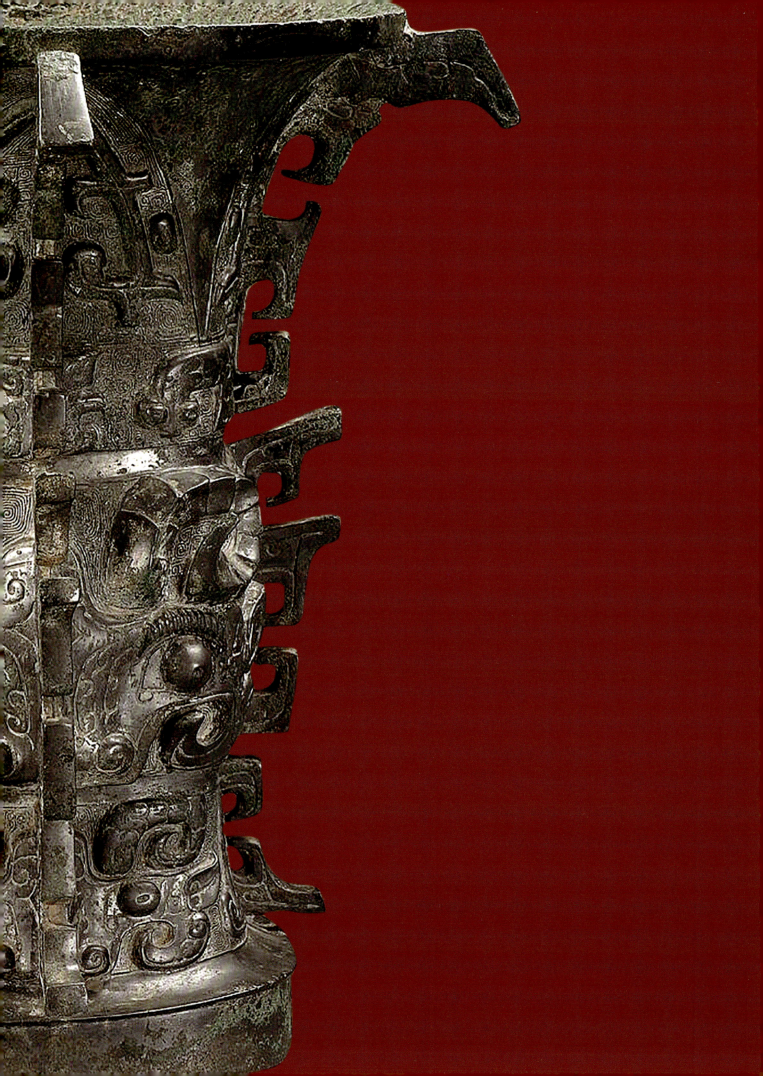

美威在久 日出东方

CRADLES OF CIVILIZATION WITNESS TO HISTORY

亚细亚洲是亚洲的全称，意为"太阳升起的地方"。亚洲是世界上面积最广袤、人口与民族最多的大陆，也是人类古老文明的重要发源地，两河流域文明、印度河文明和中华文明等都诞生于亚洲。亚洲各国各地区人民，在探索人与自然、人与社会、现实与未来的关系中，描绘了博大精深、绚丽多彩的文明画卷。

Asia, meaning 'the place where the sun rises', is a continent with the largest area, population, and most ethnic groups in the world, and is an important birthplace of ancient human civilizations. Mesopotamian civilization, Indian civilization, and Chinese civilization were all born in great river basins of Asia. While exploring the relationships between man and nature, man and society, reality and the future, people of Asian countries and regions have created a profound and colorful collection of civilizations.

阿富汗伊斯兰共和国
The Islamic Republic of Afghanistan

高脚陶杯

Goblet

公元前 3000 – 前 2000 年
3000 – 2000 B.C.

高 13.8、杯沿对角线长 4.6 厘米
Height 13.8 cm, Diameter of mouth 4.6 cm

阿富汗蒙迪加克遗址
Mundigak site, Afghanistan

阿富汗国家博物馆藏
National Museum of Afghanistan

　　蒙迪加克遗址位于现坎大哈市的西北 32 公里处，法国考古队从 1951–1958 年持续进行发掘。这一时期的陶器彩绘与印度河文明的陶器装饰类似。

银器
Silverware

公元前 3000 – 前 2000 年
3000 – 2000 B.C.
（一）长 14.7、宽 5.4 厘米；
Length 14.7 cm, Width 5.4 cm
（二）长 11.8、宽 5.3 厘米
Length 11.8 cm, Width 5.3 cm

阿富汗法罗尔丘地遗址
Tepe Fullol site, Afghanistan
阿富汗国家博物馆藏
National Museum of Afghanistan

（一）

（二）

（一面）

（另一面）

青铜斧头
Axe

公元前 3000 – 前 2000 年
3000 – 2000 B.C.
高 5.1、长 7、宽 3 厘米
Height 5.1 cm, Length 7 cm, Width 3 cm

阿富汗巴克特里亚遗址
Bactria site, Afghanistan
阿富汗国家博物馆藏
National Museum of Afghanistan

　　此斧前部饰有动物相搏的图案，是阿姆河文明青铜时代的典型器物。中亚地区的文化元素诸如驯化黄牛和绵羊、日晒土坯、权杖头、短剑、青铜管銎斧、大麦和小麦等，在新疆、甘肃、青海乃至中原地区的文化中也有所发现。

泥塑佛坐像
Buddha Statue

公元 2 世纪
2nd Century A.D.

高 23、宽 19 厘米
Height 23 cm, Width 19 cm

阿富汗哈达遗址
Hadda site, Afghanistan
阿富汗国家博物馆藏
National Museum of Afghanistan

玻璃花瓶

Vase

公元 2 世纪
2nd Century A.D.
高 12.7 厘米
Height 12.7 cm

阿富汗贝格拉姆遗址
Begram site, Afghanistan
阿富汗国家博物馆藏
National Museum of Afghanistan

石雕佛像
Buddha Statue

公元 3 世纪
3rd Century A.D.
高 125、宽 57 厘米
Height 125 cm, Width 57 cm

阿富汗沙拉 – 卡瓦加遗址
Sarai – Khwaja site, Afghanistan
阿富汗国家博物馆藏
National Museum of Afghanistan

　　此佛陀雕像身着通肩袈裟，肩膀后部有火焰冒出，脚底有水流喷涌，一般认为是表现佛教题材中的"双神变"。

　　阿富汗喀布尔周边分布着很多古代寺院遗迹，这一区域出土的片岩佛教雕刻在佛教美术史中称为"迦毕试样式"。迦毕试美术以燃灯佛授记为主要雕刻题材，与犍陀罗造型样式不同，采取五头身大小的身材比例，其正面像姿势、肩部的火焰背光也是犍陀罗样式所没有的。

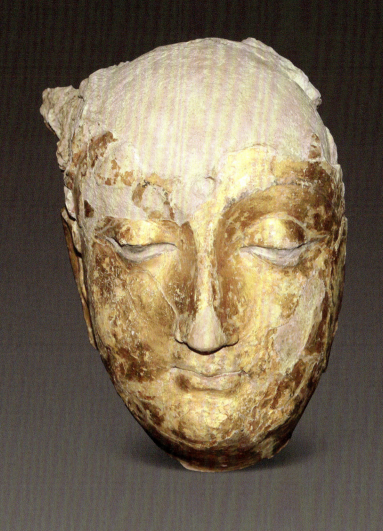

泥塑贴金佛首
Buddha Head

公元 5 世纪
5th Century A.D.

高 20、宽 13 厘米
Height 20 cm, Width 13 cm

阿富汗梅斯 – 艾纳克遗址
Mes Aynak site, Afghanistan

阿富汗国家博物馆藏
National Museum of Afghanistan

亚美尼亚共和国
Republic of Armenia

陶鸟形来通
Rhyton Bird – Shaped

公元前 8 – 前 7 世纪
8th – 7th Century B.C.

长 17、宽 15、高 21 厘米
Length 17 cm, Width 15 cm, Height 21 cm

亚美尼亚历史博物馆藏
History Museum of Armenia

　　"来通"（rhyton）是一种形状特殊的酒器，起源于西方，当时人们认为"来通"是圣物，用它注酒能防止中毒；举杯一饮而尽，则是向神灵致敬。

　　这件鸟形来通的形制特殊，制作于亚美尼亚乌拉尔图王国时期。酒液通过中空的鸟腿部注入，经过鸟身，从鸟喙流出，鸟背上的图案具有鲜明的地域特点。

　　来通传到亚洲之后，广泛流行于西亚、中亚，传入中国。西安何家村唐代窖藏中发现的镶金兽首玛瑙杯，也是一件精美的来通。

 在亚洲文明对话大会开幕式的"亚洲文物精品展"展出

祭祀用陶储存罐
Cultic Storage Vessel

公元前 10 – 前 9 世纪
10th – 9th Century B.C.

腹部直径 32、深 38 厘米
Abdominal diameter 32 cm, Depth 38 cm

亚美尼亚德芬遗址
Dvin site, Armenia

亚美尼亚历史博物馆藏
History Museum of Armenia

陶壶
Pitcher

公元前 8 世纪
8th Century B.C.

腹部直径 26.5、口径 20.5 厘米
Abdominal diameter 26.5 cm, Diameter of mouth 20.5 cm

亚美尼亚埃里温遗址
Erebuni – Yerevan site, Armenia

亚美尼亚历史博物馆藏
History Museum of Armenia

陶壶
Pitcher

公元前 7 世纪
7th Century B.C.

腹部直径 19、口径 7.5、深 20 厘米
Abdominal diameter 19 cm,
Diameter of mouth 7.5 cm, Depth 20 cm

亚美尼亚埃里温遗址
Karmir Blour – Yerevan site, Armenia
亚美尼亚历史博物馆藏
History Museum of Armenia

靴形高脚来通陶杯
Goblet in the Shape of a High Boot

公元前 8 – 前 7 世纪
8th – 7th Century B.C.

高 24.6、直径 19.5、底径 15.3 厘米
Height 24.6 cm, Diameter 19.5 cm, Bottom diameter
15.3 cm

亚美尼亚埃里温遗址
Karmir Blour – Yerevan site, Armenia
亚美尼亚历史博物馆藏
History Museum of Armenia

　　以靴筒为杯身，靴底为杯底，尖靴头微微翘起，用大块白色和黑色线条勾勒出系带长靴的结构，杯体前侧和口沿处有棋盘纹装饰。靴状来通杯常见于公元前 8 至前 7 世纪，表面抛光，敞口，多为刻花或画花装饰。

釉陶托盘
Tray

公元 9 – 10 世纪
9th – 10th Century A.D.
直径 42 厘米
Diameter 42 cm

亚美尼亚德芬遗址
Dvin site, Armenia
亚美尼亚历史博物馆藏
History Museum of Armenia

釉陶盘
Dish

公元 10 – 11 世纪
10th – 11th Century A.D.
直径 16、深 5 厘米
Diameter 16 cm, Depth 5 cm

阿尼遗址
Ani site
亚美尼亚历史博物馆藏
History Museum of Armenia

　　陶盘中央装饰着飞舞的人面神兽，其身后沿着
盘子口沿装饰了一圈如柳条状的植物纹，整体流畅
且动感强烈。

铜香炉
Censer

公元 10 – 11 世纪
10th – 11th Century A.D.
直径 12.5 厘米
Diameter 12.5 cm

阿尼遗址
Ani site
亚美尼亚历史博物馆藏
History Museum of Armenia

铜水壶
Vessel for Water

公元 12 – 13 世纪
12th – 13th Century A.D.
直径 17、深 33 厘米
Diameter 17 cm, Depth 33 cm

阿尼遗址
Ani site
亚美尼亚历史博物馆藏
History Museum of Armenia

　　该水壶最大的特征是兽足底座和顶端带有翻卷棕榈叶的流线式手柄。手柄造型源于伊朗自 7 世纪起盛行的梨形水壶。阿尼地区一直以来都是古代贸易之路的重要站点，文化交流的痕迹也体现在器物上。

带状装饰陶贮藏罐
Storage Vessel Karas With an Ornamental Band

公元 10 – 11 世纪
10th – 11th Century A.D.
直径 43、深 40 厘米
Diameter 43 cm, Depth 40 cm

亚美尼亚德芬遗址
Dvin site, Armenia
亚美尼亚历史博物馆藏
History Museum of Armenia

红色磨光陶罐
Red Polished Vessel

公元 11 – 12 世纪
11th – 12th Century A.D.
直径 17、高 15 厘米
Diameter 17 cm, Height 15 cm

亚美尼亚德芬遗址
Dvin site, Armenia
亚美尼亚历史博物馆藏
History Museum of Armenia

釉陶盘
Dish

公元 11 – 12 世纪
11th – 12th Century A.D.
直径 28 厘米
Diameter 28 cm

亚美尼亚德芬遗址
Dvin site, Armenia
亚美尼亚历史博物馆藏
History Museum of Armenia

釉陶盘
Dish

公元 11 – 12 世纪
11th – 12th Century A.D.
直径 18 厘米
Diameter 18 cm

亚美尼亚德芬遗址
Dvin site, Armenia
亚美尼亚历史博物馆藏
History Museum of Armenia

彩陶托盘
Tray

公元 11 – 12 世纪
11th – 12th Century A.D.
直径 37 厘米
Diameter 37 cm

亚美尼亚德芬遗址
Dvin site, Armenia
亚美尼亚历史博物馆藏
History Museum of Armenia

阿塞拜疆共和国
Republic of Azerbaijan

地毯

Carpet *Surakhani*

公元 19 世纪晚期
Late 19th Century A.D.

长 193、宽 130 厘米
Length 193 cm, Width 130 cm

阿塞拜疆巴库
Baku, Azerbaijan

阿塞拜疆地毯博物馆藏
Azerbaijan Carpet Museum

阿塞拜疆是古代的手工艺之都和地毯纺织中心，其纺织历史可追溯至公元前 2000 年。其地毯类型齐全，织结紧密，"寿命"长达 300 至 500 年。其中巴库地毯以材质柔软、色彩亮丽、团花装饰取胜，是最具代表性的地毯流派之一。

地毯
Carpet *Aghajli*

公元 19 世纪中期
Mid 19th Century A.D.
长 296、宽 130 厘米
Length 296 cm, Width 130 cm

阿塞拜疆地毯博物馆藏
Azerbaijan Carpet Museum

地毯
Carpet *Jayirli*

公元 19 世纪早期
Early 19th Century A.D.
长 161、宽 122 厘米
Length 161 cm, Width 122 cm

阿塞拜疆希尔万
Shirvan, Azerbaijan
阿塞拜疆地毯博物馆藏
Azerbaijan Carpet Museum

盐袋
Salt Bag

公元 19 世纪
19th Century A.D.

长 57、宽 38 厘米
Length 57 cm, Width 38 cm

阿塞拜疆地毯博物馆藏
Azerbaijan Carpet Museum

耳饰
Earrings

公元 20 世纪中期
Mid 20th Century A.D.

阿塞拜疆盖达尔·阿利耶夫基金会收藏
Heydar Aliyev Foundation

耳环
Earrings

公元 20 世纪中期
Mid 20th Century A.D.

阿塞拜疆连科兰
Lankaran, Azerbaijan

阿塞拜疆盖达尔·阿利耶夫基金会收藏
Heydar Aliyev Foundation

项链
Chechik Necklace

公元 20 世纪中期
Mid 20th Century A.D.

阿塞拜疆纳希切万
Nakhchivan, Azerbaijan

阿塞拜疆盖达尔·阿利耶夫基金会收藏
Heydar Aliyev Foundation

项链
Chechik Necklace

公元 20 世纪中期
Mid 20th Century A.D.

阿塞拜疆盖达尔·阿利耶夫基金会收藏
Heydar Aliyev Foundation

青铜马
Statuette Horses

公元 2000 年
2000 A.D.

长 80、宽 20、高 43 厘米
Length 80 cm, Width 20 cm, Height 43 cm

阿塞拜疆盖达尔·阿利耶夫基金会收藏
Heydar Aliyev Foundation

长颈琵琶萨兹
Saz - Traditional Azerbaijani Musical Instrument

公元 2000 年
2000 A.D.

长 105、宽 25、厚 22 厘米
Length 105 cm, Width 25 cm, Thickness 22 cm

阿塞拜疆盖达尔·阿利耶夫基金会收藏
Heydar Aliyev Foundation

　　萨兹是古代中亚和安纳托利亚地区乐器的综合体，主要用于阿塞拜疆游吟诗人的音乐艺术（Azerbaijani Ashiqs）中。该艺术形式是阿塞拜疆文化和国家认同的象征，传承并保存了阿塞拜疆的语言、文学和音乐等文化艺术。

传统阿塞拜疆女性服饰
Traditional Azerbaijani Women Costume

公元 2017 年
2017 A.D.

阿塞拜疆盖达尔·阿利耶夫基金会收藏
Heydar Aliyev Foundation

　　阿塞拜疆传统女性服装包括外套和内搭两部分。内搭是宽袖衫和灯笼裤。外搭长袖外套，开襟收腰，也可搭配腰带，一般选用色彩亮丽的布料；下身配及踝喇叭裙，头戴药盒帽和披巾。除服装本身，还有配套的金银珠宝和精致刺绣，如金银纽扣、腰带，吊坠、项链和华丽的滚边绣花等。

柬埔寨王国
The Kingdom of Cambodia

湿婆神的坐骑公牛南迪像
Nandin

公元 550 – 600 年（前吴哥时期）
550 – 600 A.D. (Pre-Angkorian Period)

长 53、宽 31、高 30 厘米
Length 53 cm, Width 31 cm, Height 30 cm

柬埔寨柴桢省罗密赫县巴萨克
Bassak, Rumduol, Svay Rieng, Cambodia
柬埔寨国家博物馆藏
National Museum of Cambodia

石雕毗湿奴立像
Standing Vishnu

公元 550 – 600 年（前吴哥时期）
550 – 600 A.D. (Pre–Angkorian Period)

长 40、高 95.5 厘米
Length 40 cm, Height 95.5 cm

柬埔寨国家博物馆藏
National Museum of Cambodia

　　毗湿奴是印度教中世界的维护者。常着王者衣冠，佩戴宝石和粗大的花环，四臂手持法螺贝、妙见神轮、伽陀神锤、神弓或宝剑（其所佩武器有时以拟人化的形象出现）、莲花等。他有时坐于莲花上，有时躺在一条千头蛇身上，有时骑在一只大鹏鸟迦楼罗身上。

石雕佛头像
Head of Buddha

公元 7 世纪（前吴哥时期）
7th Century A.D. (Pre-Angkorian Period)

直径 20、高 31 厘米
Diameter 20 cm, Height 31 cm

柬埔寨茶胶省吴哥波雷县
Vat Kampong Luong, Angkor Boeri, Takeo, Cambodia
柬埔寨国家博物馆藏
National Museum of Cambodia

石雕蛇王纳迦护佛像
Buddha on Naga

公元 7 世纪（前吴哥时期）
7th Century A.D. (Pre-Angkorian Period)

长 60、宽 33、高 128 厘米
Length 60 cm, Width 33 cm, Height 128 cm

柬埔寨磅湛省
Kampong Cham, Cambodia
柬埔寨国家博物馆藏
National Museum of Cambodia

石浮雕门楣
Decorated Lintel

公元 10 世纪中期（吴哥时期）
Mid 10ᵗʰ Century A.D. (Angkorian Period)
长 167、宽 43、厚 29 厘米
Length 167 cm, Width 43 cm, Thickness 29 cm

柬埔寨马德望市
Battambang, Cambodia
柬埔寨国家博物馆藏
National Museum of Cambodia

石浮雕门楣
Decorated Lintel

公元 10 世纪（吴哥时期）
10ᵗʰ Century A.D. (Angkorian Period)
长 155.5、宽 48 厘米
Length 155.5 cm, Width 48 cm

柬埔寨马德望市
Battambang, Cambodia
柬埔寨国家博物馆藏
National Museum of Cambodia

石雕迦楼罗残片
Fragment of Figure of Garuda

公元 10 世纪中期（吴哥时期）
Mid 10th Century A.D. (Angkorian Period)
长 50、高 76 厘米
Length 50 cm, Height 76 cm

柬埔寨国家博物馆藏
National Museum of Cambodia

　　大鹏金翅鸟又叫迦楼罗鸟，梵文音译苏钵刺尼，意译为羽毛美丽者、食吐悲苦声。传说其翅金色，两翼广 336 万里，住于须弥山下层，在佛教中为八部众之一。在印度教中是毗湿奴神的坐骑，其人身形象在供奉毗湿奴神的神庙中随处可见。

石狮
Lion

公元 10 世纪晚期（吴哥时期）
Late 10th Century A.D. (Angkorian Period)
长 19、宽 20、高 31 厘米
Length 19 cm, Width 20 cm, Height 31 cm

柬埔寨磅士卑省公比塞县
Kong Pisei, Kampong Speu, Cambodia
柬埔寨国家博物馆藏
National Museum of Cambodia

青铜象头神伽内什像

Ganesha

公元 12 世纪末 – 13 世纪初（吴哥时期）
End of 12th Century A.D. – Beginning
of 13th Century A.D. (Angkorian Period)
长 14.5、高 19.4 厘米
Length 14.5 cm, Height 19.4 cm

柬埔寨国家博物馆藏
National Museum of Cambodia

石雕伐楼拿神像
Varuna sitted on Hamsa

公元 10 世纪
10th Century A.D. (Angkorian Period)
长 38、宽 36、高 95 厘米
Length 38 cm, Width 36 cm, Height 95 cm

柬埔寨国家博物馆藏
National Museum of Cambodia

　　此件石雕神像，表现的是印度教中掌管天空、雨水和海洋的神灵——伐楼拿，反映了东南亚与南亚地区的文明交流。

 在亚洲文明对话大会开幕式的"亚洲文物精品展"展出

印度共和国
The Republic of India

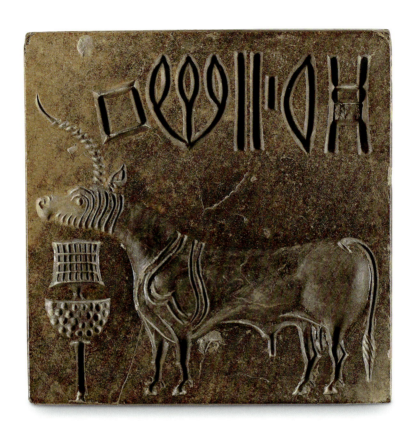

动物纹刻符印章
Seal with Animal Pattern and Engravings Pattern

公元前 25 – 前 20 世纪
25th – 20th Century B.C.

长 3.4、宽 3.2 厘米
Length 3.4 cm, Width 3.2 cm

摩亨佐·达罗遗址
Mohenjo daro site

印度新德里国家博物馆藏
National Museum, New Delhi, India

此类印章是古印度文明的重要代表性文物。刻划符号至今尚未被解读，可能表示签名或财产标记。1922 年，古印度文明的遗址首先在印度河流域的哈拉帕地区被发掘出来，所以通常也称为"哈拉帕文明"。摩亨佐·达罗遗址是古印度文明的重要遗址之一。

虎纹刻符印章
Seal with Tiger Pattern and Engravings

公元前 25 – 前 20 世纪
25th – 20th Century B.C.

长 3.1、宽 3 厘米
Length 3.1 cm, Width 3 cm

摩亨佐·达罗遗址
Mohenjo daro site

印度新德里国家博物馆藏
National Museum, New Delhi, India

铜秤
Copper Balance

公元前 2500 年
2500 B.C.

秤臂长 12、直径 0.3 厘米
Balance arm: Length 12 cm, Diameter 0.3 cm

秤板长 15.7、宽 5.7 厘米
Balance plate: Length 15.7 cm, Width 5.7 cm

秤砣最大长 2.4、宽 2.4、高 1.8，最小长 0.7、宽 0.7、高 0.6 厘米
Maximum length 2.4cm, Width 2.4cm, Height 1.8 cm
Mininum length 0.7cm, Windth 0.7cm, Height 0.6 cm

摩亨佐·达罗遗址
Mohenjo daro site

印度新德里国家博物馆藏
National Museum, New Delhi, India

铜犀牛

Copper Rhinoceros

公元前 1500 – 前 1050 年
1500 – 1050 B.C.

印度马哈拉施特拉邦代玛巴德村
Daimabad, Maharashtra, India
印度新德里国家博物馆藏
National Museum, New Delhi, India

此件铜犀牛 1974 年出土，同时出土的还有大象、水牛、两头公牛牵拉车辆等三件铜雕，显示出 3000 多年前古印度工匠高超的造型技艺与工艺水平。

压印银币
Punch Marked Coin

公元前 4 – 前 3 世纪
4ᵗʰ – 3ʳᵈ Century B.C.

直径 3.3 厘米、重 5.8 克
Diameter 3.3 cm, Weight 5.8 g

印度新德里国家博物馆藏
National Museum, New Delhi, India

压印银币
Punch Marked Coin

公元前 3 – 前 2 世纪
3ʳᵈ – 2ⁿᵈ Century B.C.

直径 3.3 厘米、重 5.8 克
Diameter 3.3 cm, Weight 5.8 g

印度新德里国家博物馆藏
National Museum, New Delhi, India

石雕猴面人身像
Head and Bust of a Grotesque Male

约公元前 324 – 约前 187 年（孔雀王朝）
Circa 324 – 187 B.C. (Maurya)

长 6、宽 5.7、高 10.2 厘米
Length 6 cm, Width 5.7 cm, Height 10.2 cm

印度新德里国家博物馆藏
National Museum, New Delhi, India

石雕伎乐像
Musical Group and Various Other Motifs

公元前 2 世纪（巽加王朝）
2nd Century B.C. (Shunga)

长 46、宽 26、高 23 厘米
Length 46 cm, Width 26 cm, Height 23 cm

印度中央邦
Madhya Pradesh, India
印度新德里国家博物馆藏
National Museum, New Delhi, India

　　这件雕刻作品整体呈长方形，原本应是柱子的一部分。方柱表面采用浮雕手法，表现包括人物、动物在内的大型场景。正面由栏楯分成上下两层，上层只剩一小部分，呈现牛羊等动物；下方车驾装饰，有马车夫、手持拂尘的随从等人，俨然是庄严的出行队伍。石柱侧面布满大量正在奏乐、听乐的人物。整件作品体现出古代印度叙事性浮雕作品技法朴拙、构图繁密的特点。

石雕骑象者

Elephant Rider

公元前 1 世纪（娑多婆诃那王朝）
1st Century B.C. (Satavahana)

长 49、宽 21.5、高 41 厘米
Length 49 cm, Width 21.5 cm, Height 41 cm

印度桑奇
Sanchi, India

印度新德里国家博物馆藏
National Museum, New Delhi, India

贵霜铜币
Kushan Coin

公元 1 世纪
1st Century A.D.

直径 2.6 厘米、重 16.6 克
Diameter 2.6 cm, Weight 16.6 g

印度新德里国家博物馆藏
National Museum, New Delhi, India

石雕龙王礼佛饰板
Buddha with Naga-Kalika

公元 2 世纪（贵霜王朝）
2nd Century A.D. (Kushan)

长 47、宽 10、高 35 厘米
Length 47 cm, Width 10 cm, Height 35 cm

印度新德里国家博物馆藏
National Museum, New Delhi, India

在贵霜时代的犍陀罗艺术中，曾出现大量表现佛传故事的浮雕饰板。这些饰板大多装饰在佛塔塔基上，通过连环的叙事方式表现佛陀的一生事迹。

这件浮雕饰板上就表现了这样的题材。浮雕右侧为一根方形隔柱，柱子左边有大量人物。场景中间为具有头光、身穿通肩式袈裟的释迦牟尼立像，周围由持金刚等眷属人物相伴，面对右边树下的夫妇。这对夫妇站在带有围栏的平台上，前方国王装扮的人物和其身后的龙女双手合十礼佛。

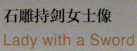

石雕持剑女士像

Lady with a Sword

公元 2 世纪（贵霜王朝）
2nd Century A.D. (Kushan)

长 19、宽 18.5、高 88 厘米
Length 19 cm, Width 18.5 cm, Height 88 cm

印度新德里国家博物馆藏
National Museum, New Delhi, India

石雕泉中浴女像

Lady Taking Bath Under A Spring

公元 2 世纪（贵霜王朝）
2nd Century A.D. (Kushan)

长 21、宽 18.5、高 91 厘米
Length 21 cm, Width 18.5 cm, Height 91 cm

印度新德里国家博物馆藏
National Museum, New Delhi, India

石雕斯基泰人头像
Scythian Head

公元 2 世纪（贵霜王朝）
2nd Century A.D. (Kushan)
底径 23、高 45 厘米
Bottom diameter 23 cm, Height 45 cm

印度秣菟罗出土
Unearthed from Mathura, India
印度新德里国家博物馆藏
National Museum, New Delhi, India

在贵霜王朝统治印度时期，犍陀罗、秣菟罗两地成为著名的造像中心。

这尊斯基泰人头像出自印度秣菟罗地区，原本应属于一尊完整的独雕人像。造像由红色的西克里石雕刻而成，人物面部圆润饱满，尤其是眉弓处及略微宽厚的嘴唇处，都体现出秣菟罗造像的特点。

石雕佛立像
Buddha

公元 2 – 3 世纪
2nd – 3rd Century A.D.

长 24、宽 14、高 56 厘米
Length 24 cm, Width 14 cm, Height 56 cm

印度新德里国家博物馆藏
National Museum, New Delhi, India

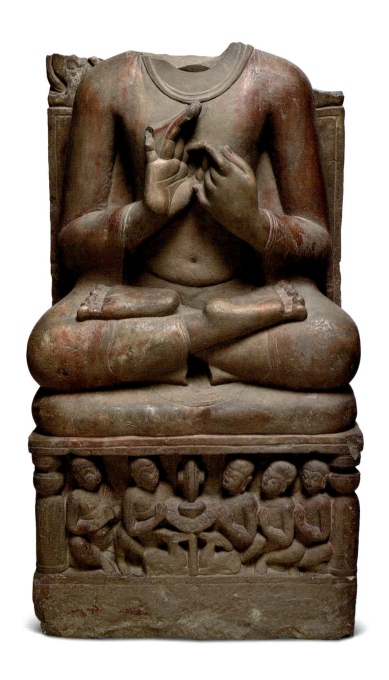

石雕无头坐佛像
Headless Buddha

公元 5 – 6 世纪（笈多王朝）
5th – 6th Century A.D. (Gupta)

长 40、高 71 厘米
Length 40 cm, Height 71 cm

印度新德里国家博物馆藏
National Museum, New Delhi, India

石雕象头神伽内什坐像
Ganesha

公元 10 世纪
10th Century A.D.
长 30、宽 14、高 60 厘米
Length 30 cm, Width 14 cm, Height 60 cm

印度中央邦
Madhya Pradesh, India
印度新德里国家博物馆藏
National Museum, New Delhi, India

　　象头神迦内什是印度教重要的神，象征智慧，同时也是"象头神派"的主神。

　　这尊雕像具有早期象头神造像的特征，其坐于低矮台座上，长有象头和人身，有一条粗长的象鼻和一根象牙；腹部圆鼓突出，双腿粗壮有力；拥有四条手臂，一手残缺，另三手分持装有蜜糖罐子、小碗、断牙。其断牙是因为它在记录广博仙人口述《摩诃婆罗多》时折断了神笔，故而拔下一颗牙齿继续书写所致；同时它正在用象鼻享受罐中的蜜糖，这也是早期象头神造像的一个重要特征。

石雕玩球女子像
Lady Playing Ball

公元 11 世纪（古希拉王朝）
11ᵗʰ Century A.D. (Guhila)

长 33、宽 21、高 105 厘米
Length 33 cm, Width 21 cm, Height 105 cm

印度新德里国家博物馆藏
National Museum, New Delhi, India

石雕迦梨女神像
Kali

公元 12 世纪（朱罗王朝晚期）
12th Century A.D. (Late Chola)

长 39、宽 20、高 61 厘米
Length 39 cm, Width 20 cm, Height 61 cm

印度新德里国家博物馆藏
National Museum, New Delhi, India

（正面）　　　　　　　　　　　（背面）

哲罗王朝 / 潘地亚王朝铜币
Pandya / Chera Coin

公元 16 世纪
16th Century A.D.

直径 1.6 厘米，重 2.2 克
Diameter 1.6 cm, Weight 2.2 g

印度新德里国家博物馆藏
National Museum, New Delhi, India

铜里沙跋那陀像
Rishabhanatha

公元 17 世纪
17th Century A.D.
长 17、高 24.38 厘米
Length 17 cm, Height 24.38 cm

印度新德里国家博物馆藏
National Museum, New Delhi, India

　　里沙跋那陀是印度耆那教二十四位祖师中的第一位，也是耆那教的创始人。根据《梵天往世书》的记载，他是刹帝利的祖先。在《湿婆往世书》中，他又是湿婆神的化身，与湿婆融为一体，但在《薄伽梵往世书》《阿耆尼往世书》中，他又被说成是毗湿奴的化身。

　　此尊祭坛式造像，主尊里沙跋那陀祖师裸身趺坐入定，他相貌年轻俊美，面容安详，两臂结禅定印置于脚上，胸前有吉祥符标志，表现了这位祖师超凡入圣的状态。

Mughal Coin During the Reign of Shah Jahan

（正面）

公元 1628 – 1658 年
1628 – 1658 A.D.
边长 2.2 厘米，重 11.4 克
Side length 2.2 cm, Weight 11.4 g

印度新德里国家博物馆藏
National Museum, New Delhi, India

（背面）

　　此币为印度莫卧儿王朝时期沙贾汗所发行的银制卢比，"沙贾汗"意为"世界的统治者"，他是莫卧儿帝国的第五任皇帝。钱币整体呈方形，两面四周边框皆为连续的乳突纹，正反两面分别印有花体阿拉伯文和波斯文铭文。

印度沙丽裙边
End of a Sari

公元 1650 年
1650 A.D.
长 87、宽 62 厘米
Length 87 cm, Width 62 cm

印度新德里国家博物馆藏
National Museum, New Delhi,
India

印度尼西亚共和国
Republic of Indonesia

玉髓斧

Pickaxe (Beliung)

新石器时代
The Neolithic Age

长 13、宽 6 厘米
Length 13 cm, Width 6 cm

印度尼西亚西爪哇省苏加武眉县帕拉干·沙腊克镇
Sukabumi, West Java, Indonesia

印度尼西亚国家博物馆藏
National Museum of Indonesia

铜佛立像

Buddha

公元 8 – 9 世纪
8th – 9th Century A.D.

长 13、高 40 厘米
Length 13 cm, Height 40 cm

印度尼西亚南苏门答腊省巨港市
Palembang, South Sumatra, Indonesia
印度尼西亚国家博物馆藏
National Museum of Indonesia

铜梵天像
Brahma

公元 14 – 15 世纪
14th – 15th Century A.D.

长 17、宽 14、高 55 厘米
Length 17 cm, Width 14 cm,
Height 55 cm

印度尼西亚南苏门答腊省巨港市
清水
Air Bersih, Palembang, South
Sumatra, Indonesia

印度尼西亚国家博物馆藏
National Museum of Indonesia

铜湿婆像
Shiva

公元 14 – 15 世纪
14th – 15th Century A.D.

长 24、宽 16、高 50.7 厘米
Length 24 cm, Width 16 cm,
Height 50.7 cm

印度尼西亚南苏门答腊省巨港市
清水
Air Bersih, Palembang, South
Sumatra, Indonesia

印度尼西亚国家博物馆藏
National Museum of Indonesia

铜毗湿奴像
Vishnu

公元 14 – 15 世纪
14th – 15th Century A.D.

长 28、宽 22、高 57 厘米
Length 28 cm, Width 22 cm,
Height 57 cm

印度尼西亚南苏门答腊省巨港市
清水
Air Bersih, Palembang, South
Sumatra, Indonesia

印度尼西亚国家博物馆藏
National Museum of Indonesia

　　这组铜制雕像表现的是印度教中的三大主神梵天、湿婆、毗湿奴。梵天是印度教的创造之神，梵文字母的创造者。他的坐骑是孔雀（或天鹅），四张脸象征四部《吠陀经》，四只手臂象征东南西北四个方向，也象征心灵、智慧、自我、自信。

湿婆兼具生殖与毁灭、创造与破坏双重性格。毗湿奴肤色绀青，佩戴宝石和花环，四臂手持不同法器，骑在大鹏鸟迦楼罗上。

巴塔拉·古鲁（天帝）皮影
Batara Guru

公元 1905 年之前
Before 1905 A.D.
长 58、宽 27.5 厘米
Length 58 cm, Width 27.5 cm

印度尼西亚巴厘岛
Bali, Indonesia
印度尼西亚国家博物馆藏
National Museum of Indonesia

　　巴塔拉·古鲁是西印度尼西亚和马来西亚的印度教神话中的诸神之首，巴厘人把他看作最高神湿婆的化身，被描绘为带有湿婆表征物的人物，外貌是骑在圣牛背上的神人，生有四臂。

谏义里国楞布阿米佐约国王面具
Mask of Prabu Kediri (Lembu Aamijoyo)

公元 1939 年之前
Before 1939 A.D.
长 20、宽 14 厘米
Length 20 cm, Width 14 cm

印度尼西亚日惹市
Yogyakarta, Indonesia
印度尼西亚国家博物馆藏
National Museum of Indonesia

伊朗伊斯兰共和国
The Islamic Republic of Iran

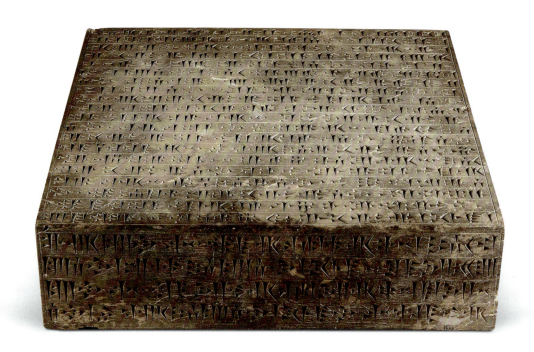

大流士一世埃兰语楔形文字石刻

Elamite Cuneiform Inscription Stone of Darius the Great, on Foundation of Apadana Palace with Name of 22 Different Nations

约公元前 520 年（波斯阿契美尼德王朝）
Circa 520 B.C. (Achaemenid Period)

长 30、宽 30 厘米
Length 30 cm, Width 30 cm

伊朗苏萨城阿帕达那宫
Apadana, Susa, Iran

伊朗国家博物馆藏
National Museum of Iran

此石碑出土于古埃兰王国的首都苏萨城址。记录了大流士一世于苏萨阿巴丹（觐见大厅）用三种文字（古波斯文、古埃兰文和古巴比伦文）刻写的碑文。在索罗亚斯德教主神阿胡拉·玛兹达庇佑下，集帝国各地之精粹，建造苏萨宫殿的过程。此石刻为古埃兰文记录。用三语铭文记录功绩是大流士一世特有的王权表达方式，此石碑是研究古代波斯帝国的重要资料。

模制玻璃盘
Mold Glass Plate

公元前 330 – 前 247 年（塞琉古时期）
330 – 247 B.C. (Seleucid Period)
高 3 厘米
Height 3 cm

伊朗胡泽斯坦省苏萨市
Susa, Khuzestan Province, Iran

伊朗国家博物馆藏
National Museum of Iran

　　伊朗开始制作玻璃容器的时间至少可以追溯到埃兰时期，到了萨珊王朝时期，玻璃制品已非常普遍。这件容器小巧玲珑，由半透明灰白色玻璃制成。容器外侧有凸起的条纹装饰，器身上饰有数十个模压图案。

彩绘陶制来通
Painted Pottery Rhyton

公元前 2 世纪晚期 – 前 1 世纪早期（安息帝国时期）
Late 2nd – Early 1st Century B.C. (Parthian Period)
高 27.5 厘米
Height 27.5 cm

伊朗德黑兰省达玛万德市维利然
Valiran, Damavand, Tehran, Iran
伊朗国家博物馆藏
National Museum of Iran

　　此来通为砖红色陶胎，表面装饰有浅棕色、红褐色几何图案。前端为伏地而坐的野山羊，在山羊的胸部可见一个乳头状的灌注孔。夸张的羊角连接着杯身，自然成为杯柄，构思奇巧。

灰泥半身像
Stucco Bust of Man

约公元 309 – 379 年（萨珊时期）
Circa 309 – 379 A.D. (Sasanian Period)
直径 37 厘米
Diameter 37 cm

伊朗法尔斯省哈吉阿巴德
Hajjiabad, Fars Province, Iran
伊朗国家博物馆藏
National Museum of Iran

吹制—切割制法玻璃容器
Blown-Cutting-Glass Container

公元 224 – 651 年（萨珊时期）
224 - 651 A.D. (Sasanian Period)
高 16 厘米
Height 16 cm

伊朗哈马丹省纳哈万德
Nahavand, Hamadan Province, Iran
伊朗国家博物馆藏
National Museum of Iran

有翼格里芬铜盘
Bronze Plate with Winged Griffin

公元 5 – 6 世纪（萨珊时期）
5th – 6th Century A.D. (Sassanid Period)
直径 32.5 厘米
Diameter 32.5 cm

伊朗哈马丹省
Hamadan, Iran
伊朗国家博物馆藏
National Museum of Iran

釉面彩绘碗
Bowl with Painting under Glaze and Black Calligraphy on the Turquoise Slip

公元 13 世纪（塞尔柱王朝）
13th Century A.D. (Seljuq Dynasty)
直径 18、高 8 厘米
Diameter 18 cm, Height 8 cm

伊朗戈勒斯坦省戈尔甘市
Gorgan, Golestan Province, Iran
伊朗国家博物馆藏
National Museum of Iran

彩绘棕地白色书法纹罐
Jug Calligraphic White on Brown Slip Lustre Painted

公元 13 世纪（伊利汗国时期）
13th Century A.D. (Ilkhanate Dynasty)
直径 9、高 18 厘米
Diameter 9 cm, Height 18 cm

伊朗戈勒斯坦省戈尔甘市
Gorgan, Golestan Province, Iran
伊朗国家博物馆藏
National Museum of Iran

　　该水罐属于在烧制时往黏土里加入了玻璃料的陶器，单柄宽腹折腰，圆柱形瓶颈。罐身呈球状，罐底为喇叭形高脚圈足，带有竖直的手柄。整体以褐色和白色为主。罐体下半部和颈部绘有链状纹，口沿、手柄处绘有红底白字阿拉伯文饰带。罐腹以缠枝叶片为主，卷云纹为辅，底未施釉。缠枝纹样与阿拉伯文相结合，是典型的伊斯兰艺术风格。

釉面瓷砖
Calligraphic Brown on White Slip Lustre Painted Star Tile

公元 13 世纪（伊利汗国时期）
13th Century A.D. (Ilkhanate Dynasty)
直径 21 厘米
Diameter 21 cm

伊朗西阿塞拜疆省苏里曼圣殿
Takht – e Soleymān, West Azerbaijan Province, Iran
伊朗国家博物馆藏
National Museum of Iran

青花花卉纹罐

Blue and White Porcelain Jar with the Omar Khayyam Poem and Date of the Jar Mading in Nastalig

公元 1466 年（帖木儿帝国时期）
1466 A.D. (Timurid Dynasty)

口径 11.5、高 29.5 厘米
Diameter of mouth 11.5 cm, Height 29.5 cm

伊朗伊斯法罕省
Isfahan Province, Iran

伊朗国家博物馆藏
National Museum of Iran

此罐罐身大片的花卉装饰带有野逸之趣，与常见的中国青花罐缠枝纹样多有不同。罐肩覆莲纹和二方连续心形饰带之间有阿拉伯文饰带，是伊斯兰特色装饰。该青花陶罐的器型和缠枝花卉都仿自中国青花而另有特色。

青花花鸟纹瓷盘

**Blue and White Porcelain Dish, Waqfnameh
of Shah Abbas on Exterior**

公元 1571 – 1629 年（萨菲王朝时期）
1571 - 1629 A.D. (Safavid Dynasty)

直径 44、高 8 厘米
Diameter 44 cm, Height 8 cm

伊朗阿尔达比勒省谢赫萨菲阿德丁墓
Sheikh Safi al – Din Khānegāh and Shrine Ensemble,
Ardabil Province, Iran

伊朗国家博物馆藏
National Museum of Iran

青花龙纹盘

**Blue and white Porcelain Dish, Waqfnameh
of Shah Abbas on Exterior**

公元 1571 – 1629 年（萨菲王朝时期）
1571 - 1629 A.D. (Safavid Dynasty)

直径 83、高 7 厘米
Diameter 83 cm, Height 7 cm

伊朗阿尔达比勒省谢赫萨菲阿德丁墓
Sheikh Safi al – Din Khānegāh and Shrine Ensemble,
Ardabil Province, Iran

伊朗国家博物馆藏
National Museum of Iran

　　盘内中央绘细密的海水云龙纹，一只三爪游龙出没于巨浪中，周围配以四季花卉，寓意四季平安。该盘画工精美，细腻的笔触勾勒出三只龙爪，威风凛凛。阿拨斯一世礼赠字样印于盘身外侧靠近盘脚处。卡塔查盖（Qarachaghay）的印章刻于底座。此件青花器为中国明代永乐至宣德时期江西省景德镇出品，所用青料应是西亚钴料苏麻离青，呈现出特有的晕散现象及铁锈斑特征，其青料深入胎骨，青花纹样呈深蓝色，幽倩典雅。

日本国
Japan

深钵形陶器
Deep Bowl

公元前 3000 – 前 2000 年
3000 – 2000 B.C.

高 56 厘米
Height 56 cm

日本东京秋留野市雨间地区墓地
Tomb site, Amema, Akiruno – shi, Tokyo, Japan

日本东京国立博物馆藏
Tokyo National Museum

流水纹铜铎
Ritual Bronze Bell

公元前 2 – 前 1 世纪
2nd – 1st Century B.C.

通高 44.3、铎身高 31.9、口径 23.1 厘米
Overall height 44.3 cm, Bell height 31.9 cm,
Diameter of mouth 23.1 cm

日本大阪府八尾市恩智中町 3 丁目
Onji Nakamachi, Yao, Osaka, Japan
日本东京国立博物馆藏
Tokyo National Museum

　　日本弥生时代开始使用可能由中国和朝鲜半岛传入的铜器和铁器。铜铎的源头可以追溯至中国的铜铃和朝鲜半岛的小铜铎，但这件铜铎尺寸更大，双面均绘有花纹，具有鲜明的日本群岛特征。用于悬挂的挂纽上绘有青蛙，下缘绘有排成一列列的鱼儿，而另一侧下缘绘的则是排成一列列的小鹿。青蛙和鱼同水稻栽种有关，鹿则与种植中的撒种和插秧有关。

陶扛锹埴轮
Terracotta Figurine of a Man Carrying a Shovel

公元 6 世纪
6th Century A.D.
高 91.9、最大宽 23、底径 17.1 厘米
Height 91.9 cm, Maximum width 23 cm, Bottom diameter 17.1cm

日本群马县伊势崎市下触
Shimofurei – cho, Isesaki – shi, Gunma Prefecture, Japan
日本东京国立博物馆藏
Tokyo National Museum

　　埴轮见于 3 世纪后半期到 6 世纪期间的日本群岛，种类多样，有屋形、器具、象形等。5 世纪，中国南朝的陪葬制度传入日本，日本仿照其人物俑制作出人物埴轮。

　　此件埴轮笑容可爱，腰间佩刀，双耳佩戴耳环。为了方便劳动，头发在耳边短短扎起。头戴头巾，斗笠的造型有所损坏，头部有所凸起。本该手握木柄、肩抗锹头的造型，现在却耷拉到肩头，这种简易造型手法也是埴轮的特征。

金耳饰
Gold Earrings

公元 6 世纪
6th Century A.D.
长 7.9 厘米
Length 7.9 cm

日本滋贺县高岛市鸭稻荷山古坟
Kamoinariyama Kofun, Takashima, Shiga Prefecture, Japan
日本东京国立博物馆藏
Tokyo National Museum

铜鎏金半跏思惟菩萨像
Gilt-bronze Bodhisattva in Meditation

公元 7 世纪
7th Century A.D.
通高 33.3 厘米
Height 33.3 cm

日本和歌山县那智胜浦町那智山
Nachi Mountain, Nachikatsuura, Wakayama Prefecture,
Japan
日本东京国立博物馆藏
Tokyo National Museum

　　菩萨右手指尖抚颊，右足搭于左膝上，做思索状。嘴角上扬，微笑怡然。菩萨像整体修长，但依然可见肌肉轮廓。上半身全裸，不着任何胸饰或璎珞的造型在日本比较罕见，更多见于朝鲜半岛三国时代。

彩绘木刻行道持国天王面具
Gyodo Mask "Dhatarattha"

公元 14 世纪
14th Century A.D.
长 26.9、宽 18.1 厘米
Length 26.9 cm, Width 18.1 cm

日本东京国立博物馆藏
Tokyo National Museum

长次郎制"尼寺"铭黑乐烧 茶碗
Black Raku Ware by Chojiro (Black Glaze)

公元 16 世纪
16th Century A.D.

高 8.2、口径 10.3、圈足直径 5 厘米
Height 8.2 cm, Diameter of mouth 10.3 cm, Diameter of ring foot 5 cm

日本东京国立博物馆藏
Tokyo National Museum

织部烧 有足方形瓷钵
Mino Ware Cornered Bowl in Oribe Type

公元 17 世纪
17th Century A.D.
高 7、长 20.2、宽 20.3 厘米
Height 7 cm, Length 20.2 cm, Width 20.3 cm

日本美浓地区
Mino province, Japan
日本东京国立博物馆藏
Tokyo National Museum

锅岛藩窑　雪景山水图青花瓷盘

Dish, Nabeshima Ware with Design of Snowscape in Underglaze Blue

公元 18 世纪
18th Century A.D.

高 7.9、口径 30.3、底径 15.2 厘米
Height 7.9 cm, Diameter of mouth 30.3 cm, Bottom diameter 15.2 cm

日本东京国立博物馆藏
Tokyo National Museum

　　1610 年左右，日本九州的有田地区从朝鲜引进制瓷技术，烧制了首批日产瓷器。锅岛府开发了技术工艺堪与中国景德镇瓷器媲美的瓷器，并敬献给将军府，这就是"锅岛烧"。锅岛烧基本形态为具有高圈足的圆盘，无论外形还是尺寸都严格遵守规格。同时，在设计构思方面也极尽洗练，与民窑风格大相径庭。

　　该盘在锅岛烧盘中属于最大款。运用上色泛黑的钴颜料，以浓淡晕染巧妙描绘出美丽的雪景。

宫川长龟 游女闲谈图

Courtesans Having a Chat by Miyagawa
Choki

公元 18 世纪
18th Century A.D.

长 55.2、宽 33.2 厘米
Length 55.2 cm, Width 33.2 cm

日本东京国立博物馆藏
Tokyo National Museum

桃源斋荣舟　太夫爱猫图
Beauty with Cat by Togensai Eishu

公元 19 世纪
19ᵗʰ Century A.D.

长 94.6、宽 29.1 厘米
Length 94.6 cm, Width 29.1 cm

日本东京国立博物馆藏
Tokyo National Museum

　　此幅作品描绘了头插许多发簪，身着华丽鲜艳
长罩衫的艺妓和其脚畔的猫，取材于日本古典文学
名作《源氏物语》中的"若菜上"卷而作。"若菜
上"卷讲的是第三皇女与柏木戏剧性邂逅的故事。
六条家院举办蹴鞠活动时，第三皇女养的猫拉开了
她房间的竹帘，正在蹴鞠的柏木与第三皇女便这样
邂逅了。艺妓的服饰上描绘了牡丹和菊花，还绘有
竹帘纹样，暗示着与"若菜上"卷故事的关系。

　　作者桃源斋荣舟师承以手绘浮世绘闻名于世
的鸟文斋荣之。荣舟传承了其师荣之描画窈窕匀称
的美人风格，本作品为其代表作之一。

约旦哈希姆王国
The Hashemite Kingdom of Jordan

妇女造型陶水壶
Small Water Jug Featuring a Female Head

约公元前 16 世纪
Circa 16th Century B.C.

高 19 厘米
Height 19 cm

约旦杰里科
Jericho, Jordan

约旦考古博物馆藏
Jordan Archaeological Museum

猴形陶壶
Monkey-shaped pottery Jug

公元前 11 – 前 10 世纪
11th – 10th Century B.C.
高 12.5、宽 7 厘米
Height 12.5 cm, Width 7 cm

约旦考古博物馆藏
Jordan Archaeological Museum

纳巴泰风格祭坛
Nabataean Altar

公元 1 世纪
1st Century A.D.
高 56、宽 30 厘米
Height 56 cm, Width 30 cm

约旦考古博物馆藏
Jordan Archaeological Museum

大理石头像
Marble Head

公元前 2 – 前 1 世纪
2ⁿᵈ – 1ˢᵗ Century B.C.

高 27、宽 23.5 厘米
Height 27 cm, Width 23.5 cm

约旦考古博物馆藏
Jordan Archaeological Museum

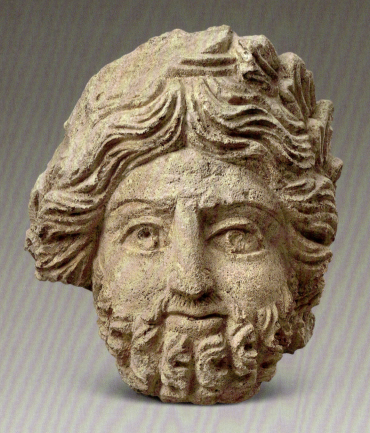

纳巴泰风格灰岩神灵头像
Limestone Head of God Hadad

公元 1 世纪
1ˢᵗ Century A.D.

高 32、宽 32 厘米
Height 32 cm, Width 32 cm

约旦考古博物馆藏
Jordan Archaeological Museum

　　此头像有浓厚的希腊化特色，波浪式的头发、直通鼻等都是希腊化的典型特征。纳巴泰人崇拜雨神哈达德，但哈达德通常有犄角，因此该头像刻画的应该是国王像而非纳巴泰人崇拜的哈达德神。

纳巴泰文铭文石碑
Nabataean Inscription

约旦考古博物馆藏
Jordan Archaeological Museum

纳巴泰时期
Nabataean Period

高 11.5、宽 19.5 厘米
Height 11.5 cm, Width 19.5 cm

纳巴泰语是古代阿拉伯半岛北部地区纳巴泰人所使用的语言。纳巴泰人于公元前 6 世纪占领约旦南部、迦南和阿拉伯半岛北部地区，他们在此地兴修水利，不断繁荣壮大。纳巴泰文从阿拉伯字母发展而来，此碑上的文字体现出早期纳巴泰文古朴的字体风格。

纳巴泰风格砂岩柱头
Sand Stone Capital (Nabataean)

公元 1 世纪
1ˢᵗ Century A.D.

高 32、宽 42 厘米
Height 32 cm, Width 42 cm

约旦考古博物馆藏
Jordan Archaeological Museum

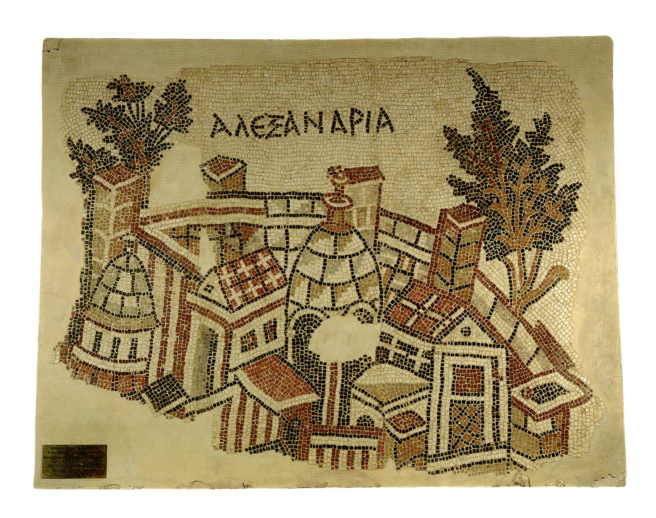

亚历山大里亚图景马赛克

Painted glazed ceramic plate Mosaic with representation of the city of Alexandria

公元 531 年
531 A.D.

高 143、宽 158 厘米
Height 143 cm, Width 158 cm

约旦杰拉什博物馆藏
Jarash Museum, Jordan

釉陶盘

Glazed Plate Decorated

公元 1250 – 1517 年（马穆鲁克时期）
1250 – 1517 A.D. (Mamluk Period)

直径 28、高 9 厘米
Diameter 28 cm, Height 9 cm

约旦考古博物馆藏
Jordan Archaeological Museum

老挝人民民主共和国
The Lao People's Democratic Republic

星形石器
Star-shaped Stone

新石器时代
The Neolithic Age

长 10、宽 6.5 厘米
Length 10 cm, Width 6.5 cm

老挝乌多姆赛省
Oudomxay Province, Laos

老挝国家博物馆藏
Lao National Museum

此物黑色砂岩质地，整体为星形，器心中空，便于穿插木杖或穿绳系挂等，磨制的 12 个芒呈中心对称分布。构思巧妙，制作精细，应与原始先民的祭祀生活有关。星形石器是东南亚地区新石器时代文化的一类特色器物，中国云南省临沧市耿马傣族佤族自治县石佛洞遗址也有类似发现。

石斧
Stone Axe

史前时代
Prehistoric Age

宽 7.2、长 16.2 厘米
Width 7.2 cm, Length 16.2 cm

老挝沙耶武里省
Sainyabuli Province, Laos
老挝国家博物馆藏
Lao National Museum

陶罐
Pottery Jar

史前时代
Prehistoric Age

宽 20.8、高 14.7 厘米
Width 20.8 cm, Height 14.7 cm

老挝沙耶武里省
Sainyabuli Province, Laos
老挝国家博物馆藏
Lao National Museum

铜鼓
Bronze Drum

史前时代
Prehistoric Age

宽 41.5、高 56.5 厘米，重 14.8 千克
Width 41.5 cm, Height 56.5 cm, Weight 14.8 kg

老挝沙湾拿吉省
Savannakhet Province, Laos
老挝国家博物馆藏
Lao National Museum

铜斧
Bronze Axe

史前时代
Prehistoric Age
长 6.5、宽 10.1 厘米
Length 6.5 cm, Width 10.1 cm

老挝乌多姆赛省
Oudomxay Province, Laos
老挝国家博物馆藏
Lao National Museum

石雕毗湿奴头像
Stone Statue of Vishnu

公元 12 世纪
12th Century A.D.
宽 25.8、高 46.6 厘米
Width 25.8 cm, Height 46.6 cm

老挝万象市
Vientiane, Laos
老挝国家博物馆藏
Lao National Museum

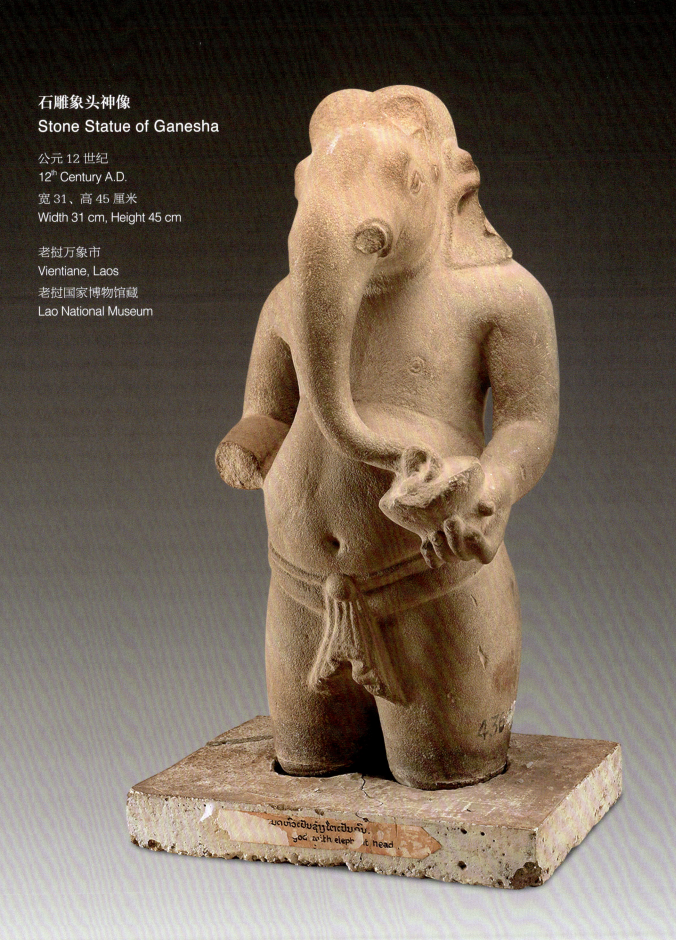

石雕象头神像
Stone Statue of Ganesha

公元 12 世纪
12th Century A.D.
宽 31、高 45 厘米
Width 31 cm, Height 45 cm

老挝万象市
Vientiane, Laos
老挝国家博物馆藏
Lao National Museum

《罗摩衍那》木制原本
Ramayana (Wood, Original)

公元 1353 – 1697 年（澜沧王国时代）
1353 – 1697 A.D. (Lan Xang)

长 55、宽 23 厘米
Length 55 cm, Width 23 cm

老挝琅勃拉邦省
Luang Prabang Province, Laos

老挝国家博物馆藏
Lao National Museum

贝叶经是用铁笔在贝多罗树叶（棕榈科乔木）上所刻写的经文，内容除佛教经典外，还有许多传说、故事、诗歌和历史记载等。东南亚各国至今保留着制作和书写贝叶经的文化传统。

最常见的巴利文贝叶经《罗摩衍那》（梵语，意为"罗摩的历险经历"），内容主要讲述阿逾陀国王子罗摩的故事。

竹质芦笙

Khaen, Musical Instrument (Bamboo)

公元 1353 – 1697 年（澜沧王国时代）
1353 – 1697 A.D. (Lan Xang)

长 85、宽 17.5 厘米
Length 85 cm, Width 17.5 cm

老挝琅勃拉邦省
Luang Prabang Province, Laos
老挝国家博物馆藏
Lao National Museum

木琴

Xylophone

公元 1353 – 1697 年（澜沧王国时代）
1353 – 1697 A.D. (Lan Xang)

长 90、宽 33 厘米
Length 90 cm, Width 33 cm

老挝琅勃拉邦省
Luang Prabang Province, Laos
老挝国家博物馆藏
Lao National Museum

铜佛坐像
Copper Buddha Statue

公元 1353 – 1697 年（澜沧王国时代）
1353 – 1697 A.D. (Lan Xang)

宽 26、高 38.5 厘米
Width 26 cm, Height 38.5 cm

老挝万象市
Vientiane, Laos

老挝国家博物馆藏
Lao National Museum

　　此为佛陀成道像，左手平伸结禅定印，右手下垂触地结降魔印，表现佛陀在菩提树下战胜了魔王各种诱惑和攻击后，证得无上菩提的瞬间。与大乘佛像不同，东南亚地区的南传上座部佛像，往往只表现佛传和佛本生故事形象。

　　此尊佛像肉髻高隆，火焰顶受到了斯里兰卡艺术影响，但整体造像风格为老挝本地特色。佛陀身着袒右式袈裟，薄衣透体，弯眉长目，面相清秀却不失庄严。

金佛坐像
Buddha

公元 1353 – 1697 年（澜沧王国时代）
1353 – 1697 A.D. (Lan Xang)
宽 8.6、高 17.3 厘米
Width 8.6 cm, Height 17.3 cm

老挝万象市
Vientiane, Laos
老挝国家博物馆藏
Lao National Museum

木饭篓
Wooden Food Container

公元 1353 – 1697 年（澜沧王国时代）
1353 – 1697 A.D. (Lan Xang)
宽 89.8、高 52 厘米，重 358 克
Width 89.8 cm, Height 52 cm, Weight 358 g

老挝万象市
Vientiane, Laos
老挝国家博物馆藏
Lao National Museum

黎巴嫩共和国
The Lebanese Republic

彩绘陶头像
Ceramic Painted Head

青铜时代
Bronze Age

长 22.5、宽 14.5、厚 1.2 厘米
Length 22.5 cm, Width 14.5 cm, Thickness 1.2 cm

黎巴嫩吉耶
Jiyeh, Lebanon

黎巴嫩文物局藏
Directorate General of Antiquities – Lebanon

象形文字石碑
Stela with Hieroglyphic Inscription

青铜时代
Bronze Age
宽 32、高 60、厚 14 厘米
Width 32 cm, Height 60 cm, Thickness 14 cm

黎巴嫩毕步勒
Byblos, Lebanon
黎巴嫩文物局藏
Directorate General of Antiquities – Lebanon

　　石碑中的人物为埃及风格，侧面正身站立，双手抬起，做供奉姿势。
　　毕步勒是古代腓尼基最主要的三个城市之一，黎巴嫩雪松便是通过毕步勒这唯一的港口运往古代埃及和世界各地的。

红陶杯
Cup

青铜时代
Bronze Age
高 7.4、直径 6.8 厘米
Height 7.4 cm, Diameter 6.8 cm

黎巴嫩泰尔阿卡
Tell Arka, Lebanon
黎巴嫩文物局藏
Directorate General of Antiquities – Lebanon

雪花石膏瓶
Bottle

青铜时代
Bronze Age

高 17.5、厚 4、直径 14.5 厘米
Height 17.5 cm, Thickness 4 cm, Diameter 14.5 cm

黎巴嫩卡梅尔埃洛兹
Kamed el Loz, Lebanon

黎巴嫩文物局藏
Directorate General of Antiquities – Lebanon

单耳瓶
Jug with Handle

青铜时代
Bronze Age

高 26.2、厚 2.1、直径 17 厘米
Height 26.2 cm, Thickness 2.1 cm, Diameter 17 cm

黎巴嫩卡梅尔埃洛兹
Kamed el Loz, Lebanon

黎巴嫩文物局藏
Directorate General of Antiquities – Lebanon

此瓶表面光滑，瓶颈较高，瓶身呈球状，体现出较高的制作工艺。卡梅尔埃洛兹即是阿玛尔纳文书（Amarna Letter）中所提到的库米底（Kumidi）城，替埃及法老监管南黎凡特王的督察官便驻扎于此。

红陶罐

Pottery

铁器时代 II
Iron Age II
高 37、直径 31 厘米
Height 37 cm, Diameter 31 cm

黎巴嫩泰尔拉希迪
Tell Rachidieh, Lebanon
黎巴嫩文物局藏
Directorate General of Antiquities – Lebanon

红陶雕像

Figurine

希腊化时期
Hellenistic Period
高 13.2、宽 4.7、厚 0.9 厘米
Height 13.2 cm, Width 4.7 cm, Thickness 0.9 cm

黎巴嫩哈拉耶布
Kharayeb, Lebanon
黎巴嫩文物局藏
Directorate General of Antiquities – Lebanon

大理石雕孩童像
Marble Statue of a Child

公元前 4 世纪中期
Mid 4th Century B.C.

长 47、宽 21、高 40 厘米
Length 47 cm, Width 21 cm,
Height 40 cm

黎巴嫩厄舒蒙神庙
Temple of Eshmun, Lebanon

黎巴嫩文物局藏
Directorate General of Antiquities
– Lebanon

高浮雕祭祀神王朱庇特像
High Relief of Jupiter
Heliopolitan

公元 573 年（罗马时期）
573 A.D. (Roman Period)

长 42.5、宽 45、厚 29 厘米
Length 42.5 cm, Width 45 cm,
Thickness 29 cm

黎巴嫩贝卡
Bekaa, Lebanon

黎巴嫩文物局藏
Directorate General of Antiquities
– Lebanon

椰枣形玻璃瓶
Flask in the Shape of a Date

罗马时期
Roman Period
高 7.3、厚 0.3、直径 3.1 厘米
Height 7.3 cm, Thickness 0.3 cm, Diameter 3.1 cm

黎巴嫩贝鲁特
Beirut, Lebanon
黎巴嫩文物局藏
Directorate General of Antiquities – Lebanon

长颈锥形底座玻璃瓶
Unguentarium

罗马时期
Roman Period
高 10.1、厚 0.5、直径 5.9 厘米
Height 10.1 cm, Thickness 0.5 cm, Diameter 5.9 cm

黎巴嫩贝鲁特
Beirut, Lebanon
黎巴嫩文物局藏
Directorate General of Antiquities – Lebanon

长颈葫芦形底座玻璃瓶
Unguentarium

罗马时期
Roman Period
高 11.6、厚 0.5、直径 2.7 厘米
Height 11.6 cm, Thickness 0.5 cm, Diameter 2.7 cm

黎巴嫩贝鲁特
Beirut, Lebanon
黎巴嫩文物局藏
Directorate General of Antiquities – Lebanon

蓝色玻璃迷你双耳瓶
Unguentarium

罗马时期
Roman Period
高 10.3、厚 0.5、直径 5 厘米
Height 10.3 cm, Thickness 0.5 cm, Diameter 5 cm

黎巴嫩贝鲁特
Beirut, Lebanon
黎巴嫩文物局藏
Directorate General of Antiquities – Lebanon

　　罗马盛行的香水瓶，除了细长颈平底型外，还有双耳细颈尖底瓶，被称为 Amphorisko，意思是"迷你双耳瓶"，器形源于希腊彩陶瓶，其用途是盛放香水、油和化妆品。古埃及人发明了蓝色玻璃，古罗马时期进一步提升了其制作技术，使得玻璃透亮细腻，此瓶是蓝玻璃器中的精品。

玻璃瓶
Unguentarium

罗马时期
Roman Period
高 11.3、厚 0.4、直径 6.8 厘米
Height 11.3 cm, Thickness 0.4 cm, Diameter 6.8 cm

黎巴嫩贝鲁特
Beirut, Lebanon
黎巴嫩文物局藏
Directorate General of Antiquities – Lebanon

千花玻璃碗

Millefiori

罗马时期
Roman Period
高 2.9、厚 0.4、直径 7.8 厘米
Height 2.9 cm, Thickness 0.4 cm, Diameter 7.8 cm

黎巴嫩贝鲁特
Beirut, Lebanon
黎巴嫩文物局藏
Directorate General of Antiquities – Lebanon

Millefiori 是意大利语，意思是"千万朵花"，特指古埃及人发明的玻璃制作技术，该技术在古罗马时期尤为流行。棕色为主色调，以白色点缀的千花模仿天然玛瑙的质感和花纹，也有模仿马赛克质地的多彩千花玻璃盘。古罗马千花玻璃器远销各地，阿富汗贝格拉姆宝藏中也有一件千花玻璃盘。千花玻璃器见证了古代世界的审美和文化交流的轨迹。

马来西亚
Malaysia

布玛布
Pua Kumbu

公元 1939 年
1939 A.D.

马来西亚国家博物馆藏
National Museum of Malaysia

金线刺绣桲叶盒（一套）

Betel-nut Box Embroidered in Gold

公元 1949 年
1949 A.D.

长 33.5、宽 19、通高 17.5 厘米
Length 33.5 cm, Width 19 cm, Height 17.5 cm

马来西亚国家博物馆藏
National Museum of Malaysia

　　该桲叶盒为木制，全身由红色绒布包裹，上面绣以金丝。一套桲叶盒里由四个金属盒、一个钳剪、槟郎臼和槟郎杵构成。桲叶盒因刺绣而闻名，常出现在婚礼的开场等重要仪式中。

伊班刀
Mandau (Traditional Weapon)

公元 1969 年
1969 A.D.

马来西亚砂捞越
Sarawak, Malaysia

马来西亚国家博物馆藏
National Museum of Malaysia

木雕墨阳虾祖
Moyang Udang

公元 1969 年
1969 A.D.

长 21、宽 11、通高 57 厘米
Length 21 cm, Width 11 cm, Height 57 cm

马来西亚国家博物馆藏
National Museum of Malaysia

银链刻花烟盒
Tobacco Box

公元 1974 年
1974 A.D.

长 17、宽 7、通高 3.5 厘米
Length 17 cm, Width 7 cm, Height 3.5 cm

马来西亚国家博物馆藏
National Museum of Malaysia

婴儿背篓
Baby Carrier

公元 1982 年
1982 A.D.

长 37、宽 17、通高 34.5 厘米
Length 37 cm, Width 17 cm,
Height 34.5 cm

马来西亚国家博物馆藏
National Museum of Malaysia

娘惹高跟珠鞋
Beaded High Heels

公元 1989 年
1989 A.D.

长 24、宽 9、通高 6 厘米
Length 24 cm, Width 9 cm, Height 6 cm

马来西亚国家博物馆藏
National Museum of Malaysia

娘惹上装

Kebaya

公元 1989 年
1989 A.D.

长 111、宽 71 厘米
Length 111 cm, Width 71 cm

马来西亚国家博物馆藏
National Museum of Malaysia

伴随着海外贸易活动，早期移民马来半岛的华人娶当地女子为妻，其男性后裔被称为"峇峇（Baba）"，女性后裔被称为"娘惹（Nyonya）"。娘惹服（可芭雅服）是土生华人常穿的服饰，通常绣有金鱼、海浪和玫瑰花图案，能突显身材，颇受年轻人喜爱。

（两面）

峇迪布
Sarong Cloth

公元 1989 年
1989 A.D.

长 105、宽 96.5 厘米
Length 105 cm, Width 96.5 cm

马来西亚国家博物馆藏
National Museum of Malaysia

热瓦普
Rebab

公元 1999 年
1999 A.D.
琴，通高 109、长 20.5、宽 8 厘米
Rebab: Height 109 cm, Length 20.5 cm, Width 8 cm
琴杆，通高 79、宽 6.5、长 1.5 厘米
Neck of Rebab: Height 79 cm, Width 6.5 cm,
Length 1.5 cm

马来西亚国家博物馆藏
National Museum of Malaysia

　　热瓦普是一种流行于马来地区的弦乐器，主体通常由菠萝蜜木制成，内部镂空，上部较宽，下部呈锥形。热瓦普琴箱蒙牛肚皮，琴头上部雕刻成嫩笋状。在马来西亚的吉兰丹州，常用其为玛蓉舞等传统艺术表演伴奏。

马来短剑

Keris Semenanjung (Traditional Malay Weapon)

公元 2004 年
2004 A.D.

通高 15、长 38、宽 8 厘米
Height 15 cm, Length 38 cm, Width 8 cm

马来西亚国家博物馆藏
National Museum of Malaysia

玛赫玛丽族面具

Wooden Mask

公元 2006 年
2006 A.D.

长 37、宽 26 厘米
Length 37 cm, Width 26 cm

马来西亚国家博物馆藏
National Museum of Malaysia

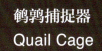

鹌鹑捕捉器
Quail Cage

公元 2009 年
2009 A.D.
长 23.5、宽 22、通高 30 厘米
Length 23.5 cm, Width 22 cm, Height 30cm

马来西亚国家博物馆藏
National Museum of Malaysia

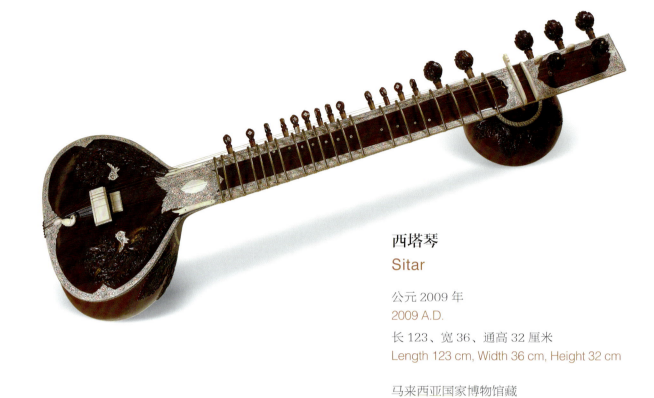

西塔琴
Sitar

公元 2009 年
2009 A.D.

长 123、宽 36、通高 32 厘米
Length 123 cm, Width 36 cm, Height 32 cm

马来西亚国家博物馆藏
National Museum of Malaysia

沙巴葫芦笙
Sompoton

公元 2014 年
2014 A.D.

长 40、宽 20.5 厘米
Length 40 cm, Width 20.5 cm

马来西亚国家博物馆藏
National Museum of Malaysia

丰收陶罐

Harvest Pottery

公元 2014 年
2014 A.D.
通高 21.5、直径 25 厘米；
Height 21.5 cm, Diameter 25 cm;
通高 10、直径 20.5 厘米
Height 10 cm, Diameter 20.5 cm

马来西亚国家博物馆藏
National Museum of Malaysia

　　丰收陶罐多在庆祝丰收节时使用，以祭拜太阳神，乞求丰收。过节时，人们将米和牛奶装入该陶器中，制成甜牛奶米粥并煮沸溢出，祈祷新的一年获得大丰收。

蒙古国
Mongolia

银碗
Silver Bowl

公元 20 世纪早期
Early 20th Century A.D.

高 6.7、直径 24.4、底径 15.2 厘米，重 1105 克
Height 6.7 cm, Diameter 24.4 cm, Diameter of base 15.2 cm, Weight 1105 g

蒙古国家博物馆藏
National Museum of Mongolia

银碗
Large Silver Bowl

公元 20 世纪早期
Early 20th Century A.D.

高 8.9、直径 23.4、底径 13.9 厘米，重 1375 克
Height 8.9 cm, Diameter 23.4 cm, Diameter of base 13.9 cm, Weight 1375 g

蒙古国家博物馆藏
National Museum of Mongolia

该碗平沿直壁，木胎，用银包裹，周身饰有花纹，碗底浮雕出五只动物图案。包银木碗通常为蒙古族上层人物、贵族家庭所用，既是吃饭的餐具，又是饮用奶茶的茶皿，是家庭富有和身份高贵的象征。

奶茶壶
Jug

公元 20 世纪早期
Early 20th Century A.D.

高 37、底径 16 厘米
Height 37 cm, Diameter of base 16 cm

蒙古国家博物馆藏
National Museum of Mongolia

烙铁
Branding Iron

公元 20 世纪早期
Early 20th Century A.D.

长 55、直径 8 厘米
Length 55 cm, Diameter 8 cm

蒙古国家博物馆藏
National Museum of Mongolia

马鞭
Riding Crop (whip)

公元 20 世纪
20th Century A.D.

长 72 厘米
Length 72 cm

蒙古国家博物馆藏
National Museum of Mongolia

马鞍
Saddle

公元 1939 年
1939 A.D.

高 90、宽 45 厘米
Height 90 cm, Width 45 cm

蒙古国家博物馆藏
National Museum of Mongolia

　　这种马鞍又叫巴托诺夫鞍，包括一片黄色皮革马鞍布，一块鞍下红色毡垫和 10 个压制的银盘。银盘的中心饰有方形图案，两侧饰有雕刻的角状图案。鞍尾用骨头制成，饰有银制角状图案。

　　巴托诺夫（Batnorov）制鞍法是由著名工匠托吉尔（Tojil）发明的，融合了独特的银冶炼技术、雕刻技术和压花技术。

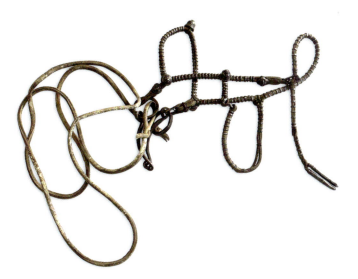

缰绳
Bridle

公元 20 世纪早期
Early 20ᵗʰ Century A.D.

长 29 厘米
Length 29 cm

蒙古国家博物馆藏
National Museum of Mongolia

套索
Lasso

公元 20 世纪中期
Mid 20ᵗʰ Century A.D.

长 1200 厘米
Length 1200 cm

蒙古国家博物馆藏
National Museum of Mongolia

刮板（马刷）
Scrapers (curry comb)

公元 20 世纪中期
Mid 20ᵗʰ Century A.D.

长 33、宽 4 厘米
Length 33 cm, Width 4 cm

蒙古国家博物馆藏
National Museum of Mongolia

　　该马刷为木质，雕刻有马匹的图案，流露出草原游牧文化的气息。

缅甸联邦共和国

The Republic of the Union of Myanmar

竖琴

Harp

当代
Contemporary
高 36、长 34 厘米
Height 36 cm, Length 34 cm

缅甸宗教与文化部藏
The Ministry of Religious Affairs and Culture, the Republic
of the Union of Myanmar

在缅甸，竖琴被尊称为弦乐器之王，在骠国时代被广泛使用。一般弦乐器可弹奏五声音阶，但缅甸竖琴却可弹奏七声音阶。此琴共鸣腔由花梨木制成，琴颈与琴箱交汇处的形状酷似黄兰叶片，船形琴箱的尾部呈碗状。琴颈顶端即为琴头，呈菩提叶状。琴颈由儿茶木制成，琴箱外裹有一层鹿皮。

印有一百名仕女的折纸

Folding Parabike depicting 100 Number of Ladies in Waiting

当代
Contemporary

未折叠：长约 109.7、宽约 36.6 厘米
Unfolded: Length 109.7 cm, Width 36.6 cm

折叠后：长约 36.6、宽约 12.2 厘米
Folded: Length 36.6 cm, Width 12.2 cm

缅甸宗教与文化部藏
The Ministry of Religious Affairs and Culture, Republic of the Union of Myanmar

　　此件作品，画家用缅甸传统绘画手法描绘了亚达纳邦时代曼同王统治时期百位侍女的肖像。侍女的名字、着装和仪态皆被记录其上。当时的画家并没有在作品中署名的传统，但人们推测这是宫廷画家乌卡尼尤特（U Kyar Nyunt）的作品。此件是原作的复制品。

木偶
Puppets

当代
Contemporary

高 26、宽 11 厘米，重 3 千克
Height 26 cm, Width 11 cm, Weight 3 kg

缅甸宗教与文化部藏
The Ministry of Religious Affairs and Culture,
Republic of the Union of Myanmar

木琴
Xylophone

当代
Contemporary

高 25、长 57 厘米，重 11.4 千克
Height 25 cm, Length 57 cm, Weight 11.4 kg

缅甸宗教与文化部藏
The Ministry of Religious Affairs and Culture,
Republic of the Union of Myanmar

巴奥定音鼓
Pa-Oh Pot Drum

当代
Contemporary

直径 24、高 60 厘米，重 60 千克
Diameter 24 cm, Height 60 cm, Weight 60 kg

缅甸宗教与文化部藏
The Ministry of Religious Affairs and Culture, Republic
of the Union of Myanmar

定音鼓
Pot Drum

当代
Contemporary

直径 16、高 62 厘米，重 12 千克
Diameter 16 cm, Height 62 cm, Weight 12 kg

缅甸宗教与文化部藏
The Ministry of Religious Affairs and Culture, Republic
of the Union of Myanmar

巴基斯坦伊斯兰共和国
The Islamic Republic of Pakistan

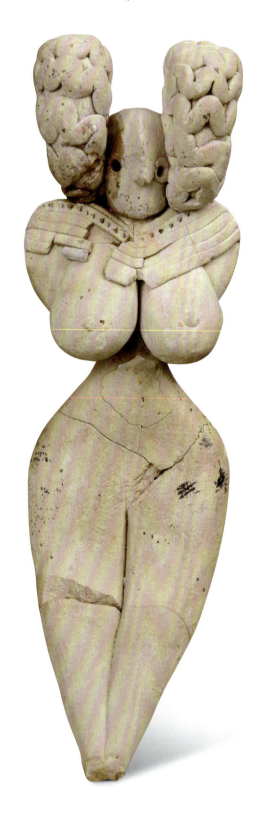

女性陶塑像
Terracotta Female Human Figurine

公元前 3000 年
3000 B.C.

高 10.3、宽 3.5 厘米
Height 10.3 cm, Width 3.5 cm

巴基斯坦美赫尕尔
Mehrgarh, Pakistan

巴基斯坦考古与博物馆司藏
Department of Archaeology and Museums,
Government of Pakistan

　　早在公元前 8000 年左右，巴基斯坦西南部俾路支省的美赫尕尔（Mehrgarh）已经出现了人类定居点，是南亚留有农耕和放牧生活痕迹的最古老的遗址之一。

　　这尊陶制女神像丰满的乳房和宽大的臀部暗示其与生育力、创造力有关。她端庄的仪态、丰满的胸部和繁复的发型体现了当地流行的风格。神像立体感十足，长发垂下，五官逼真，发髻之间的发饰清晰可见。女神突起的双目，高挺的鼻梁，微微翘起的嘴唇引人注目。

彩绘陶罐

Terracotta Painted Jar

公元前 2700 – 前 2400 年
2700 – 2400 B.C.

直径 12.9、深 13 厘米
Diameter 12.9 cm, Depth 13 cm

巴基斯坦俾路支省宁道瑞遗址
Nindowari site, Balochistan, Pakistan

巴基斯坦考古与博物馆司藏
Department of Archaeology and Museums,
Government of Pakistan

库里文化盛行于公元前 2700 至前 2400 年，俾路支省的宁道瑞 (Nindowari) 遗址是最大的库里文化遗址之一。

此罐上绘有被拴在树前植物上公牛。陶罐上的空白处绘有各种符号，这是库里文化常见的风格。陶罐表面的图案由菩提树叶装饰的两栏分为两个部分。陶罐肩部绘有黑色线条环绕的波浪线，颈部、肩部和腹部上还绘有三条棕色宽带。图案展现出丰富的农业景观。

彩绘陶罐
Terracotta Painted Jar

公元前 2600 – 前 1800 年
2600 - 1800 B.C.
直径 38、深 35 厘米
Diameter 38 cm, Depth 35 cm

巴基斯坦瑙哈罗
Nausharo, Pakistan
巴基斯坦考古与博物馆司藏
Department of Archaeology and Museums,
Government of Pakistan

石雕男性半身残像
Headless Male Sculpture in Stone

公元前 2500 – 前 1800 年
2500 – 1800 B.C.
长 28、高 22 厘米
Length 28 cm, Height 22 cm

摩亨佐·达罗
Moenjo daro
巴基斯坦考古与博物馆司藏
Department of Archaeology and Museums,
Government of Pakistan

马形柄器盖
Lid with Horse Shaped Handle

公元前 1000 年
1000 B.C.
直径 32.5 厘米
Diameter 32.5 cm

巴基斯坦考古与博物馆司藏
Department of Archaeology and Museums,
Government of Pakistan

陶瓮棺
Terracotta Burial Pot

公元前 1000 年
1000 B.C.
直径 37.5、深 36 厘米
Diameter 37.5 cm, Depth 36 cm

巴基斯坦扎里夫科鲁纳
Zarif Koruna, Pakistan
巴基斯坦考古与博物馆司藏
Department of Archaeology and Museums,
Government of Pakistan

犍陀罗墓葬文化的陶像大多制作简单，其他饰品也只做简单的点状装饰。这件陶器形状浑圆，体形较大，有开口，底部变窄。陶器有三个装饰孔，分别代表死者的眼睛和嘴巴，配有黏土捏制而成的鼻子和眉毛。

女性陶塑像
Terracotta Female Figurine

公元前 3 – 前 2 世纪
3rd – 2nd Century B.C.
长 11、宽 4 厘米
Length 11 cm, Width 4 cm

巴基斯坦塔克西拉遗址比尔丘
Bhir Mound, Taxila site, Pakistan
巴基斯坦考古与博物馆司藏
Department of Archaeology and Museums,
Government of Pakistan

青铜勺
Bronze Spoon

公元前 2 – 前 1 世纪
2nd – 1st Century B.C.
长 23、宽 10.5 厘米
Length 23 cm, Width 10.5 cm

巴基斯坦塔克西拉遗址锡尔卡波
Sirkap, Taxila site, Pakistan
巴基斯坦考古与博物馆司藏
Department of Archaeology and Museums,
Government of Pakistan

双耳陶罐
Terracotta Double Handled Pot

公元前 2 – 前 1 世纪
2nd – 1st Century B.C.
底径 12.5、高 29 厘米
Bottom diameter 12.5 cm, Height 29 cm

巴基斯坦塔克西拉遗址锡尔卡波
Sirkap, Taxila site, Pakistan
巴基斯坦考古与博物馆司藏
Department of Archaeology and Museums,
Government of Pakistan

灰片岩佛立像
Grey Schist Standing Buddha

公元 2 – 3 世纪
2nd – 3rd Century A.D.
长 39、高 85 厘米
Length 39 cm, Height 85 cm

犍陀罗遗址中部
Central Gandhara site
巴基斯坦考古与博物馆司藏
Department of Archaeology and Museums,
Government of Pakistan

　　这尊站佛头部带有光环，脸向左偏转。
佛像头部长有硕大、平滑的肉髻，头发浓密。
五官深刻，长长的耳垂和双眼引人注目。
佛身着僧袍，双腿隐于僧袍之下，长袍的
层层褶皱以线条的方式体现，清晰可见。

刻有运送佛陀遗骨图样的绿片岩石板
Panel in Green Schist, Depicting Transportation of the Relics of Buddha

公元 2 – 3 世纪
2nd – 3rd Century A.D.

长 31、宽 28 厘米
Length 31 cm, Width 28 cm

巴基斯坦斯瓦特
Swat, Pakistan

巴基斯坦考古与博物馆司藏
Department of Archaeology and Museums, Government of Pakistan

绿片岩丘比特浮雕建筑构件
Architectural Panel in Green Schist
Depicting a Cupid

公元 1 – 3 世纪
1st – 3rd Century A.D.

长 31、宽 28.5 厘米
Length 31 cm, Width 28.5 cm

巴基斯坦斯瓦特县布特卡拉遗址
Butkara site, Swat, Pakistan

巴基斯坦考古与博物馆司藏
Department of Archaeology and Museums,
Government of Pakistan

灰泥佛坐像
Buddha in Meditation
(Stucco)

公元 2 – 3 世纪
2nd – 3rd Century A.D.

长 46、宽 47 厘米
Length 46 cm, Width 47 cm

犍陀罗遗址中部
Central Gandhara site

巴基斯坦考古与博物馆司藏
Department of Archaeology and
Museums, Government of Pakistan

灰泥菩萨头像
Bodhisattva Head (Stucco)

公元 3 – 4 世纪
3rd – 4th Century A.D.
直径 13、高 10.5 厘米
Diameter 13 cm, Height 10.5 cm

巴基斯坦塔克西拉遗址
Taxila site, Pakistan
巴基斯坦考古与博物馆司藏
Department of Archaeology and Museums,
Government of Pakistan

灰泥佛陀头像
Buddha Head (Stucco)

公元 3 – 4 世纪
3rd – 4th Century A.D.
直径 12.5、高 19 厘米
Diameter 12.5 cm, Height 19 cm

巴基斯坦塔克西拉遗址
Taxila site, Pakistan
巴基斯坦考古与博物馆司藏
Department of Archaeology and Museums,
Government of Pakistan

大理石女供养人像
Female Donor (Marble)

公元 10 世纪
10th Century A.D.
宽 18.5、高 29 厘米
Width 18.5 cm, Height 29 cm

巴基斯坦卡塔斯
Katas, Pakistan
巴基斯坦考古与博物馆司藏
Department of Archaeology and Museums,
Government of Pakistan

青铜油灯
Oil Lamp in Bronze

公元 11 世纪
11th Century A.D.
直径 12、高 12.5 厘米
Diameter 12 cm, Height 12.5 cm

巴基斯坦乌迪格姆
Udigram, Pakistan
巴基斯坦考古与博物馆司藏
Department of Archaeology and Museums,
Government of Pakistan

沙特阿拉伯王国
Kingdom of Saudi Arabia

石雕动物头颈
Head and Neck of an Animal Figurine

公元前 7000 – 前 6000 年
7000 - 6000 B.C.

长 21、宽 14、厚 5 厘米
Length 21 cm, Width 14 cm, Thickness 5 cm

沙特阿拉伯阿尔马卡
Almaqar, Saudi Arabia

沙特阿拉伯旅游及民族遗产总机构藏
Saudi Arabia Commission for Tourism and National
Heritage

　　2010 年，考古学家在沙特阿拉伯的中心地带发现了距今 9000 年的阿尔马卡文化。阿尔马卡文化遗址出土了众多动物雕像，有马、山羊、鸵鸟、猎狗、鹰隼和鱼等，这些雕像残片和一起出土的生活器具有明显的人工制作痕迹。

石雕动物头颈
Head and Neck of an Animal Figurine

公元前 7000 – 前 6000 年
7000 – 6000 B.C.
长 52、宽 23、厚 5.8 厘米
Length 52 cm, Width 23 cm, Thickness 5.8 cm

沙特阿拉伯阿尔马卡
Almaqar, Saudi Arabia
沙特阿拉伯旅游及民族遗产总机构藏
Saudi Commission for Tourism and National Heritage

石雕动物头颈
Head and Neck of an Animal Figurine

公元前 7000 – 前 6000 年
7000 – 6000 B.C.
长 27.5、宽 13、厚 5.5 厘米
Length 27.5 cm, Width 13 cm, Thickness 5.5 cm

沙特阿拉伯阿尔马卡
Almaqar, Saudi Arabia
沙特阿拉伯旅游及民族遗产总机构藏
Saudi Commission for Tourism and National Heritage

石雕人像
A Part of a Human Figurine

公元前 7000 年
7000 B.C.
长 65、宽 41、高 12 厘米
Length 65 cm, Width 41 cm, Height 12 cm

沙特阿拉伯塔布克地区
Tabuk, Saudi Arabia
沙特阿拉伯旅游及民族遗产总机构藏
Saudi Commission for Tourism and National Heritage

  沙特阿拉伯塔布克地区的古代遗存和考古遗迹众多，有岩画、铭文、堡垒、宫殿等。
  该人像是在打磨的石头表面做浅浮雕，着重勾勒了面部轮廓和五官。

石雕头像
A Figurine Head with Complexion

公元前 650 – 公元 600 年
650 B.C. – 600 A.D.
长 18.5、宽 11 厘米
Length 18.5 cm, Width 11 cm

沙特阿拉伯奈季兰
Najran, Saudi Arabia
沙特阿拉伯旅游及民族遗产总机构藏
Saudi Commission for Tourism and National Heritage

砂岩人像
A Human Figurine

公元前 300 – 前 100 年
300 – 100 B.C.
长 23、宽 11.5 厘米
Length 23 cm, Width 11.5 cm

沙特阿拉伯欧拉遗址
Al–Ula site, Saudi Arabia
沙特阿拉伯旅游及民族遗产总机构藏
Saudi Commission for Tourism and National Heritage

　　欧拉城始建于公元前 6 世纪，是沙漠中的绿洲，土壤丰沃，水源充足，连接阿拉伯半岛和美索不达米亚的"香料之路"贯穿其间。随着香料等珍贵资源的来往贸易，不同的文化也在此地交融。

　　这件人物塑像头大肩宽，下身娇小，眼睛涂白，应为举行仪式时所用之物。

带流口的金属器
A Small Vessel with a Spout

公元前 4 – 公元 4 世纪
4ᵗʰ Century B.C. – 4ᵗʰ Century A.D.
长 7、宽 4.2、深 0.5 厘米
Length 7 cm, Width 4.2 cm, Depth 0.5 cm

沙特阿拉伯法奥
Alfaw, Saudi Arabia
沙特阿拉伯旅游及民族遗产总机构藏
Saudi Commission for Tourism and National Heritage

铜眼线笔

A Kohl Copper Eyeliner

公元前 4 – 公元 4 世纪
4th Century B.C. – 4th Century A.D.
长 5、直径 0.3 厘米
Length 5 cm, Diameter 0.3 cm

沙特阿拉伯法奥
Alfaw, Saudi Arabia
沙特阿拉伯旅游及民族遗产总机构藏
Saudi Commission for Tourism and National Heritage

古也门铭文方形石香炉

A Square Incense Burner Adorned with Musnad Inscription

公元前 4 – 公元 4 世纪
4th Century B.C. – 4th Century A.D.
长 10、宽 9.5、深 1.2 厘米
Length 10 cm, Width 9.5 cm, Depth 1.2 cm

沙特阿拉伯法奥
Alfaw, Saudi Arabia
沙特阿拉伯旅游及民族遗产总机构藏
Saudi Commission for Tourism and National Heritage

立方型香炉的使用在古代近东历史悠久，在当时的黎凡特和阿拉伯地区尤为盛行，专用于焚烧天然香料。此香炉的四面铭文可能是指四种不同的香料。

吹制玻璃瓶

A Cylinderical Bottle, Hand-blown

公元 7 – 10 世纪
7th – 10th Century A.D.

腹部直径 7.5、口径 3、深 6.5 厘米
Abdominal diameter 7.5 cm, Diameter of mouth 3 cm,
Depth 6.5 cm

沙特阿拉伯拉巴达遗址
Alrabadha site, Saudi Arabia

沙特阿拉伯旅游及民族遗产总机构藏
Saudi Commission for Tourism and National Heritage

吹制玻璃瓶

An Oval Bottle, Hand-blown

公元 7 – 10 世纪
7th – 10th Century A.D.

腹部直径 6.5、口径 1、深 5.8 厘米
Abdominal diameter 6.5 cm, Diameter of mouth 1 cm,
Depth 5.8 cm

沙特阿拉伯拉巴达遗址
Alrabadha site, Saudi Arabia

沙特阿拉伯旅游及民族遗产总机构藏
Saudi Commission for Tourism and National Heritage

新加坡共和国
Republic of Singapore

陶碗
Bowl

公元 9 世纪
9th Century A.D.

高 5.5、直径 20.3 厘米
Height 5.5 cm, Diameter 20.3 cm

伊拉克
Iraq

新加坡亚洲文明博物馆藏
Asian Civilisations Museum, Singapore

公元 8 世纪至 9 世纪，阿拔斯陶工试图仿制中国进口的瓷器，为了达到半透明瓷器般的效果，他们使用了锡基釉。经过烧制后，氧化锡使陶瓷表面呈现出奶油般的乳白色，随后再加以装饰。

这件陶碗的内部刻有用库法体写成的阿拉伯短语，第一个单词"amal"的意思是"某某人的作品"，其后字迹已无法辨别。

铜壶
Jug

公元 12 世纪晚期 – 13 世纪
Late 12th – 13th Century A.D.
高 26.5、宽 23 厘米
Height 26.5 cm, Width 23 cm

伊朗东北部大呼罗珊
Khurasan, Northeast Iran
新加坡亚洲文明博物馆藏
Asian Civilisations Museum, Singapore

青铜五头湿婆像
Shiva as Sadashiva or Mahesha

公元 12 世纪晚期 – 13 世纪早期
Late 12th – early 13th Century A.D.
长 14.5、宽 9.5、高 37.3 厘米
Length 14.5, Width 9.5 cm, Height 37.3 cm

柬埔寨
Cambodia
新加坡亚洲文明博物馆藏
Asian Civilisations Museum, Singapore

陶碗

Bowl

公元 15 世纪
15th Century A.D.
高 9.3、直径 20.3 厘米
Height 9.3, Diameter 20.3 cm

伊朗或中亚
Iran or Central Asia
新加坡亚洲文明博物馆藏
Asian Civilisations Museum, Singapore

　　伊朗和中亚盛产制作蓝色颜料需要的自然资源，例如青金岩、钴矿石和靛蓝。因此，蓝色在该地区的艺术品中很常见，如这只陶碗。这些资源随着贸易流入中国，成为制作中国青花瓷的重要着色剂。

　　伊斯兰陶瓷的发展受到中国陶工的影响，公元 13 世纪的伊利汗国（Il-khanids），与中国的元朝统治者同出一族，进一步推动了两个区域之间的贸易和文化交流。伊斯兰陶瓷风格上的变化多体现在更为厚重的形状、对中国元素的改编，以及更为繁复的装饰。

青花五彩碗
Bowl

公元 19 世纪中后期
Mid late 19th Century A.D.
直径 21、深 9 厘米
Diameter 21 cm, Depth 9 cm

Lee Kip Lee 夫妇赠
Gift of Mr and Mrs Lee Kip Lee
新加坡亚洲文明博物馆藏
Asian Civilisations Museum, Singapore

"邱裕美" 款瓷盘
Plate with Mark of Khoo Joo Bee

公元 1821 – 1850 年 (清·道光)
1821 – 1850 A.D. (the reign of Daoguang, Qing Dynasty)
直径 19.7、高 2.5 厘米
Diameter 19.7 cm, Height 2.5 cm

新加坡亚洲文明博物馆藏
Asian Civilisations Museum, Singapore

和合器
Chupu

公元 1875 – 1908 年 (清·光绪)
1875 – 1908 A.D. (the reign of Guangxu, Qing Dynasty)
直径 8 厘米
Diameter 8 cm

新加坡亚洲文明博物馆藏
Asian Civilisations Museum, Singapore

粉彩盖盅

Kamcheng

公元 19 世纪晚期
Late 19th Century A.D.

盖子直径 35.5、高 15 厘米，底座直径 36、高 21.5 厘米
Cover: Diameter 35.5 cm, Height 15 cm;
Base: Diameter 36 cm, Height 21.5 cm

新加坡亚洲文明博物馆藏
Asian Civilisations Museum, Singapore

　　此件粉彩盖盅是新加坡土生华人从中国瓷都景德镇定制的，用于婚礼、寿宴、春节等喜庆场合。它反映了中新两国的历史文化渊源，也见证了海上丝绸之路繁盛的贸易往来。

"陈"字款和合器
Chupu with the Surname "Chen"

公元 1875 – 1908 年（清·光绪）
1875 – 1908 A.D. (the reign of Guangxu, Qing Dynasty)

直径 19.2、深 19.3 厘米
Diameter 19.2 cm, Depth 19.3 cm

新加坡亚洲文明博物馆藏
Asian Civilisations Museum, Singapore

　　和合器是"娘惹瓷"的一种代表器形，有多种尺寸、颜色和图案，盖顶酒杯状纽。在婚礼上，人们用和合器盛装燕窝，或糯米汤圆等吉祥美食，供新娘和新郎享用，祝福新婚夫妇拥有幸福美满的婚姻。

　　这件和合器刻有"锦庆珍藏"四个字，表明其是陈锦庆的收藏品。陈锦庆（1904 年逝世）生前是马来半岛港口城市槟城一位德高望重的领袖人物。

粉彩盘

Plate

公元 1909 – 1911 年 (清 · 宣统)
1909 – 1911 A.D. (the reign of Xuantong,
Qing Dynasty)

通高 3、直径 19.7 厘米
Height 3 cm, Diameter 19,7 cm

新加坡亚洲文明博物馆藏
Asian Civilisations Museum, Singapore

斯里兰卡民主社会主义共和国
The Democratic Socialist Republic of Sri Lanka

郑和布施锡兰山佛寺碑（复制品）
Galle Trilingual Inscription Installed by Zheng He (Replica)

公元 1368–1644 年（明代）
1368 – 1644 A.D. (Ming Dynasty)
高 144.88、宽 76.2、厚 12.7 厘米
Height 144.88 cm, Width 76.2 cm, Thickness 12.7 cm

斯里兰卡科伦坡国家博物馆藏
Sri Lanka National Museum of Colombo

此碑是海上丝绸之路的重要见证物，由中国明代著名航海家、外交家郑和在访问斯里兰卡时树立的。斯里兰卡古称锡兰山国，是海上丝绸之路贸易中枢。

此碑是郑和第二次下西洋前在明朝首都南京刻制的，碑上刻有中文、泰米尔文和波斯文三种文字，分别是郑和代表明朝皇帝向佛教、印度教、伊斯兰教神灵的祈愿和供养。反映了海上丝绸之路上不同族群、语言和宗教共存的现象，也体现了古代中斯两国人民不远万里的友好交往。

 在亚洲文明对话大会开幕式的"亚洲文物精品展"展出

阿拉伯叙利亚共和国
The Syrian Arab Republic

女性石雕像
Female Figurine

公元前 9200 – 前 8800 年
9200 – 8800 B.C.

长 19.2、宽 7.8、厚 5.7 厘米
Length 19.2 cm, Width 7.8 cm, Thickness 5.7 cm

叙利亚大马士革国家博物馆藏
National Museum of Damascus

　　此像类似于史前雕刻母神。脸部特征抽象，站立姿势，双手背后，腰部、臀部及腿部以波浪弯曲和宽阔的线条形方式展示。

黑石残件
Black Stone (Fragment)

公元前 9200 – 前 8800 年
9200 – 8800 B.C.

长 4.8、宽 4.3、厚 1.8 厘米
Length 4.8 cm, Width 4.3 cm, Thickness 1.8 cm

叙利亚大马士革国家博物馆藏
National Museum of Damascus

金属色近方形石刻
Metallic-colored Squarish Stone

公元前 9200 – 前 8800 年
9200 – 8800 B.C.

长 5.5、宽 3.4、厚 0.7 厘米
Length 5.5 cm, Width 3.4 cm, Thickness 0.7 cm

叙利亚大马士革国家博物馆藏
National Museum of Damascus

石雕动物像
Stone Statue of an Animal

公元前 8200 – 前 7500 年
8200 – 7500 B.C.

高 3.2、宽 2、厚 1.3 厘米
Length 3.2 cm, Width 2 cm, Thickness 1.3 cm

叙利亚大马士革国家博物馆藏
National Museum of Damascus

石雕动物残像
Stone Statue of an Animal with a Broken Horn

公元前 8200 – 前 7500 年
8200 - 7500 B.C.

高 3.2、宽 2、厚 1.3 厘米
Length 3.2 cm, Width 2 cm, Thickness 1.3 cm

叙利亚大马士革国家博物馆藏
National Museum of Damascus

锥形人像
Pyramid-like Human Figurine

公元前 8200 – 前 7500 年
8200 – 7500 B.C.

长 3.3、宽 2、厚 1.5 厘米
Length 3.3 cm, Width 2 cm, Thickness 1.5 cm

叙利亚大马士革国家博物馆藏
National Museum of Damascus

石斧
Stone Axe
公元前 7500 – 前 5500 年
7500 - 5500 B.C.

长 7、宽 4、厚 2 厘米
Length 7 cm, Width 4 cm, Thickness 2 cm

叙利亚大马士革国家博物馆藏
National Museum of Damascus

矩形印章
Rectangular Seal

公元前 7500 – 前 5500 年
7500 - 5500 B.C.

长 2.5、宽 2.1、厚 2 厘米
Length 2.5 cm, Width 2.1 cm, Thickness 2 cm

叙利亚大马士革国家博物馆藏
National Museum of Damascus

灰色印章
Triangular Gray Seal

公元前 7500 – 前 5500 年
7500 - 5500 B.C.

长 4.1、宽 2.7、厚 1.2 厘米
Length 4.1 cm, Width 2.7 cm, Thickness 1.2 cm

叙利亚大马士革国家博物馆藏
National Museum of Damascus

近方形印章
Squarish Seal

公元前 7500 – 前 5500 年
7500 – 5500 B.C.

长 1.6、宽 1.7、厚 1.1 厘米
Length 1.6 cm, Width 1.7 cm, Thickness 1.1 cm

叙利亚大马士革国家博物馆藏
National Museum of Damascus

祈祷者雕像
Prayer Figurine

公元前 3000 年
3000 B.C.
长 22.2、宽 7.5 厘米
Length 22.2 cm, Width 7.5 cm

叙利亚玛丽
Mary, Syria
叙利亚大马士革国家博物馆藏
National Museum of Damascus

　　幼发拉底河沿岸的庙宇中有很多正在祈祷中的男女小雕像，置于庙宇内墙边的椅上。这些小雕像，双手放在胸前，他们分别代表了行政官、登记员、办事员，以及商人等社会富裕阶层的人士。

镶嵌人物画
A Pieced-together Painting

公元前 2500 年
2500 B.C.

长 30、宽 22 厘米
Length 30 cm, Width 22 cm

叙利亚玛丽
Mary, Syria

叙利亚大马士革国家博物馆藏
National Museum of Damascus

这幅装饰画是玛丽城邦寺庙中发现的众多画作之一，由象牙、贝壳、红石灰和片岩组成。动物祭祀是当时在寺庙或庭院举行的庆祝活动的重要组成部分。画面中描绘了两位庆祝者在宗教仪式中准备宰杀一只公羊，将它拍打在地上屠宰用于祭祀的场景。不参与屠宰的人可观看，他们紧握双手表示祷告。

无底足釉陶盘
Baseless Porcelain Plate

公元前 1600 – 前 1200 年
1600 – 1200 B.C.
高 4.5、直径 13 厘米
Height 4.5 cm, Diameter 13 cm

叙利亚乌加里特
Ugarit, Syria
叙利亚大马士革国家博物馆藏
National Museum of Damascus

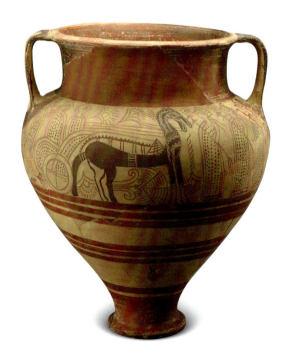

彩绘马车纹陶罐
Painted Pottery Jar Featuring a Cart

公元前 1600 – 前 1200 年
1600 - 1200 B.C.
高 43、直径 37.6 厘米
Height 43 cm, Diameter 37.6 cm

叙利亚乌加里特
Ugarit, Syria
叙利亚大马士革国家博物馆藏
National Museum of Damascus

楔形文字泥板
Clay Tablet with Cuneiform

公元前 1600 – 前 1200 年
1600 - 1200 B.C.
长 8、宽 5.1 厘米
Length 8 cm, Width 5.1 cm

叙利亚乌加里特
Ugarit, Syria
叙利亚大马士革国家博物馆藏
National Museum of Damascus

　　此泥板双面都刻有楔形文字，记录了乌加里特国王致塞浦路斯"古代亚洲"的信。乌加里特是古老的国际港都，位于北叙利亚、沿地中海都市拉塔奇亚北方数公里处。考古学家在发掘乌加里特遗址时，发现了大量刻有文字的泥板。这些泥板记录了乌加里特辉煌一时的文明，确认了乌加里特不仅和塞浦路斯有贸易外交关系，还向埃及纳贡。

（正面）　　　　　　　　　　　（背面）

双面泥板文书
Clay Tablet with double-sided Cuneiform

公元前 1600 年 – 前 1200 年
1600 – 1200 B.C.

长 6.8、宽 5.7 厘米
Length 6.8 cm, Width 5.7 cm

叙利亚大马士革国家博物馆藏
National Museum of Damascus

（正面）　　　　　　　　　　　（背面）

双面楔形文字泥版
Clay Tablet with double-sided Cuneiform

公元前 1600 年 – 前 1200 年
1600 – 1200 B.C.

长 5.5、宽 4.7 厘米
Length 5.5 cm, Width 4.7 cm

叙利亚大马士革国家博物馆藏
National Museum of Damascus

双耳铜罐
Glazed Pottery Jar

公元前 1000 年
1000 B.C.
长 7.6、宽 2.6 厘米
Length 7.6 cm, Width 2.6 cm

叙利亚阿姆里特
Amrit, Syria
叙利亚大马士革国家博物馆藏
National Museum of Damascus

陶女性头像香炉
Female Head Shaped Pottery Censer

公元 100 年
100 A.D.
长 12.5、宽 5 厘米
Length 12.5 cm, Width 5 cm

叙利亚大马士革国家博物馆藏
National Museum of Damascus

陶灯罩
Pottery Lampshade

公元 100 年
100 A.D.

长 20、宽 12.5 厘米
Length 20 cm, Width 12.5 cm

叙利亚大马士革
Damascus, Syria

叙利亚大马士革国家博物馆藏
National Museum of Damascus

釉陶双耳罐
Double-Handled Glazed Ceramic Jar

公元 200 年
200 A.D.

长 27、宽 18 厘米
Length 27 cm, Width 18 cm

叙利亚多拉奥布斯
Douraa Oroubos, Syria

叙利亚大马士革国家博物馆藏
National Museum of Damascus

灰岩泰德穆尔墓碑雕像
Tadmur Limestone Gravestone Figurine

公元 200 年
200 A.D.
长 55、宽 43、厚 25 厘米
Length 55 cm, Width 43 cm, Thickness 25 cm

叙利亚泰德穆尔
Tadmur, Syria
叙利亚大马士革国家博物馆藏
National Museum of Damascus

长方形人物石雕像
Rectangular Stone Board

公元 200 年
200 A.D.
长 21、宽 12、厚 9 厘米
Length 21 cm, Width 12 cm, Thickness 9 cm

叙利亚贾巴尔
Jabbar, Syria
叙利亚大马士革国家博物馆藏
National Museum of Damascus

灰岩泰德穆尔墓碑雕像
Tadmur Limestone Gravestone Figurine

公元 200 年
200 A.D.

长 53.5、宽 43.5、厚 25 厘米
Length 53.5 cm, Width 43.5 cm, Thickness 25 cm

叙利亚泰德穆尔
Tadmur, Syria

叙利亚大马士革国家博物馆藏
National Museum of Damascus

泰德穆尔纺织品
Tadmur Textiles

公元 200 年
200 A.D.

长 33、宽 25 厘米
Length 33 cm, Width 25 cm

叙利亚泰德穆尔
Tadmur, Syria

叙利亚大马士革国家博物馆藏
National Museum of Damascus

这批纺织品残片发现于叙利亚泰德穆尔（阿拉伯语，意为"椰枣丰盛的土地"）——即帕尔米拉城（Palmyra）。帕尔米拉是丝绸之路上的重要商贸城市。公元 2 世纪，叙利亚贸易城市佩特拉被罗马人攻陷后逐渐衰落，帕尔米拉逐渐取代了其在商贸中的地位。此地干燥的气候使大量的纺织品得以保存。根据对当地出土织物材质和纺织技术的研究，发现不少来自中国的丝织品在此地被拆解并重新编织，以制作出符合西方需求的织物，一些织物上还能看到中国、伊朗等地的纹样元素。这些织物残片无疑显示出丝绸在东西方交流方面的重要意义。

灰岩泰德穆尔墓碑雕像

Tadmur Limestone Gravestone
Featuring Two Women

公元 200 年
200 A.D.

长 58、宽 63、厚 20 厘米
Length 58 cm, Width 63 cm, Thickness 20 cm

叙利亚泰德穆尔
Tadmur, Syria

叙利亚大马士革国家博物馆藏
National Museum of Damascus

灰岩石雕板
Limestone Board

公元 200 年
200 A.D.

长 57、宽 50、厚 23 厘米
Length 57 cm, Width 50 cm, Thickness 23 cm

叙利亚泰德穆尔
Tadmur, Syria

叙利亚大马士革国家博物馆藏
National Museum of Damascus

釉陶碗
Ceramic Bowl

公元 1200 年
1200 A.D.

高 9、直径 20 厘米
Height 9 cm, Diameter 20 cm

叙利亚大马士革国家博物馆藏
National Museum of Damascus

青花釉陶壶
Ceramic Blue-and-white Jar

公元 1200 年
1200 A.D.

高 20、直径 10 厘米
Height 20 cm, Diameter 10 cm

叙利亚大马士革国家博物馆藏
National Museum of Damascus

釉陶碗
Ceramic Bowl

公元 1200 – 1300 年
1200 – 1300 A.D.
高 20、直径 9 厘米
Height 20 cm, Diameter 9 cm

叙利亚大马士革国家博物馆藏
National Museum of Damascus

釉陶油灯
Ceramic Oil Lamp

公元 1200 – 1300 年
1200 – 1300 A.D.
长 20、宽 9 厘米
Length 20 cm, Width 9 cm

叙利亚大马士革国家博物馆藏
National Museum of Damascus

釉陶壶
Glazed Ceramic Pitcher

公元 1200 – 1300 年
1200 – 1300 A.D.
高 14、直径 12.5 厘米
Height 14 cm, Diameter 12.5 cm

叙利亚大马士革国家博物馆藏
National Museum of Damascus

彩绘釉陶碗
Painted Glazed Pottery Bowl

公元 1300 年
1300 A.D.
高 10、直径 20 厘米
Height 10 cm, Diameter 20 cm

叙利亚大马士革国家博物馆藏
National Museum of Damascus

伊斯兰式单耳釉陶壶
Islamic Single Handled Ceramic Pitcher

公元 1300 – 1400 年
1300 – 1400 A.D.
高 22、直径 17 厘米
Height 22 cm, Diameter 17 cm

叙利亚大马士革国家博物馆藏
National Museum of Damascus

　　此壶为低温烧制而成的粗陶材质，窄口，收肩，圆腹，小底，单把手。壶整体造型简洁质朴，又不乏装饰性。壶身中下部较为光滑，上部装饰阿拉伯文书法，可能为模具压制而成。此类器皿通常作为盛水器。

釉陶盘
Ceramic Plate

公元 1300 – 1400 年
1300 – 1400 A.D.
高 7.5、直径 27 厘米
Height 7.5 cm, Diameter 27 cm

叙利亚大马士革国家博物馆藏
National Museum of Damascus

梨状陶球
Pear-shaped Clay Ball

公元 1300 – 1400 年
1300 – 1400 A.D.
高 11.1、直径 8.9 厘米
Height 11.1 cm, Diameter 8.9 cm

叙利亚大马士革国家博物馆藏
National Museum of Damascus

黑线条纹釉陶碗
Ceramic Bowl with Black Lines

约公元 1300 – 1400 年
Circa 1300 – 1400 A.D.
高 24.5、直径 11.3 厘米
Height 24.5 cm, Diameter 11.3 cm

叙利亚大马士革国家博物馆藏
National Museum of Damascus

土库曼斯坦
Turkmenistan

镶宝石镀金银饰
Female Accessory

公元 19 – 20 世纪
19th – 20th Century A.D.

通高 15 厘米（不含垂饰），重 212 克
Height 15 cm (without hangings), Weight
212 g

土库曼斯坦国家博物馆与国家文化中心藏
The State Museum of the State Cultural
Centre of Turkmenistan

　　此件被称为"Dagdan"的银饰，形制如童裙。银片上镀金并镶有红、绿、蓝等色宝石，下端挂坠镶嵌红色宝石的银链穗带。这种银饰是结婚时新娘佩戴的装饰品，绣满花纹且镶有数排寓意驱恶辟邪的珠宝。据土库曼人的传说，年轻貌美的女子容易招引邪灵滋扰，新娘穿着礼服行走时，衣服上的装饰发出清亮响声能够驱散邪灵。

五节镀金银臂钏

Bracelets

公元 19 – 20 世纪
19th – 20th Century A.D.
高 11.2 厘米，重 614 克
Height 11.2 cm, Weight 614 g

土库曼斯坦国家博物馆与国家文化中心藏
The State Museum of the State Cultural Centre
of Turkmenistan

女性圆形镀金银饰

Female Accessory

公元 19 – 20 世纪
19th – 20th Century A.D.
直径 15.7 厘米，重 145 克
Diameter 15.7 cm, Weight 145 g

土库曼斯坦国家博物馆与国家文化中心藏
The State Museum of the State Cultural Centre of
Turkmenistan

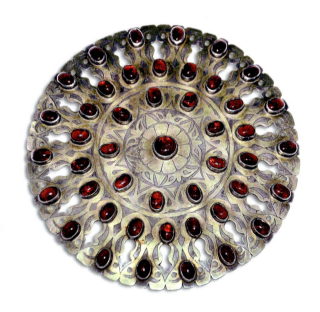

有垂饰的女性镀金银饰
Female Accessory with Hangings

公元 19 – 20 世纪
19th – 20th Century A.D.

宽 23 厘米，重 411 克
Width 23 cm, Weight 411 g

土库曼斯坦国家博物馆与国家文化中心藏
The State Museum of the State Cultural Centre of Turkmenistan

三角形镀金银饰
Female Accessory with Hangings

公元 19 – 20 世纪
19th – 20th Century A.D.

宽 32 厘米，重 1113 克
Width 32 cm, Weight 1113 g

土库曼斯坦国家博物馆与国家文化中心藏
The State Museum of the State Cultural Centre of Turkmenistan

　　此类饰品被称为"Tumar"，在三角形镀金银牌上镶满红色宝石，底端挂有 17 条珠饰挂坠。这种三角形饰物，是包括土库曼人在内的中亚多民族的护身符，既可置于房屋内，也可随身携带，用于驱鬼辟邪。

镀金银吊坠

Female Accessory

公元 19 – 20 世纪
19th – 20th Century A.D.

长 25.2 厘米，重 338 克
Length 25.2 cm, Weight 338 g

土库曼斯坦国家博物馆与国家文化中心藏
The State Museum of the State Cultural
Centre of Turkmenistan

女性带提手方形银饰

Female Accessory

公元 19 – 20 世纪
19th – 20th Century A.D.

立面长 15.3、宽 14.1 厘米，重 629 克
Length of facade 15.3 cm, Width 14.1 cm,
Weight 629 g

土库曼斯坦国家博物馆与国家文化中心藏
The State Museum of the State Cultural
Centre of Turkmenistan

白色披肩

White Cape

公元 19 – 20 世纪
19th – 20th Century A.D.

长 105、宽 69 厘米
Length 105 cm, Width 69 cm

土库曼斯坦国家博物馆与国家文化中心藏
The State Museum of the State Cultural Centre of Turkmenistan

披肩呈扇形，以白色布为地，挂坠红色宝石、珍珠等饰品。披肩底端缀有红、蓝、绿线组成的穗带。这种华贵典雅的披肩，是新娘婚礼上穿着的传统服饰。

蓝紫色大方巾
Purplish Blue Big Scarf

公元 20 世纪
20th Century A.D.

长 284、宽 189 厘米
Length 284 cm, Width 189 cm

土库曼斯坦国家博物馆与国家文化中心藏
The State Museum of the State Cultural Centre
of Turkmenistan

绿色丝质地毯
Green Silk Carpet

公元 21 世纪
21st Century A.D.

长 78、宽 59 厘米
Length 78 cm, Width 59 cm

土库曼斯坦国家博物馆与国家文化中心藏
The State Museum of the State Cultural Centre
of Turkmenistan

阿拉伯联合酋长国
The United Arab Emirates

燧石箭头

Flint Arrowhead

公元前 5000 – 前 4000 年
5000 – 4000 B.C.

阿拉伯联合酋长国乌姆盖温 2 号遗址
Umm Al Quwain No. 2 site, United Arab Emirates
阿拉伯联合酋长国乌姆盖温国家博物馆藏
National Museum of Umm Al Quwain

（印章）

（印纹）

石圆筒印章
Schist Stone

公元前 3000 – 前 2000 年
3000 – 2000 B.C.

长 4.1、直径 1.2 厘米
Length 4.1 cm, Diameter 1.2 cm

阿拉伯联合酋长国泰尔·阿布拉克遗址
Tell Abraq site, United Arab Emirates

阿拉伯联合酋长国乌姆盖温国家博物馆藏
National Museum of Umm Al Quwain

　　此印章于 1989 年出土于阿拉伯联合酋长国泰尔·阿布拉克遗址，为圆筒形。上图左为印章，右为印纹。印章表面刻有连续的图案纹样，使用者可以通过推滚印章盖印。这种圆筒形印章于公元前 4000 至前 1000 年间在近东地区广泛流行，苏萨等伊朗西南地区也有类似的实物。此印章图案与伊朗苏萨发现的埃兰中期（公元前 1500– 前 1000 年）大批印章上的图案相似。

绿泥石容器
Chlorite Vessel

铁器时代
Iron Age

高 7.2、口部直径 6.2 厘米
Height 7.2 cm, Diameter of mouth 6.2 cm

阿拉伯联合酋长国泰尔·阿布拉克遗址
Tell Abraq site, United Arab Emirates

阿拉伯联合酋长国乌姆盖温国家博物馆藏
National Museum of Umm Al Quwain

石水槽形器
Stone Spout

公元 1 世纪
1st Century A.D.
高 10、直径 25.5 厘米
Height 10 cm, Diameter 25.5 cm

阿拉伯联合酋长国艾杜尔遗址
Ed–Dour site, United Arab Emirates
阿拉伯联合酋长国乌姆盖温国家博物馆藏
National Museum of Umm Al Quwain

青铜灯
Bronze Lamp

公元 1 世纪
1st Century A.D.
长 13.3 厘米
Length 13.3 cm

阿拉伯联合酋长国艾杜尔遗址
Ed–Dour site, United Arab Emirates
阿拉伯联合酋长国乌姆盖温国家博物馆藏
National Museum of Umm Al Quwain

　　此铜灯出自阿拉伯联合酋长国乌姆盖温海岸的港口城市艾杜尔。铜灯由灯柄、灯身与灯嘴组成，整体形状如一件小茶壶。灯身顶部有圆形注油孔，原本应配盖。灯体一头有突出的灯口，开口较宽，用于安插连接灯体内灯油的灯芯。环形灯柄上还附加了 U 字形结构。从整体造型上看，这盏青铜灯与古罗马时期的早期油灯极为相似。古罗马文献曾记载艾杜尔是当时重要的对外贸易城市之一，艾杜尔的考古遗存证实了当地与地中海地区有着广泛的物质文化交流。

玛瑙挂饰

Gemstone Stone

公元 1 世纪
1ˢᵗ Century A.D.
长 20.5 厘米
Length 20.5 cm

阿拉伯联合酋长国艾杜尔遗址
Ed-Dour site, United Arab Emirates
阿拉伯联合酋长国乌姆盖温国家博物馆藏
National Museum of Umm Al Quwain

釉陶杯

Beaker

后祖尔法时期
Post Julfar

高 15、直径 7、圈足直径 7.05、圈足高 1.05 厘米
Height 15 cm, Diameter 7 cm, Diameter of ring foot 7.05 cm,
Height of ring foot 1.05 cm

阿拉伯联合酋长国拉斯海马国家博物馆藏
National Museum of Ras Al Khaimah

葬礼铭文石膏板（复制品）

Lime Plaster Block with Funerary Inscription (Replica)

公元前 3 世纪末
Late 3rd Century B.C.

宽 87、高 52、厚 16 厘米
Width 87 cm, Height 52 cm, Thickness 16 cm

阿拉伯联合酋长国米雷哈
Mleiha, United Arab Emirates
阿拉伯联合酋长国沙迦考古总机构藏
Sharjah Archaeology Authority

　　这块刻有铭文的石膏板是在米雷哈的一座大型墓穴中被发现的。其中央的铭文用阿拉伯北部方言写就，内容是一个名叫阿穆德（Amud）的人为其父建造了一座墓碑。其父名字同样是阿穆德（Amud），是戈尔（Gur）的儿子，阿里（Ali）的孙子。父子俩都曾是阿曼国王手下的检察官。石膏板边缘的亚拉姆语铭文基本是重复上述内容，但多了一个日期 90 或 97。该墓志铭首次提到了阿曼王国。

双耳釉陶瓶
Pottery Vase

公元前 2 – 前 1 世纪
2nd – 1st Century B.C.

直径 35.1、底径 15.28、高 52.80、口径 18.37 厘米
Diameter 35.1 cm, Bottom diameter 15.28 cm,
Height 52.80 cm, Diameter of mouth 18.37 cm

阿拉伯联合酋长国米雷哈
Mleiha, United Arab Emirates

阿拉伯联合酋长国沙迦考古总机构藏
Sharjah Archaeology Authority

此类大型釉陶瓶，配有装饰性手柄、瓶颈和瓶肩带有罗纹和条纹装饰。这种绿黄渐进色的釉面花瓶在阿曼半岛很受欢迎，多发现于米雷哈地区的陪葬品中，有时一起出土的还有滤酒器、长柄勺或碗。这类陶瓶可能是用于盛酒的容器。与米雷哈的多数釉面陶器一样，这类陶瓶也是从美索不达米亚南部（伊拉克）进口的。

银币
Coin

公元 1 世纪
1st Century A.D.
直径 2.5、厚 0.5 厘米，重 15 克
Diameter 2.5 cm, Thickness 0.5 cm, Weight 15 g

阿拉伯联合酋长国米雷哈
Mleiha, United Arab Emirates
阿拉伯联合酋长国沙迦考古总机构藏
Sharjah Archaeology Authority

银币
Coin

公元 1 世纪
1st Century A.D.
直径 1.09、厚 0.2 厘米
Diameter 1.09 cm, Thickness 0.2 cm

阿拉伯联合酋长国米雷哈
Mleiha, United Arab Emirates
阿拉伯联合酋长国沙迦考古总机构藏
Sharjah Archaeology Authority

银币
Coin

公元 1 世纪
1st Century A.D.
直径 1.54、厚 0.31 厘米
Diameter 1.54 cm, Thickness 0.31 cm

阿拉伯联合酋长国米雷哈
Mleiha, United Arab Emirates
阿拉伯联合酋长国沙迦考古总机构藏
Sharjah Archaeology Authority

　　此枚银币是根据亚历山大大帝及其塞琉古帝国一脉的继业者们发行的硬币仿造的。银币正面的赫拉克勒斯头裹尼米亚狮皮，背面是右手托举着一匹马的宙斯神坐像。

德拉克马银币
Drachma Coin

公元 1 世纪
1st Century A.D.
直径 2.44、厚 0.45 厘米
Diameter 2.44 cm, Thickness 0.45 cm

阿拉伯联合酋长国迪巴希森
Dibba al Hisn, United Arab Emirates
阿拉伯联合酋长国沙迦考古总机构藏
Sharjah Archaeology Authority

德拉克马银币
Drachma Coin

公元 1 世纪
1st Century A.D.
直径 2.52、厚 0.45 厘米
Diameter 2.52 cm, Thickness 0.45 cm

阿拉伯联合酋长国迪巴希森
Dibba al Hisn, United Arab Emirates
阿拉伯联合酋长国沙迦考古总机构藏
Sharjah Archaeology Authority

石罐
Jar

公元 1 – 2 世纪
1st – 2nd Century A.D.
直径 10 厘米
Diameter 10 cm

阿拉伯联合酋长国米雷哈
Mleiha, United Arab Emirates
阿拉伯联合酋长国沙迦考古总机构藏
Sharjah Archaeology Authority

　　此石罐采用当地的筋脉石制成，颇有分量。其形状并不完全对称，表明其为当地生产的仿制品。而其仿制的对象是那些从阿拉伯半岛南部（也门）进口的，用于盛装昂贵的芳香剂或油膏，由方解石或所谓的"雪花石膏"制成的花瓶。这些仿制品很可能也是用来装芳香剂或油膏的。

石罐
Jar

公元 1 – 2 世纪
1st – 2nd Century A.D.
宽 6.5、高 16.5 厘米
Width 6.5 cm, Height 16.5 cm

阿拉伯联合酋长国米雷哈
Mleiha, United Arab Emirates
阿拉伯联合酋长国沙迦考古总机构藏
Sharjah Archaeology Authority

石雕像
Statue

公元 1 – 3 世纪
1st – 3rd Century A.D.
宽 6.44、高 14.82、厚 4.97 厘米
Width 6.44 cm, Height 14.82 cm, Thickness 4.97 cm

阿拉伯联合酋长国米雷哈
Mleiha, United Arab Emirates
阿拉伯联合酋长国沙迦考古总机构藏
Sharjah Archaeology Authority

绿色玻璃瓶
Bottle/Unguentarium

公元 1 – 3 世纪
1st – 3rd Century A.D.
直径 8.55、高 12.4 厘米
Diameter 8.55 cm, Height 12.4 cm

阿拉伯联合酋长国迪巴
Dibba, United Arab Emirates
阿拉伯联合酋长国沙迦考古总机构藏
Sharjah Archaeology Authority

青瓷碗
Celadon Dish

公元 13 世纪
13th Century A.D.
直径 21.2、底径 5.41、高 9 厘米
Diameter 21.2 cm, Bottom diameter 5.41 cm, Height 9 cm

阿拉伯联合酋长国迪巴希森
Dibba al Hisn, United Arab Emirates
阿拉伯联合酋长国沙迦考古总机构藏
Sharjah Archaeology Authority

青瓷碟
Celadon Dish

公元 15 世纪
15th Century A.D.
直径 34.5、底径 19、高 7 厘米
Diameter 34.5 cm, Bottom diameter 19 cm, Height 7 cm

阿拉伯联合酋长国豪尔费坎
Khor Fakkan, United Arab Emirates
阿拉伯联合酋长国沙迦考古总机构藏
Sharjah Archaeology Authority

青花盘
Blue and White Dish

公元 16 世纪
16th Century A.D.
直径 33、底径 17.2、高 6.1 厘米
Diameter 33 cm, Bottom diameter 17.2 cm, Height 6.1 cm

阿拉伯联合酋长国豪尔费坎
Khor Fakkan, United Arab Emirates
阿拉伯联合酋长国沙迦考古总机构藏
Sharjah Archaeology Authority

中华人民共和国
The People's Republic of China

文明初现

距今 10000 年前后，中国进入新石器时代。距今 5800 年前后，黄河、长江中下游以及西辽河等流域出现了文明起源迹象。距今 3800 年前后，中原地区形成了更为成熟的文明形态，并向四方辐射文化影响。中华文明在起源与早期发展阶段形成的多元一体格局、兼容革新能力，以及从中孕育出的共同文化积淀、心理认同、礼制传统，奠定了中华文明绵延不断发展的基础。

THE DAWN OF CIVILIZATION

Around 10,000 years ago, ancient China entered the Neolithic Age. Nearly 5,800 years ago, the buds of civilization sprouted in the middle and lower reaches of the Yellow River, Yangtze River and Xiliao River Basin. Around 3,800 years ago, a more mature form of civilization appeared in the Central Plain region of ancient China, whose cultural influence radiated outward. The pluralistic form of Chinese civilization at its birth and early stages of development, and the ability to innovate yet maintain a common culture, psychological identity and system of ritual traditions, laid the foundation for the continuous development of Chinese civilization.

人面鱼纹彩陶盆

Colored Clay Basin Painted with
Human Face and Fish

约公元前5000 – 前3000年（新石器时代仰韶文化）
Circa 5000 – 3000 B.C. (Yangshao Culture, Neolithic
Period)

高 16、口径 41 厘米
Height 16 cm, Diameter of mouth 41 cm

1974 年陕西省西安市临潼区姜寨遗址出土
Unearthed from Jiangzhai site, Lintong District, Xi 'an,
Shaanxi Province, 1974

陕西历史博物馆藏
Shaanxi History Museum

　　人面鱼纹图案是仰韶文化众多陶器纹饰中最
有特色的纹饰，应与当时的信仰和经济生活有关。
姜寨史前居民过着以农业生产为主的定居生活，
兼营采集和渔猎，这种鱼纹装饰应是他们生活的
写照。

玉猪龙
Jade Animal

约公元前 4500 – 前 3000 年（新石器时代红山文化）
Circa 4500 – 3000 B.C. (Hongshan Culture, Neolithic Period)
高 14.1、宽 10.4 厘米
Height 14.1 cm, Width 10.4 cm

天津博物馆藏
Tianjin Museum

玉琮
Jade Cylinder

约公元前 3300 – 前 2300 年(新石器时代良渚文化）
Circa 3300 – 2300 B.C. (Liangzhu Culture, Neolithic Period)
高 5.2、射径 8.2、孔径 6.4 厘米
Height 5.2 cm, Outer Diameter 8.2 cm,
Inner Diameter 6.4 cm

1996 – 1998 年浙江省杭州市余杭瑶山遗址出土
Unearthed from Yao hill site in Yuhang District, Hangzhou, Zhejiang Province, 1996 – 1998

浙江省博物馆藏
Zhejiang Provincial Museum

玉琮是新石器时代最具代表性的玉礼器之一，也是神人兽面纹神徽的主要载体之一。其主要功能是祭祀与随葬。晚期玉琮节数增多，神人兽面纹大为简化，仅用突起的带状纹饰表现眼和嘴，随葬数量明显增多，象征财富的功能日益突出。

彩绘陶盆

Painted Clay Basin

约公元前 2500 – 前 2000 年（新石器时代陶寺文化）
Circa 2500 – 2000 B.C. (Longshan Culture, Neolithic Period)

高 19.3、口径 46.5 厘米
Height 19.3 cm, Diameter of mouth 46.5 cm

1978 – 1985 年山西襄汾陶寺遗址出土
Unearthed from Taosi site, Xiangfen, Shanxi Province, 1978 – 1985

中国社会科学院考古研究所藏
Institute of Archaeology, Chinese Academy of Social Sciences

玉钺

Jade Yue (Axe)

约公元前 2300 – 前 2000 年（新石器时代陶寺文化晚期）
Circa 2300 – 2000 B.C. (Late Stage of Longshan Culture, Neolithic Period)

长 10、宽 9.7 厘米
Length 10 cm, Width 9.7 cm

1979 年陕西省神木县石峁遗址附近采集
Collected from Shimao site near Shenmu County, Shaanxi Province, 1979

陕西历史博物馆藏
Shaanxi History Museum

镶嵌绿松石兽面纹青铜牌饰

Bronze Turquoise-inlaid Plaque with an Animal Face

约公元前 21 – 前 17 世纪
Circa 21st – 17th century B.C.

高 14.6、宽 10.1 厘米
Height 14.6 cm, Width 10.1 cm

1987 年河南省偃师县二里头遗址出土
Unearthed from Erlitou site, Yanshi County, Henan Province,1987

中国社会科学院考古研究所藏
Institute of Archaeology, Chinese Academy of Social Sciences

　　此牌饰是一种极具二里头文化特色的器物，它在圆角束腰形青铜薄片上铸出兽面纹，再以细小的绿松石片镶嵌其中。随葬这种牌饰的都是贵族墓，一般放置在墓主人胸腹部附近。二里头文化镶嵌绿松石牌饰上的兽面纹，开创了商周青铜器兽面纹的先河。

刻辞卜甲

Oracular Turtle Shell

约公元前 1600 – 前 1046 年（商代）
Circa 1600 – 1046 B.C. (Shang Dynasty)

长 19.3、宽 12.0 厘米
Length 19.3 cm, Width 12 cm

1991 年河南省安阳市花园庄东地出土
Unearthed from the eastern area of Huayuanzhuang, Anyang, Henan Province, 1991

中国社会科学院考古研究所藏
Institute of Archaeology, Chinese Academy of Social Sciences

　　占卜用的龟甲。刻在龟甲兽骨上的卜辞、验辞等文字，即为甲骨文。占卜时先钻凿、再火灼。据灼烧之裂纹推测吉凶，决定行止。殷墟出土的甲骨已有 15 万片左右，对甲骨的研究已成为中国考古学的一门分支学科——甲骨学。甲骨文释读对中国古代社会史、科技史和古文字学、语言学研究具有重要意义。

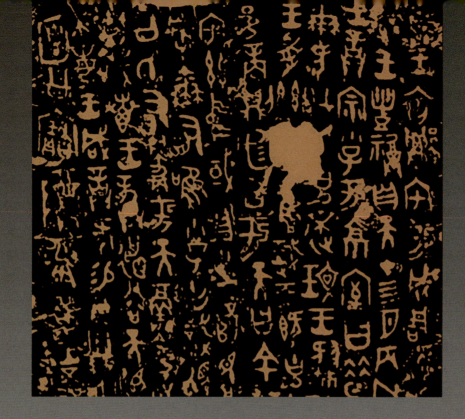

青铜何尊

Bronze He Zun (Ritual Wine Vessel)

公元前 1046 – 前 771 年（西周）
1046 – 771 B.C. (Western Zhou Dynasty)

通高 39、口径 28.6 厘米
Height 39 cm, Diameter of mouth 28.6 cm

1963 年出土于陕西省宝鸡市贾村
Unearthed from Jia Village, northeast suburb of Baoji, Shaanxi Province, 1963

宝鸡青铜器博物院藏
Baoji Bronze Ware Museum

此尊是距今 3000 年前一个名叫"何"的贵族为了纪念周王对自己的训诰而铸造的青铜礼器。

器内底部铸有 122 字铭文，讲述的是周成王（姬诵）不忘初心，继承父志，在"天下之中"的洛阳，营建都城（成周）的历史。其中有一句"余其宅兹中国，自兹乂民"，意思是：我要住在中央地区，从这里治理民众。这是"中国"一词最早的文字记录。

 在亚洲文明对话大会开幕式的"亚洲文物精品展"展出

礼制与思想

　　约 3000 多年前，以宗法制为基础的礼乐制度逐渐形成。2000 多年前的春秋战国时期，中国出现百家争鸣的盛况，老子、孔子、墨子等都创建了博大精深的思想体系。几千年来，孔子创立的儒家学说以及在此基础上发展起来的儒家思想，对中华文明和中国社会产生了深刻的影响。

THE RITUAL SYSTEM AND WAY OF THINKING

　　More than 3,000 years ago, a formal patriarchal system for music and ritual gradually came into being. More than 2,000 years ago, during the Spring and Autumn Period and the Warring States Period, the Hundred Schools of Thought sprang up all over China. Great representative thinkers such as Laozi, Confucius, and Mozi proposed extensive and profound ideological systems. For thousands of years, the Confucian Doctrine, created by Confucius, and the system of Confucianism, which developed from his way of thinking, has deeply influenced Chinese civilization and Chinese society.

铜甬钟（3 件）

Bronze Bells with Long Handles (3 Pieces)

西周（公元前 1046 – 前 771 年）
1046 – 771 B.C. (Western Zhou Dynasty)

通高 39.4、铣间 16.3 厘米
Height 39.4 cm, Width of mouth 16.3 cm

通高 31.3、铣间 15.6 厘米
Height 31.3 cm, Width of mouth 15.6 cm

通高 21、铣间 10 厘米
Height 21 cm, Width of mouth 10 cm

1958 年湖北省钟祥市花山水库窖藏出土
Unearthed near Huashan reservoir, Zhongxiang, Hubei
Province, 1958

湖北省博物馆藏
Hubei Provincial Museum

四十三年逨铜鼎

Bronze "Lai Ding" (Cauldron) in the 43rd
Year of King Xuan of Zhou

约公元前 1046 – 前 771 年（西周）
Circa 1046 – 771 B.C. (Western Zhou Dynasty)

高 57、宽 52 厘米
Height 57 cm, Width 52 cm

2003 年陕西省宝鸡市眉县杨家村出土
Unearthed from Yangjia Village, Mei County, Baoji,
Shaanxi Province, 2003

宝鸡青铜器博物院藏
Baoji Bronze Ware Museum

　　此鼎造型敦厚，口沿下饰变形兽面纹，腹部有
宽大的波曲纹，足上部饰有浮雕兽面。纹饰上皆设
宽厚的扉棱。鼎内铸有铭文 31 行，共计 316 字，
讲述了功臣逨为答谢王的赏赐，为祭祀亡父制作此
鼎的经过。铭文为研究西周册封制度和历法提供了
极其重要的资料。

马车（复原）
Carriage (Replica)

原件为公元前 475 – 前 221 年（战国）
The original: 475 – 221 B.C. (Warring States Period)

长 360、宽 296、高 180 厘米
Length 360 cm, Width 296 cm, Height 180 cm

原件于 2006 – 2008 年出土于甘肃省张家川马家塬墓地
The original was unearthed from Majiayuan tombs, Zhangjiachuan, Gansu Province, 2006 – 2008

甘肃省文物考古研究所藏
Gansu Provincial Institute of Archaeology and Cultural Relics

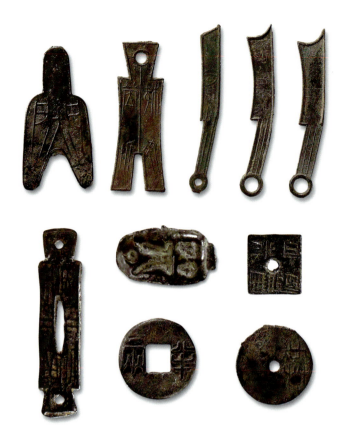

钱币（一组）
A Set of Ancient Coins

公元前 475 – 前 206 年（战国 – 秦）
475 – 206 B.C. (Warring States Period – Qin Dynasty)

征集
Collected

中国国家博物馆藏
National Museum of China

铜诏铁权
Iron Weight and Bronze Imperial Edict

公元前 221 – 前 206 年（秦代）
221 – 206 B.C. (Qin Dynasty)

通高 19、底径 25，诏版长 9、宽 9 厘米
Height 19 cm, Bottom diameter 25cm; Bronze Imperial Edict: Length 9 cm, Width 9 cm

1983 年甘肃省天水市秦城区出土
Unearthed from Qincheng District, Tianshui, Gansu Province, 1983

甘肃省博物馆藏
Gansu Provincial Museum

　　权为衡（天平）上使用的砝码。此铁权一侧镶嵌一青铜诏版，上阴刻篆书 6 行 40 字："廿六年，皇帝尽并兼天下诸侯，黔首大安，立号为皇帝，乃诏丞相状、绾，法、度、量，则不壹、歉疑者，皆明壹之。"这是秦代统一度量衡法令得以实施的直接证物。

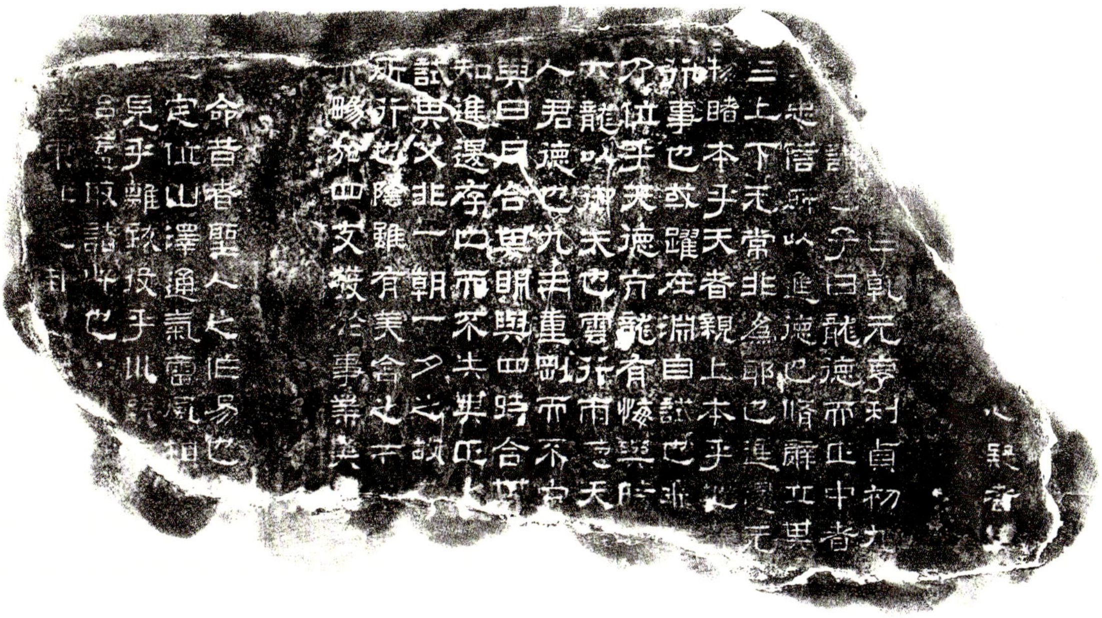

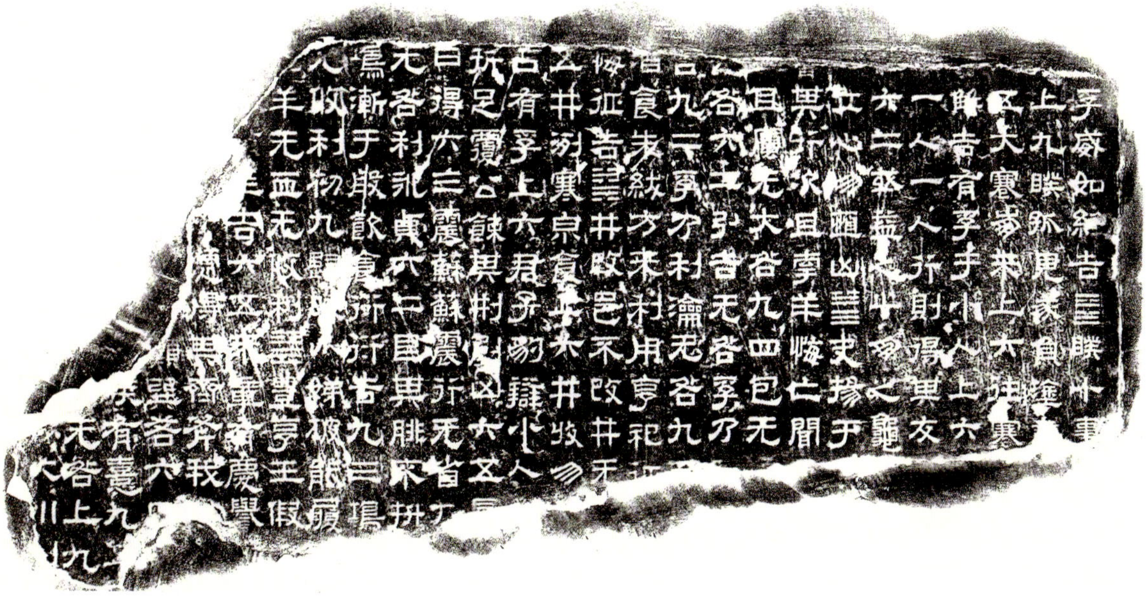

熹平石经拓片

Rubbing of Stone Tablet Recording the Confucian Classics during the Reign of Emperor Xiping

公元 25 – 220 年（东汉）

25 – 220 A.D. (Eastern Han Dynasty)

原石高 33、宽 62 厘米

Original stone: Height 33 cm, Width 62 cm

原石经 1929 年出土于河南省洛阳市大交村

Unearthed from Dajiao Village, Luoyang, Henan Province, 1929

西安碑林博物馆藏

Xi'an Beilin Museum

孔子圣迹图
Painting of *Traces of the Sage Confucius*

公元 1368 – 1644 年（明代）
1368 – 1644 A.D. (Ming Dynasty)
长 66、宽 41 厘米
Length 66 cm, Width 41 cm

孔子博物馆藏
Confucius Museum

孔子胜迹图以图画形式表现孔子一生事迹，此三张分别描绘的是"命名荣贶""夹谷会齐"和"职司乘田"。

职司乘田：孔子幼时丧父，家境贫寒。少年时丧母，曾在季氏手下任乘田吏，主管苑囿，放牧牛羊，工作尽心尽力，所牧养的牲畜茁壮，数量增多。

命名荣贶：孔子成婚之后，在第二年生了儿子，鲁昭公赐给他一条鲤鱼，孔子为了显耀国君的赏赐，给儿子取名孔鲤，字伯鱼，用志不忘君恩。

夹谷会齐：鲁定公十年（公元前 500 年），齐鲁两国国君相会于夹谷。齐国演奏四方之乐，孔子说两君相会，不能用夷狄之乐，迫使齐景公撤走乐舞。齐国又演奏宫中之乐，孔子批评说匹夫惑乱诸侯，迫使齐景公处罚乐人。因孔子的智慧，使鲁国在外交上取得了一次胜利。

铜关公立像
Bronze Statue of General Guan Yu

公元 1368 – 1644 年（明代）
1368 – 1644 A.D. (Ming Dynasty)
通高 56 厘米
Height 56 cm

武当博物馆藏
Wudang Museum

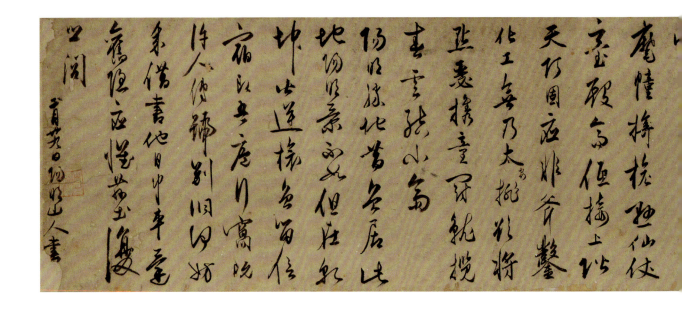

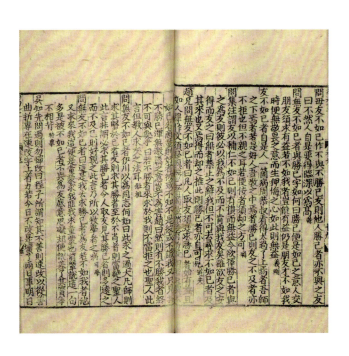

《朱子语类》 陈炜刻本

The Analects of Chu Hsi (Copied by Chen Wei on the Ninth Year under the Reign of Chenghua Emperor)

公元 1473 年（明成化九年）
1473 A.D. (9th year of Chenghua in Ming Dynasty)

纵 29.4、横 17.5 厘米
Height 29.4 cm, Width 17.5 cm

中国国家图书馆藏
National Library of China

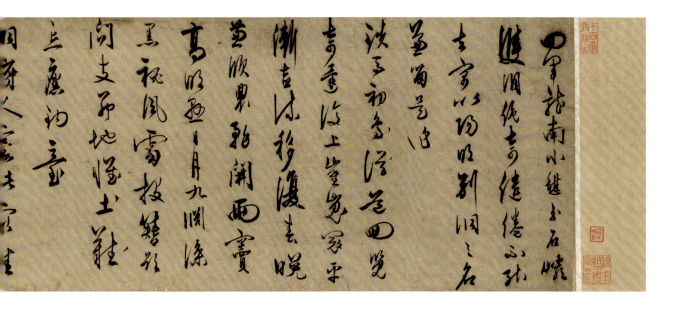

王守仁行草书《题阳明别洞三首》卷
Three Poems Written on *"Yangming Cave"*

公元 1518 年（明正德十八年）
1518 A.D. (18th year of Zhengde in Ming Dynasty)

纵 27、横 129.5 厘米
Height 27 cm, Width 129.5 cm

天津博物馆藏
Tianjin Museum

科学与技术

中国在古代天文学、地理学、数学、物理学、化学、生物学和医学等诸多领域取得了不朽的成就。指南针、火药、造纸和印刷术四大发明，以及十进位制、瓷器、丝绸等重大发明，不仅塑造了古代中国的面貌，也推动了世界历史的前进。

SCIENCE AND TECHNOLOGY

China made immortal achievements in ancient astronomy, geography, mathematics, physics, chemistry, biology and medicine. The Four Great Inventions (the compass, gunpowder, papermaking and printing) as well as other major inventions such as the decimal system, porcelain, and silk, not only displayed the features of ancient China, but also advanced the progress of human history.

铃形铜器
Bronze Bell-Shaped Implement

约公元前 2300 – 前 1900 年（新石器时代陶寺文化）
Circa 2300 - 1900 B.C. (Taosi Culture, Neolithic Period)

高 2.6、长 6.3 厘米
Height 2.6 cm, Length 6.3 cm

1983 年山西省襄汾县陶寺遗址出土
Unearthed from Taosi site, Xiangfen County, Shanxi
Province, 1983

中国社会科学院考古研究所藏
Institute of Archaeology, Chinese Academy of Social
Sciences

　　此为考古发现的年代最早的铜制礼乐器。其器
壁厚度不均，有铸造气孔。采用比较复杂的两块外
范与一块泥芯相组合的双合范技术铸造而成。

铜神兽
Bronze Mythical Beast

公元前 770 – 前 476 年（春秋）
770 – 476 B.C. (Spring and Autumn Period)

通高 48、长 47、宽 27 厘米
Height 48 cm, Length 47 cm, Width 27 cm

1990 年河南省淅川县徐家岭墓地 M9 出土
Unearthed from Xujialing tombs M9,
Xichuan County, Henan Province, 1990
河南省文物考古研究院藏
Henan Provincial Institute of Cultural
Heritage and Archaeology

曾侯乙铜尊盘

Bronze Zun (Ritual Wine Vessel) and Pan (Plate) of Marquis Yi of State Zeng

公元前 475 – 前 221 年（战国）
475 – 221 B.C. (Warring States Period)

盘高 23.5、盘口径 58 厘米，尊高 30.1、尊口径 25 厘米
Pan: Height 23.5 cm, Diameter of mouth 58 cm;
Zun: Height 30.1 cm, Diameter of mouth 25 cm

1978 年湖北省随州市曾侯乙墓出土
Unearthed from the tomb of Marquis Yi of State Zeng, Suizhou, Hubei Province, 1978

湖北省博物馆藏
Hubei Provincial Museum

此尊盘由上尊下盘两件器物组成。尊敞口，呈喇叭状，上饰蟠虺镂空花纹。颈部饰蕉叶形蟠虺纹，四只圆雕豹形伏兽攀附其上。躯体由透雕的蟠螭纹构成。腹、高足皆饰细密的蟠虺纹，其上加饰高浮雕虬龙四条，层次丰富，主次分明。盘直壁平底，四龙形蹄足，口沿上附有四只方耳，皆饰蟠虺纹，与尊口风格相同。四耳下各有两条扁形镂空夔龙，龙首下垂。四龙之间各有一圆雕式蟠龙，首伏于口沿，与盘腹蟠虺纹相互呼应。

此尊盘铸造工艺复杂，采用了陶范法、失蜡法、钎焊、铆接等多种工艺精工制作而成，造型优美，纹饰繁复。尊和盘上均有铭文，显示其为曾侯乙生前用器，故称为曾侯乙尊和曾侯乙盘，合称曾侯乙尊盘，是战国时期最复杂、最精美的青铜器之一。

错金银龙纹铜方案
Bronze Table Inlaid with Golden and Silver Dragon Pattern

公元前 475 – 前 221 年（战国）
475 – 221 B.C. (Warring States Period)

通高 36、长 47 厘米
Height 36 cm, Length 47 cm

1977 年河北省平山县中山王墓出土
Unearthed from the tomb of the King of Zhongshan State, Pingshan County, Hebei Province, 1977

河北省文物研究所藏
Cultural Relics Institute of Hebei Province

方案由底座、龙凤和框架三部分组成，底部是两雄两雌跪卧的梅花鹿，四龙四凤组成案身。四龙单首双尾，上吻托住斗拱，双尾向两侧盘环反勾住头上双角。其造型内收而外敞，动静结合，疏密得当，突破了商、周以来青铜器动物造型以浮雕或圆雕为主的传统手法。此外，四条龙头上各有一个斗拱，是战国时期的斗拱造型第一次以实物面貌生动再现。

此方案周身饰错金银花纹，集铸造、镶嵌、焊接等多种工艺于一体，复杂精致、巧夺天工。

青铜错银双翼神兽

Bronze inlaid with silver Mythical Winged Animal

公元前 475 – 前 221 年（战国）
475 – 221 B.C. (Warring States Period)

长 40、高 24 厘米
Length 40 cm, Height 24 cm

1977 年河北省平山县中山王墓出土
Unearthed from the tomb of the King of Zhongshan State,
Pingshan County, Hebei Province, 1977

河北省文物研究所藏
Cultural Relics Institute of Hebei Province

龙凤虎纹绣罗单衣衣袖

Single-layered Gusset Embroidered with Dragon, Phoenix and Tiger Patterns

公元前 475 – 前 221 年（战国）
475 – 221 B.C. (Warring States Period)

长 123.9、袖口宽 31.9、袖肩宽 67.7 厘米
Length 123.9 cm, Width of cuff 31.9 cm, Width of shoulder 67.7 cm

1982 年湖北省荆州市马山一号楚墓出土
Unearthed from Mashan Chu tomb No.1, Jingzhou, Hubei Province, 1982

荆州博物馆藏
Jingzhou Museum

鎏金铜蚕

Gilt Bronze Silk Worm

公元前 206 – 公元 220 年（汉代）
206 B.C. – 220 A.D. (Han Dynasty)

长 7.5 厘米
Length 7.5 cm

1969 年河北省静志寺塔基地宫出土
Unearthed from the Underground Chamber of the Pagoda in Jingzhi Temple, Hebei Province, 1969

定州博物馆藏
Dingzhou Museum

　　铜蚕呈仰头吐丝状，刻画精细，造型逼真，说明当时人们通过长期的桑蚕生产已熟悉蚕的生理结构。此件铜蚕制作于汉代，又在近千年后的北宋塔基地宫中被发现，说明丝织业在古代社会经济中一直备受重视。

鎏金铜长信宫灯
Gilt Bronze Human-shaped Lamp

公元前 206– 公元 25 年（西汉）
206 B.C. – 25 A.D. (Western Han Dynasty)

通高 48 厘米
Height 48 cm

1968 年出土于河北省满城县窦绾（中山靖王刘胜之妻）墓
Unearthed from the tomb of Dou Wan, wife of Liu Sheng, Prince Jing of Zhongshan, Mancheng County, Hebei Province, 1968

河北博物院藏
Hebei Museum

  此件铜鎏金宫灯的外形是一个跽坐执灯的宫女，左手托灯座，右手提灯罩，中空的衣袖和身体作为排烟管道，灯座底部盛水可以吸收烟尘，保持室内清洁。

  圆形灯盘可以转动开合，调节灯光照射方向和亮度。同时，宫灯的各个构件可以拆卸和清洗。

  此灯的结构造型，体现了 2000 多年前中国古人的环保理念和精巧工艺。

 在亚洲文明对话大会开幕式的"亚洲文物精品展"展出

 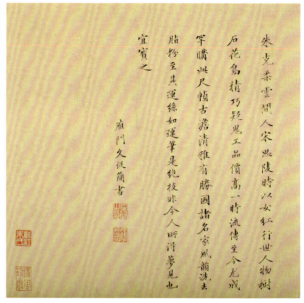

缂丝山茶蛱蝶图册

Ko-ssu (a technique used in weaving Chinese silk tapestry) Silk Painting with Camellia and Butterfly Patterns

公元 1127 – 1279 年（南宋）
1127 – 1279 A.D. (Southern Song Dynasty)

纵 25.6、横 25.3 厘米
Height 25.6 cm, Width 25.3 cm

辽宁省博物馆藏
Liaoning Provincial Museum

石日晷

Stone Sundial

公元前 206 – 公元 220 年（汉代）
206 B.C. – 220 A.D. (Han Dynasty)

高 3.5、正方形边长 27.6 厘米
Height 3.5 cm, Side length of the square 27.6 cm

1897 年内蒙古自治区呼和浩特市南托克托出土
Unearthed from Tokto County in the south of Hohhot, Inner Mongolia Autonomous Region, 1897

中国国家博物馆藏
National Museum of China

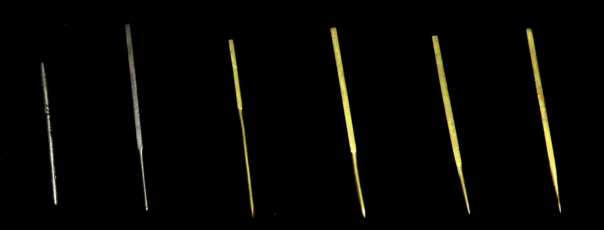

金医针、银医针
Gold Acupuncture Needle, Sliver Acupuncture Needle

公元前 206– 公元 25 年（西汉）
206 B.C. – 25 A.D. (Western Han Dynasty)

通长 7 厘米
Length 7 cm

1968 年河北省满城县汉中山靖王刘胜墓出土
Unearthed from tomb of Liu Sheng (Prince Jing of Western Han Dynasty), Mancheng County, Baoding, Hebei Province, 1968

河北博物院藏
Hebei Museum

医用长流银匜
Sliver Yi (Vessel Used for Feeding Children Medicine)

公元前 206– 公元 25 年（西汉）
206 B.C. – 25 A.D. (Western Han Dynasty)

高 3、口径 6.4、流长 6.6 厘米
Height 3 cm, Diameter of mouth 6.4 cm, Length of spout 6.6 cm

1968 年河北省满城县汉中山靖王刘胜墓出土
Unearthed from tomb of Liu Sheng (Prince Jing of Western Han Dynasty), Mancheng County, Baoding, Hebei Province, 1968

河北博物院藏
Hebei Museum

马圈湾纸

Maquanwan Paper

公元前 206 – 公元 25 年（西汉）
206 B.C. – 25 A.D. (Western Han Dynasty)

长 19、宽 10.5 厘米
Length 19 cm, Width 10.5 cm

1979 甘肃省敦煌市马圈湾烽燧出土
Unearthed from Maquanwan, Fengsui, Dunhuang,
Gansu Province, 1979

甘肃简牍博物馆藏
Gansu Bamboo Slips Museum

越窑凤头小执壶
Yue Kiln Phoenix Head Ewer

公元 618 – 907 年（唐代）
618 – 907 A.D. (Tang Dynasty)

高 6.8、腹围 4、底径 2.5 厘米
Height 6.8 cm, Abdominal perimeter 4 cm, Bottom diameter 2.5 cm

捐赠
Donated

浙江省博物馆藏
Zhejiang Provincial Museum

汝窑天青釉圆洗
Ru Kiln Glazed Sky-Blue Writing-brush Washer

公元 960 – 1279 年（宋代）
960 – 1279 A.D. (Song Dynasty)

口径 13、底径 8.9、高 3.3 厘米
Diameter of mouth 13 cm, Bottom diameter 8.9 cm, Height 3.3cm

故宫博物院藏
The Palace Museum

哥窑青釉双螭耳炉
Ge Kiln Celadon Censer with Two Dragon-shaped Handles

公元 960 – 1279 年（宋代）
960 – 1279 A.D. (Song Dynasty)

口径 11.9、底径 9.5、高 8.3 厘米
Diameter of mouth 11.9 cm, Foot diameter 9.5 cm, Height 8.3 cm

故宫博物院藏
The Palace Museum

青花釉里红开光贴塑盖罐
Blue and White Underglaze-Red Jar with Hallowed-out Lid

公元 1206 年 – 1368 年（元代）
1206 – 1368 A.D. (Yuan Dynasty)

通高 41、口径 15.5、足径 18.5 厘米
Height 41 cm, Diameter of mouth 15.5 cm, Foot diameter 18.5 cm

1964 年河北省保定市元代窖藏出土
Unearthed from Yuan Dyansty Hoard, Baoding, Hebei Province, 1964

河北博物院藏
Hebei Museum

此罐纹饰层次鲜明，综合绘画、堆塑、贴花等多种技法，是少有的把青花和釉里红、绘画和雕塑融于一体的元代青花瓷器。工匠们先模压成形，后组合粘贴完成。由于青花钴料高温下相对稳定，而釉里红主要着色剂是氧化铜，高温下容易挥发，同时烧制需要高超的技术手段和成熟的烧窑经验，这也是青花釉里红瓷器比较少见的原因。

元代瓷器器形多样，装饰手法繁多，釉彩各异，烧制技术有着革命性的创造，开创了明清和现代瓷器的新格局，以至于影响到世界陶瓷的发展。

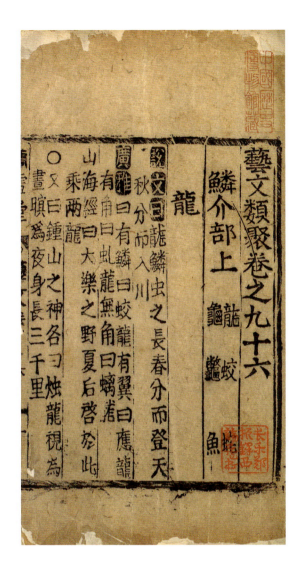

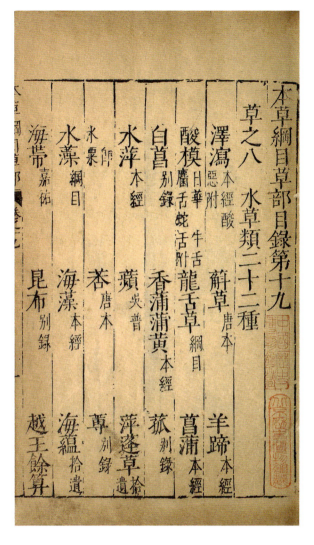

《艺文类聚》

Yiwen Leiju (A Chinese *Leishu* Encyclopedia)

公元 1368 – 1644 年（明代）
1368 – 1644 A.D. (Ming Dynasty)

长 24.5、宽 15 厘米
Length 24.5 cm, Width 15 cm

中国国家博物馆藏
National Museum of China

《本草纲目》

Compendium of Material Medica

公元 1368 – 1644 年（明代）
1368 – 1644 A.D. (Ming Dynasty)

长 27、宽 17 厘米
Length 27 cm, Width 17 cm

中国国家博物馆藏
National Museum of China

　　此著作共 52 卷，明代李时珍撰于嘉靖三十一年
(1552 年) 至万历六年 (1578 年)。此书采用"目随
纲举"的编写体例，故以"纲目"名书。书中收载
药物 1892 种，附药图 1000 余幅，阐明药物的性味、
主治、用药法则、产地、形态、采集、炮制、方剂
配伍等，并载附方 10000 余，是我国 16 世纪之前
药学集大成之作。

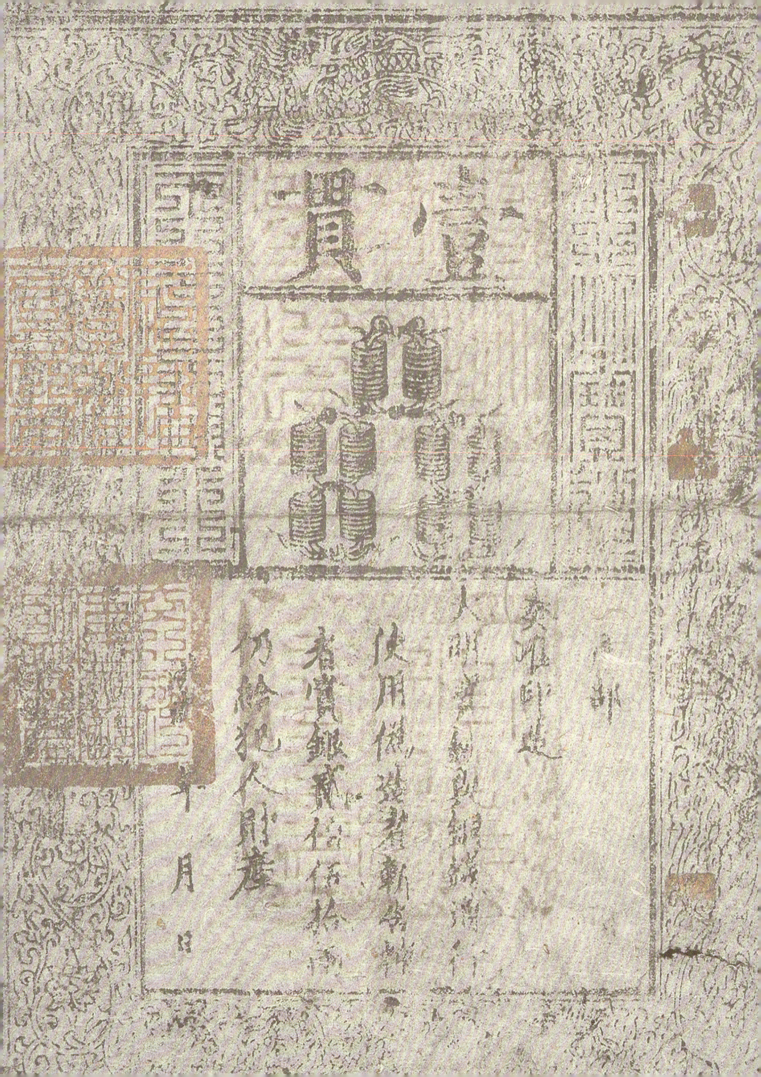

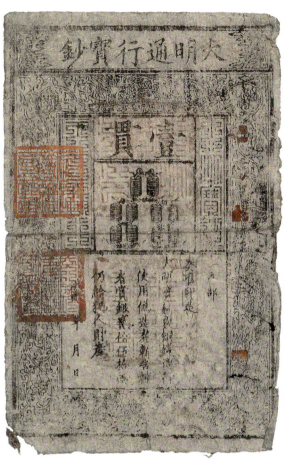

大明通行宝钞及印钞铜板

Da Ming Baochao Banknote and Its Printing
Plate

公元 1368 – 1644 年（明代）
1368 – 1644 A.D. (Ming Dynasty)

长 33、宽 22 厘米
Length 33 cm, Width 22 cm

中国国家博物馆藏
National Museum of China

文化与艺术

　　中华文化积淀着中华民族最深沉的精神追求，是中华民族生生不息、发展壮大的丰厚滋养。世代流传下来的美玉佳配、文房器玩、诗词戏曲、琴棋书画、典籍文献等，不仅是中华文化与艺术的凝结，更是人类文明宝库中的重要财富。

CULTURE AND ART

　　Chinese culture is the accumulation of Chinese people's most profound pursuits, which has generously nurtured China's endless growth and prosperity. All the fine jade, jewelry, treasures of scholar's studio, poetry, dramas, music, paintings, ancient books and records that were handed down from generation to generation, are not only a manifestation of Chinese culture and art, but also a treasure—trove of human civilization.

玉熊镇
Jade Bear Paperweight

公元前 206– 公元 25 年（西汉）
206 B.C. – 25 A.D. (Western Han Dynasty)

长 20.3、宽 8.3、高 6.6 厘米
Length 20.3 cm, Width 8.3 cm, Height 6.6 cm

1994 – 1995 年江苏省徐州市狮子山楚王墓出土
Unearthed from King of Chu's tomb in Lion Hill,
Xuzhou, Jiangsu Province, 1994 – 1995

徐州博物馆藏
Xuzhou Museum

龙形玉佩
Dragon-shaped Jade Pendant

公元前 206– 公元 25 年（西汉）
206 B.C. – 25 A.D. (Western Han Dynasty)

长 17.5、宽 10.2、厚 0.6 厘米
Length 17.5 cm, Width 10.2 cm, Thickness 0.6 cm

1994 – 1995 年江苏省徐州市狮子山楚王墓出土
Unearthed from King of Chu's tomb in Lion Hill,
Xuzhou, Jiangsu Province, 1994 – 1995

徐州博物馆藏
Xuzhou Museum

　　此件龙形玉佩呈"S"形，和田白玉，玉质温
润细腻。它继承了战国玉龙的雕琢风格，采用阴线
刻、浮雕和局部透雕等技法，把龙潜深渊、蛰伏待
时的意蕴刻划得淋漓尽致。玉龙眼睛下方有一钻
孔，为佩戴时的系穿用孔，表明这件玉龙为佩饰。

龙凤纹玉环
Jade Bracelet with Dragon and Phoenix Designs

公元前 206– 公元 25 年（西汉）
206 B.C. – 25 A.D. (Western Han Dynasty)

直径 7.9、孔径 4.1、厚 0.3 厘米
Diameter 7.9 cm, Inner diameter 4.1 cm,
Thickness 0.3 cm

1994 – 1995 年江苏省徐州市东洞山楚
王墓出土
Unearthed from King of Chu's tomb in
Dongdong Mountain, Xuzhou, Jiangsu
Province, 1994 – 1995

徐州博物馆藏
Xuzhou Museum

戏剧俑砖雕
Brick Featuring Opera Performers

公元 1115 – 1234 年（金代）
1115 – 1234 A.D. (Jin Dynasty)

俑高 20 – 22 厘米
Height of figurine 20 – 22 cm

1959 年山西省侯马市董氏墓出土
Unearthed from Dong Family tomb in Houma,
Shanxi Province, 1959

山西博物院藏
Shanxi Museum

　　侯马金代董氏墓以其精彩的砖雕戏俑闻名于
世，戏台上戏俑共五件，平均高约 20 厘米，并列
一排，从左至右分别为副净、末泥、装孤、引戏（装
旦）和副末五个角色。五个戏俑均经彩绘，色彩绚
丽，形象生动，具有代表性。

古琴

Guqin

公元 1127 – 1279 年（南宋）
1127 – 1279 A.D. (Southern Song Dynasty)

通长 123.9 厘米
Length 123.9 cm

天津博物馆藏
Tianjin Museum

围棋棋盘、棋子、棋罐

Go Board, Go Pieces, and Go Pieces Jar

公元 1368 – 1644 年（明代）
1368 – 1644 A.D. (Ming Dynasty)

棋盘边长 40.6 厘米，棋子直径 1.8 – 2.2 厘米
Side length of chessboard 40.6 cm, Diameter of go
pieces 1.8 – 2.2 cm

1971 年山东省邹县鲁荒王墓出土
Unearthed from Luhuang tomb in Zou County,
Shandong Province, 1971

山东博物馆藏
Shandong Museum

围棋，在中国古代称为弈，是古代棋类之鼻祖。春秋战国时期已在社会上流传，东汉中晚期开始盛行。南北朝时，文人尚清谈，因而弈风更盛，称为"手谈"。唐宋时，由于帝王喜爱，风行全国，发展成为中国的"国棋"。围棋作为一种文明的象征，流传至今的棋书、棋谱很多，但存世完整实物很少，鲁荒王的这副围棋是难得一见的珍品。

端砚

Inkstone Produced in Zhaoqing

公元 1368 – 1644 年（明代）
1368 – 1644 A.D. (Ming Dynasty)
高 4、长 22、宽 25.7 厘米
Height 4 cm, Length 22 cm, Width 25.7 cm

天津博物馆藏
Tianjin Museum

程君房仿古玉妙品墨

Ink Cake in Imitation of a Magnificent Ancient Jade

公元 1368 – 1644 年（明代）
1368 – 1644 A.D. (Ming Dynasty)
直径 5、高 0.9 厘米
Diameter 5 cm, Height 0.9 cm

天津博物馆藏
Tianjin Museum

紫檀木马尾大抓笔

Burmese Rosewood Thick Writing Brush Made of Horsetail Hair

公元 1368 – 1644 年（明代）
1368 – 1644 A.D. (Ming Dynasty)
长 43.5 厘米
Length 43.5 cm

天津博物馆藏
Tianjin Museum

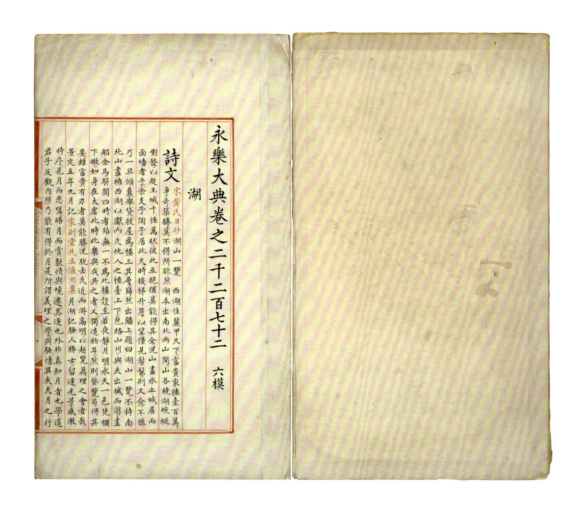

《永乐大典》（"湖"字卷）嘉靖内府录副写本

Yongle Dadian (The Yongle Encyclopedia), Hand-copied by Household Office during the Reign of Emperor Jiajing of Ming Dynasty

公元 1522 – 1566 年（明·嘉靖）
1522 – 1566 A.D. (the reign of Jiajing, Ming Dynasty)

长 50、宽 30 厘米
Length 50 cm, Width 30 cm

中国国家图书馆藏
National Library of China

《永乐大典》是明永乐元年（1403 年）至六年（1408 年）解缙等奉敕编纂的大型类书，全书共 22877 卷，是中国古代最大的"百科全书"。它汇集了明初以前的图书七八千种，保存了大量珍贵的古籍文献。现仅存约 400 册，星散于 8 个国家和地区的 30 个单位。清乾隆年间，四库馆臣编纂《四库全书》时，曾有从《永乐大典》中辑录文献资料的记录。

此卷 2272 至 2274，为"模"字韵"湖"字一册。原藏海外，2009 年回归。是明代嘉靖内府录副写本。国家图书馆原藏"湖"字两册，此册恰为中间部分，可使内容前后相缀。

金彩龙纹纸
Hand Scroll of Gold-painted Paper
with Dragon Designs

公元 1644 – 1911 年（清代）
1644 – 1911 A.D. (Qing Dynasty)

长 144、宽 44.2 厘米
Length 144 cm, Width 44.2 cm

天津博物馆藏
Tianjin Museum

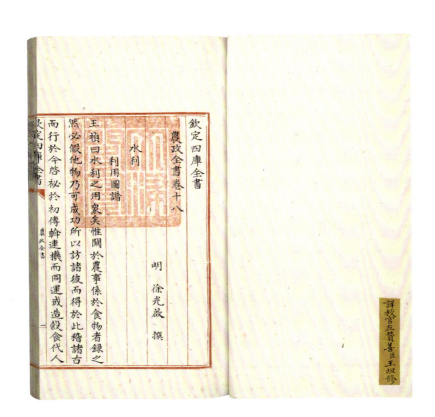

**《钦定文津阁四库全书》（《农政全书》
六十卷）清乾隆内府写本**

*Complete Library in Four Sections
(Nongzheng Quanshu, 60 Volumes)*
Hand-copied by Household Office during
the Reign of Emperor Qianlong of Qing
Dynasty

公元 1736 – 1795 年（清·乾隆）
1736 – 1795 A.D. (the reign of Qianlong, Qing Dynasty)

长 31.7、宽 20 厘米
Length 31.7 cm, Width 20 cm

中国国家图书馆藏
National Library of China

马麟《荷乡清夏图卷》

Painting Scroll of Lotus Fragrance Refreshing the Summer

公元 1127 – 1279 年（南宋）
1127 – 1279 A.D. (Southern Song Dynasty)

纵 41.7、横 495 厘米
Height 41.7 cm, Width 495 cm

辽宁省博物馆藏
Liaoning Provincial Museum

马麟是南宋马派画风的主要传人，其父马远与李唐、刘松年、夏珪并称"南宋四大家"。

此卷是马麟重要作品之一，再现了南宋时期杭州西湖的夏日盛景。画面绘垂柳拂岸，木桥横于碧波之上，四人散步其间。湖中船只穿梭，远方烟霭出没，山峦树木，隐约可见。构图为平远散点式，山石为斧劈皴，用墨有浓淡干湿变化，人物线条用笔中锋，赋色以汁绿为主，并用多种颜色，均显示出画家高超的艺术技巧。

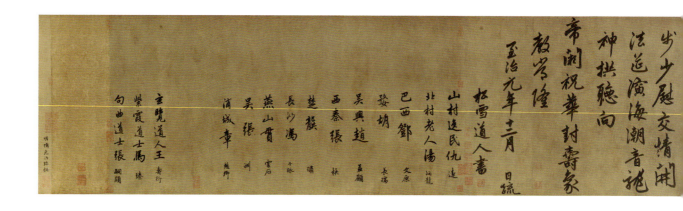

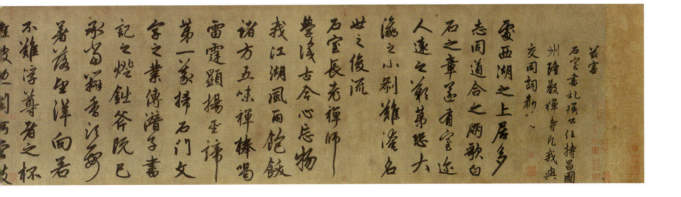

赵孟頫行书《为隆教禅寺石室长老疏卷》
Zhao Mengfu's Semi-cursive Calligraphic Work: *For the Abbot of Longjiao Temple*

公元 1321 年
1321 A.D.

纵 47.5、横 333.5 厘米
Height 47.5 cm, Width 333.5 cm

天津博物馆藏
Tianjin Museum

　　此卷书于元代至治元年（1321 年）十二月，时年赵孟頫 68 岁。用笔精致圆润厚重，线条粗细对比强烈，字体取势丰富和谐，结体疏朗宛转流美，气韵遒劲潇洒飘逸，通篇充溢着赵氏老年书法的姿媚雄健之气。

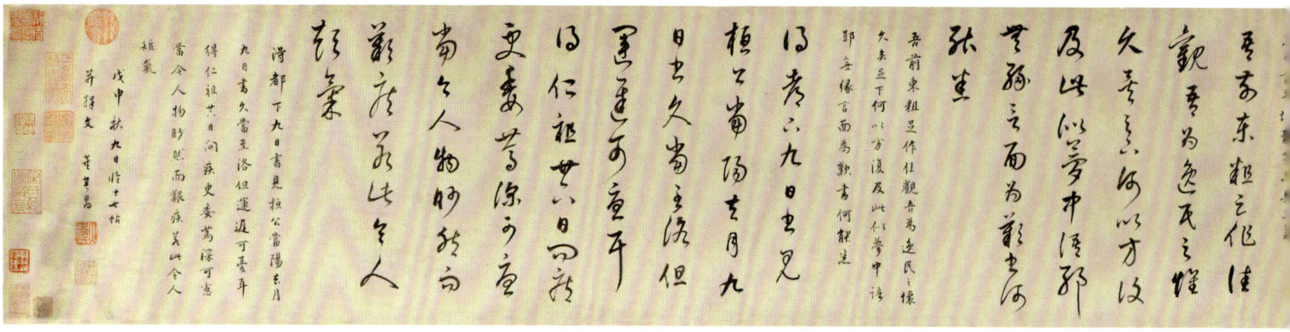

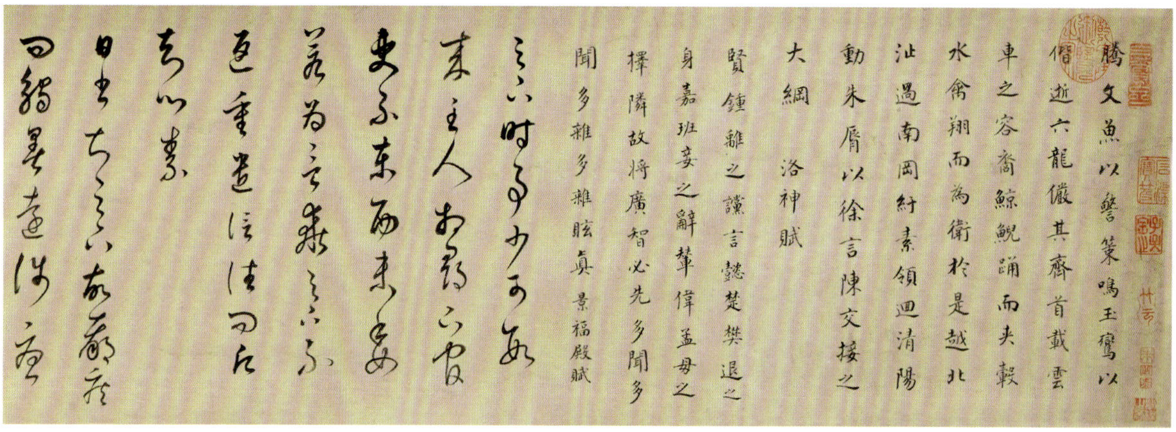

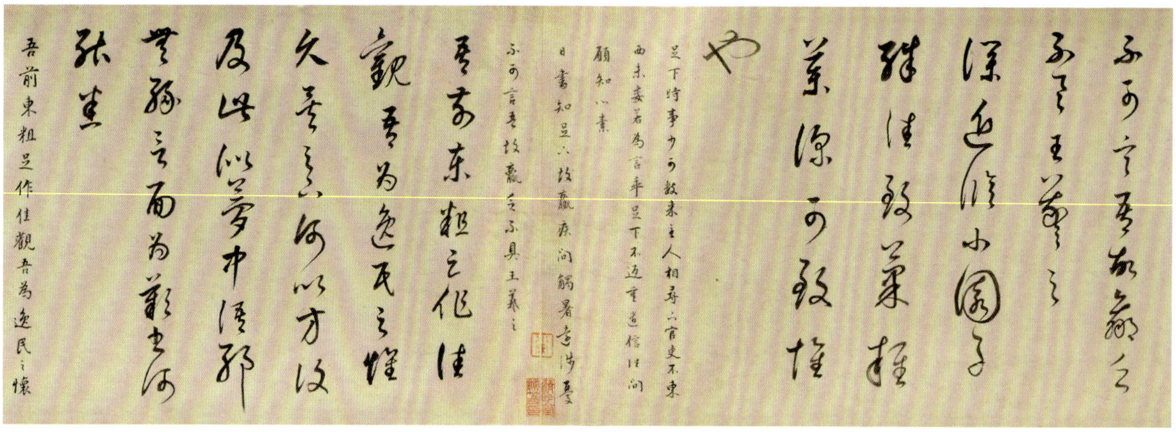

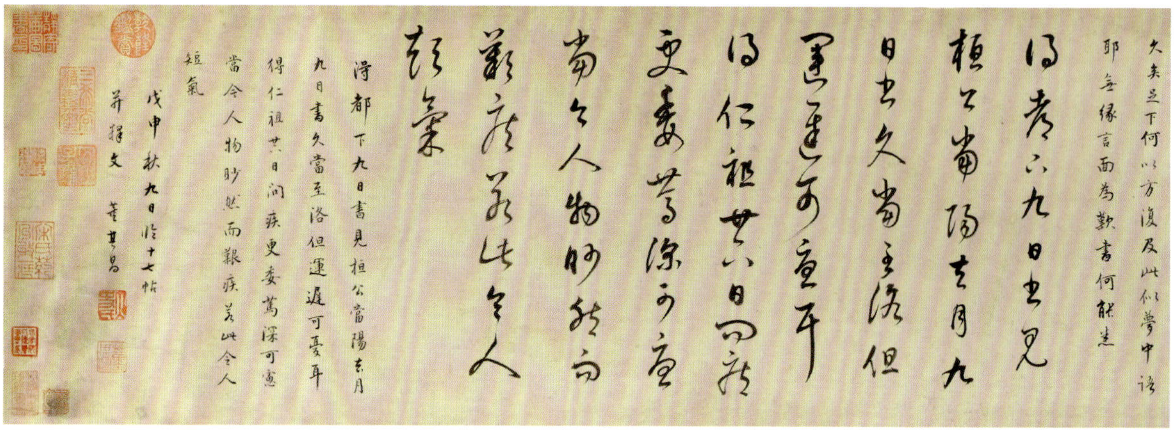

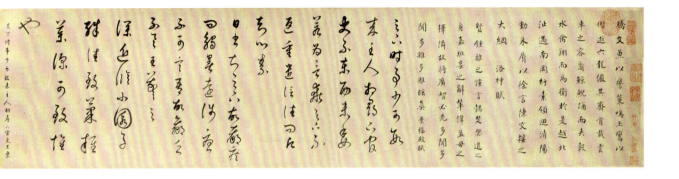

董其昌行草书《临十七帖卷》

Dong Qichang's Calligraphic Work: *A Copy of Wang Xizhi's Shiqi (Seventeen) Modelbook*

公元 1368 – 1644 年（明代）
1368 – 1644 A.D. (Ming Dynasty)

纵 24.6、横 216 厘米
Height 24.6 cm, Width 216 cm

天津博物馆藏
Tianjin Museum

沈周《虎丘送客图》

Shen Zhou's *Seeing off a Guest at Huqiu (Tiger Hill)*

公元 1368 – 1644 年（明代）
1368 – 1644 A.D. (Ming Dynasty)

纵 173.1、横 64.2 厘米
Height 173.1 cm, Width 64.2 cm

天津博物馆藏
Tianjin Museum

斗彩勾莲纹开光粉彩诗句花卉纹瓶

Painted Vase with Colorful Flowers
and Poems

公元 1616 – 1911 年（清代）
1616 – 1911 A.D. (Qing Dynasty)

高 36.8、口径 11、足径 11.3 厘米
Height 36.8 cm, Diameter of mouth 11 cm, Foot
diameter 11.3 cm

故宫博物院藏
The Palace Museum

（局部）

青花四爱图梅瓶
Blue-and-white "Four Predilections" Meiping (Plum Bottle)

公元 1206 – 1368 年（元代）
1206 – 1368 A.D. (Yuan Dynasty)

高 38.7、口径 6.4、底径 13 厘米
Height 38.7 cm, Diameter of mouth 6.4, Bottom diameter 13 cm

2006 年出土于湖北省钟祥市明郢靖王朱栋（朱元璋第 23 子）墓
Unearthed from the tomb of Prince Ying, Zhongxiang, Hubei Province, 2006

湖北省博物馆藏
Hubei Provincial Museum

　　元青花体现了不同文化的融合：蓝色颜料"苏麻离青"产自中亚、西亚；器形根据各地需要定制；图案纹饰具有不同地域特色。

　　此件青花梅瓶，瓶身绘出四幅古代人物故事，表现了中华民族崇尚修为、淡泊名利的美好品格。分别是：

　　东晋书法家王羲之喜爱兰花，以幽谷之兰隐喻君子之风，将兰亭作为会友修禊之所，留下书

法名篇《兰亭集序》；

　　宋代哲学家周敦颐酷爱莲花，其佳作《爱莲说》中有"独爱莲之出淤泥而不染"的名句；

　　北宋诗人林和靖痴爱梅花的高雅和白鹤的飘逸，一生与梅、鹤为伴，人称"梅妻鹤子"，所作"疏影横斜水清浅，暗香浮动月黄昏"被誉为千古咏梅绝唱；

东晋诗人陶渊明深爱菊花的傲霜品性，向往怡然自如的田园生活，写下流传千古的《桃花源记》和"采菊东篱下，悠然见南山"的名句。

 在亚洲文明对话大会开幕式的"亚洲文物精品展"展出

经济与社会

　　中国春秋晚期铁农具、牛耕的使用和推广，为中华文明的持续发展奠定了坚实的物质基础。自给自足的农耕经济，与周边国家、地区的贸易融合，宗法制和君主制结合的家国制度，中华文化的包容和凝聚力，这些因素推动了中国古代经济社会的不断发展。

ECONOMY AND SOCIETY

　　During the late Spring and Autumn Period and the Warring States Period, the use and promotion of iron farming tools and cattle farming laid a solid material foundation for the sustainable development of Chinese civilization. The continuous development of ancient Chinese economy and society was due to many factors, including a self-sufficient farming economy, trade and integration with surrounding countries and regions, the combining of a patriarchal clan system with a monarchical system, and the inclusiveness and cohesive power of Chinese culture.

铁农具（3件）
Iron Farming Tools (3 Pieces)

公元前 206 – 公元 220 年（汉代）
206 B.C. – 220 A.D. (Han Dynasty)

铧冠高 14、宽 25 厘米
Spade crown: Height 14 cm, Width 25 cm

犁铧长 30、宽 27 厘米
Plough beryllium: Length 30 cm, Width 27 cm

犁长 28、宽 26 厘米
Plough: Length 28 cm, Width 26 cm

1974 年河南省三门峡市渑池火车站古代铁器窖藏出土
Unearthed from a hoard storing ancient iron tools, Mianchi Railway Station, Sanmenxia, Henan Province, 1974

河南省文物考古研究院藏
Henan Provincial Institute of Cultural Heritage and Archaeology

　　汉代时，犁上的铧一般为全铁制，比战国时期的铁口木铧进步很多。同时，采用在前端套铧冠的方法防止铧的口刃磨损。为提高翻土效率，还在铧上装置犁镜。汉代铁器的制造和使用量很大，已遍及全国。铁农具的普遍使用，使得汉代农业生产效率有了显著提高。

"长乐未央"瓦当
Eaves Tile Engraved with Four Characters "Chang Le Wei Yang"

公元前 206 – 公元 220 年（汉代）
206 B.C. – 220 A.D. (Han Dynasty)

直径 6.8、厚 2.45 厘米
Diameter 6.8 cm, Thickness 2.45 cm

1997 年陕西省咸阳市汉阳陵南阙门遗址出土
Unearthed from ruins of the South Gate Tower of Hanyangling, Xianyang, Shaanxi Province, 1997

汉景帝阳陵博物院藏
Hanyangling Museum

"千秋万岁"瓦当
Eaves Tile Engraved with Four Characters "Qian Qiu Wan Sui"

公元前 206 – 公元 220 年（汉代）
206 B.C. – 220 A.D. (Han Dynasty)

直径 17.4、厚 2.9 厘米
Diameter 17.4 cm, Thickness 2.9 cm

1997 年陕西省咸阳市汉阳陵南阙门遗址出土
Unearthed from ruins of the South Gate Tower of Hanyangling, Xianyang, Shaanxi Province, 1997

汉景帝阳陵博物院藏
Hanyangling Museum

彩绘木六博俑
Painted Wooden Figurines Playing Liubo

公元前 206 – 公元 220 年（汉代）
206 B.C. – 220 A.D. (Han Dynasty)

棋盘长 29.2、宽 19.3 厘米；木俑一高 27.5 厘米，一高 28.5 厘米
Chessboard: Length 29.2 cm, Width 19.3 cm; Wooden figurine: Height 27.5 cm, 28.5 cm

1972 年甘肃省武威市磨咀子汉墓出土
Unearthed from Han Dynasty tomb, Mozuizi, Wuwei, Gansu Province, 1972

甘肃省博物馆藏
Gansu Provincial Museum

五层彩绘陶仓楼
Han Dynasty Five-floor Color-painted Clay Building Complex

公元前 206 – 公元 220 年（汉代）
206 B.C. – 220 A.D. (Han Dynasty)

高 145、面阔 81、进深 77 厘米
Height 145 cm, Width 81 cm, Depth 77 cm

2009 年河南省焦作白庄汉墓出土
Unearthed from Han Dynasty tombs, Baizhuang Village, Jiaozuo, Henan Province, 2009

焦作市博物馆藏
Jiaozuo Museum

　　汉代是中国古代建筑艺术发展的第一个高峰。河南地区是汉代的中心地区，建筑成就更为突出。东汉陶仓楼作为当时建筑的实物模型，真实反映了当时的建筑水平和技艺。此陶仓楼以其古朴的造型、雄伟的气势、高超的技艺，深厚的内涵在数以万计的汉代陶制冥器中脱颖而出。

彩绘耕织壁画砖

Painted Mural Brick with People Farming and Weaving

公元 220 – 420 年（魏晋）
220 – 420 A.D. (Wei & Jin Dynasties)

长 35、宽 17、厚 5 厘米
Length 35 cm, Width 17 cm, Thickness 5 cm

甘肃省嘉峪关市魏晋 1 号墓出土
Unearthed from Wei and Jin Dynasties tomb No. 1, Jiayuguan, Gansu Province

甘肃省博物馆藏
Gansu Provincial Museum

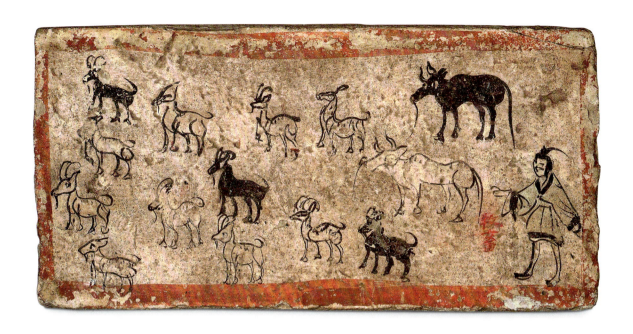

彩绘畜牧壁画砖
Painted Mural Brick with a Man Herding

公元 220 – 420 年（魏晋）
220 – 420 A.D. (Wei & Jin Dynasties)

长 35、宽 17、厚 5 厘米
Length 35 cm, Width 17 cm, Thickness 5 cm

1972 年甘肃省嘉峪关市新城第五号墓出土
Unearthed from tomb No.5, Xincheng Village,
Jiayuguan, Gansu Province, 1972

甘肃省博物馆藏
Gansu Provincial Museum

　　此壁画砖描绘了一位身着窄袖短袍的牧民，正守护着一群羊和马自由自在，悠闲游走的场景。画面呈现出河西地区古代牧民在荒原上放牧的情景，形象地再现了"河西畜牧为天下饶"的景象。

木牛车
Wooden Cart

公元 265 – 589 年（晋 – 南北朝）
265 – 589 A.D. (Jin Dynasty – Southern and Northern
Dynasties)

牛通高 18.1、体宽 8.6、长 27.9 厘米；车通长 52、宽 34.4、高 46 厘米
Cattle: Height 18.1 cm, Width 8.6 cm, Length 27.9 cm;
Cart: Length 52 cm, Width 34.4 cm, Height 46 cm

1973 年新疆维吾尔自治区吐鲁番哈拉和卓墓地 19 号墓出土
Unearthed from tomb No.19, Karakhoja Ancient
tombs, Turpan, Xinjiang Uygur Autonomous Region,
1973
新疆维吾尔自治区文物考古研究所藏
Institute of Xinjiang Uygur Autonomous Region for
Cultural Property and Archaeology

彩绘乐舞陶女俑

Painted Clay Figurines of Female Dancers

公元 618 – 907 年（唐代）

618 – 907 A.D. (Tang Dynasty)

坐俑高 19、宽 12.5 厘米；立俑高 30、宽 10 厘米

Sitting figurine: Height 19 cm, Width 12.5 cm;
Standing figurine: Height 30 cm, Width 10 cm

1991 年河南省洛阳市孟津唐墓出土

Unearthed from Tang Dynasty tombs, Mengjin
County, Luoyang, Henan Province, 1991

洛阳博物馆藏

Luoyang Museum

三彩打马球俑
Tri-colored Glazed Pottery Figurine of Polo Player

公元 618 – 907 年（唐代）
618 – 907 A.D. (Tang Dynasty)

长 33、高 35.5 厘米
Length 33 cm, Height 35.5 cm

2012 年河南省洛阳华山北路出土
Unearthed from Huashan North Road, Luoyang, Henan Province, 2012

洛阳市文物考古研究院藏
Luoyang City Cultural Relics and Archaeology Research Institute

　　马球是唐代喜闻乐见的体育运动，表现打马球活动的唐三彩俑十分常见。此俑神情专注，形象逼真，生动地反映了盛唐时期的社会习俗和文化风貌。

陶舞蹈俑

Pottery Figurine of a Dancer

公元 1206 – 1368 年（元代）
1206 – 1368 A.D. (Yuan Dynasty)

高约 37 厘米
Height 37 cm

1971 年河南省焦作西冯封村出土
Unearthed from Xifengfeng Village, Jiaozuo, Henan
Province, 1971

河南博物院藏
Henan Museum

焦秉贞《耕织图》册页

Picture of Farming and Weaving by Jiao Bingzhen

公元 1616 – 1911 年（清代）
1616 – 1911 A.D. (Qing Dynasty)

高 24.9 厘米
Height 24.9 cm

中国国家博物馆藏
National Museum of China

此册页是画家焦秉贞奉康熙旨，依楼璹《耕织图》样，用西洋画法绘制了耕、织图各 23 张后，康熙皇帝亲自为其作序作诗，命刻版印发。

《耕织图》是用绘画的艺术表现形式反映农桑劳作过程的一大创举，被称为"世界首部农业科普画册"，是解读中国农业史、纺织史、艺术史的珍贵文献。

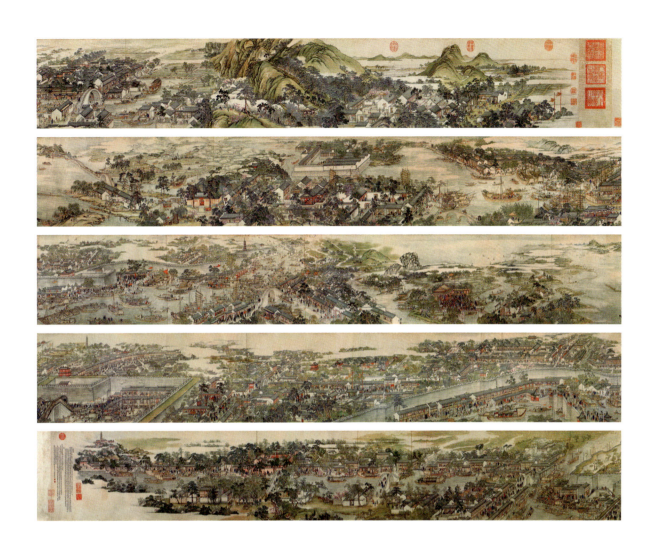

姑苏繁华图卷
Painting Scroll: *The Prosperous Suzhou*

公元 1759 年（清乾隆二十四年）
1759 A.D.

纵 36.5、全长 1241 厘米
Height 36.5 cm, Width 1241 cm

辽宁省博物馆藏
Liaoning Provincial Museum

画面自西向东，由乡入城，展现了连绵数十里内的湖光山色、水乡田园、村镇城池及社会风情。布局精妙严谨，气势恢宏，笔触细致，以长卷形式和散点透视技法，形象地反映了 18 世纪中叶苏州风景秀丽、物产富饶、百业兴旺、人文荟萃的繁盛景象，具有很高的艺术鉴赏价值。

美在通途
行久致远

VOYAGE OF DISCOVERY
BRIDGE OF COMMUNICATION

亚洲文明在峥嵘岁月中生长繁衍，在大山大川、江河湖海间投射激荡。苍茫大地的驼马印记与水际天边的海岸帆影，印刻在延绵不绝的旅途，铃声悠扬，八方回响。数千年来，中国与其他亚洲各国克服高山大海的阻隔，开辟出连接彼此、横跨欧亚的陆上、海上丝绸之路。

Asian civilization has grown and proliferated over a long period of time, and has spread through great mountains and valleys as well as surging rivers and seas. The imprint camels and horses left on the vast expanse of land they traversed over the years and the trace of ships on the horizon of the ocean making their unending journeys, cannot be forgotten as camel bells still ring melodiously and echo in all directions. For thousands of years, China and other Asian countries have overcome geographic barriers and co-constructed the Silk Road by land and sea to connect Europe and Asia.

驼铃悠扬——陆上丝绸之路

　　陆上丝绸之路是一条连接亚洲、非洲和欧洲的商业贸易路线。它东起中国的古都长安（今西安）、洛阳，穿河西走廊，出玉门关、阳关，经天山南北，通过中亚、西亚和北非，最终抵达非洲和欧洲。陆上丝路也是不同文化融合、交流和对话的通道，为人类文明的共同繁荣作出重要贡献。

Melodious Camel Bells
—— The Silk Road on Land

　　The ancient Silk Road was a commercial and trade route that connected Asia, Africa and Europe. The overland route began in Chang'an (present–day Xi'an) and Luoyang, passed through the Hexi Corridor, through Yumen Pass and Yangguan Pass, and the Tianshan Mountain range, and then made its way through Central Asia, West Asia and North Africa before finally arriving in Africa and Europe. The Silk Road also allowed different cultures to mix together, and was a passage of exchange and dialogue, which contributed greatly to the prosperity of human civilization.

陆上丝绸之路正式形成于西汉。公元前2世纪，西汉武帝两次派张骞出使西域，开辟了东西方文化交流的新纪元。数千年来，各国使节、商队、游客、学者、工匠和教徒等沿着丝绸之路互通有无，川流不息。

《张骞出使西域图》敦煌莫高窟唐初壁画摹本

Copy of Cave Painting *Zhang Qian's Travel to the Western Regions* from Early Tang Dynasty in Mogao Caves, Dunhuang

画心纵 136、横 163 厘米
Image: Height 136 cm, Width 163 cm

原作位于甘肃省敦煌莫高窟第 323 窟
Original work from the 323th Cave of Mogao Caves in Dunhuang, Gansu Province

壁画共 5 组画面，每组画面都有榜题，以全景连环画形式详细描绘了汉武帝派遣张骞出使西域的故事。通过出使西域，张骞一行获得了邦国分布、山川地形、道里行程，以及风土人情等宝贵信息。

蓝地人首马身纹毛布
Woolen Cloth Featuring a Man's Head and a Horse's Body

公元前 206 – 公元 220 年（汉代）
206 B.C. – 220 A.D. (Han Dynasty)

长 116、宽 48 厘米
Length 116 cm, Width 48 cm

1984 年新疆维吾尔自治区山普拉墓地出土
Unearthed from Shanpula tombs, Xinjiang Uygur Autonomous Region, 1984

新疆维吾尔自治区博物馆藏
Xinjiang Uygur Autonomous Region Museum

　　此件毛布以蓝色为主，还有红、黄及晕染效果，构成了丰富的色彩。纹样为上缀毛织的人首马身图案，下缀毛织的武士像。毛布原为两条灯笼裤裤腿，经拆洗拼对而成，或作为壁挂。

人物印染花布

Cloth Featuring Human Figures

公元 25 – 220 年（东汉）
25 – 220 A.D. (Eastern Han Dynasty)

长 85、宽 48 厘米
Length 85 cm, Width 48 cm

1959 年新疆维吾尔自治区民丰县尼雅 1 号墓出土
Unearthed from Tomb No.1 of Niya Ruins in Minfeng
County, Xinjiang Uygur Autonomous Region, 1959

新疆维吾尔自治区博物馆藏
Xinjiang Uygur Autonomous Region Museum

锦饰绢手套

Silk Gloves

公元前 206 – 公元 420 年（汉晋）
206 B.C. – 420 A.D. (Han Dynasty – Jin Dynasty)

通长 33.8、宽 15 厘米
Length 33.8 cm, Width 15 cm

新疆维吾尔自治区民丰县尼雅遗址出土
Unearthed from Niya Ruins in Minfeng County, Xinjiang
Uygur Autonomous Region

新疆维吾尔自治区文物考古研究所藏
Institute of Xinjiang Uygur Autonomous Region for
Cultural Property and Archaeology

"五星出东方利中国"护膊（复制品）
"Five Stars Rise in the East" Brocade Arm Protecter (Replica)

原件公元前 206 – 公元 420 年（汉晋）
Date of the Original piece: 206 B.C. – 420 A.D.
(Han Dynasty – Jin Dynasty)

长 18.5、13.2 厘米
Length 18.5 cm, 13.2 cm

原件 1995 年出土于新疆维吾尔自治区民丰县尼雅遗址 1 号墓地
Unearthed from Niya Ruins in Minfeng County, Xinjiang Uygur Autonomous Region, 1995

新疆维吾尔自治区博物馆藏
Xinjiang Uygur Autonomous Region Museum

　　护膊材质为蜀地织锦。锦为蓝色地，以蓝、黄、绿、白、红五组彩色经线和两组纬线交织而成的经二重平纹织物。花纹主体为平行排列的孔雀、仙鹤、辟邪、夔龙和虎等祥禽瑞兽，以卷曲的蔓藤及两蕾一花做间隔。在花纹中间织出汉字隶书"五星出东方利中国"，"五"字后起每隔三字织有三色同心圆饰。"五星出东方利中国"是中国古代星占用辞，《史记·天宫书》就有详细记载及翻译。

佉卢文木牍

Wooden Slips with Letters in Kharosthi Script

公元前 206 – 公元 420 年（汉晋）
206 B.C. – 420 A.D. (Han Dynasty – Jin Dynasty)

上页长 14.2、宽 8.1、最厚 1.1；
下页长 22.4、宽 8.1、最厚 1.1 厘米
Above page: Length 14.2cm, Width 8.1 cm,
Maximum thickness 1.1 cm;
Under page: Length 22.4 cm, Width 8.1 cm,
Maximum thickness 1.1 cm

1959 年新疆维吾尔自治区民丰县尼雅遗址出土
Unearthed from Niya Ruins in Minfeng County,
Xinjiang Uygur Autonomous Region, 1959

新疆维吾尔自治区文物考古研究所藏
Institute of Xinjiang Uygur Autonomous Region for
Cultural Property and Archaeology

此木牍为胡杨木加工制成，分上下两页，上页为盖，下页为函。函盒中部下切凹槽，内墨书佉卢文字，函盖置于函盒凹槽内，背部隆起，有三道捆扎用的槽沟和一长方形封泥凹槽，用以捆扎的绳索和封泥已脱落。函盖两端亦横书佉卢文字。

此木牍类似于当今的信函，当为精绝国人发送的信件。一般情况下，函盖书写的是收件人的姓名、地址和寄件人的信息，下页则书写信件内容，也有部分木牍书写的是买卖或租赁契约。

蘑菇状立耳圈足铜镬

Bronze Pot with Mushroom-shaped Ears and Round Base

公元前 206 – 公元 420 年（汉晋）
206 B.C. – 420 A.D. (Han Dynasty – Jin Dynasty)

通高 57、口径 39 厘米
Height 57 cm, Diameter of mouth 39 cm

1976 年新疆维吾尔自治区乌鲁木齐市南山出土
Unearthed from Nanshan, Urumqi, Xinjiang Uygur Autonomous Region, 1976

新疆维吾尔自治区博物馆藏
Xinjiang Uygur Autonomous Region Museum

局部

狩猎纹鎏金银盘

Gilded Silver Plate with Hunting Scenes

公元 504 年（北魏正始元年）
504 A.D. (the 1st year of the Zhengshi period, Northern Wei Dynasty)

直径 18、高 4 厘米
Diameter 18 cm, Height 4 cm

1981 年山西省大同市封和突墓出土
Unearthed from tomb of Fenghetu in Datong, Shanxi Province, 1981

山西博物院藏
Shanxi Museum

　　这是一件典型的波斯萨珊器物。盘内沿刻有弦纹三圈，中央捶揲狩猎场景，左腿站立的狩猎者持长枪刺向身侧的一头野猪，右脚踏向另一头野猪。猎人络腮胡须，头戴半弧形冠，项饰联珠项链，头后饰飘带两道。这件银盘是研究萨珊金属工艺史及中国与西亚地区文化交流史的珍贵资料。

鎏金银壶
Gilded Silver Pitcher

公元 557 – 581 年（北周）
557 – 581 A.D. (Northern Zhou Dynasty)
底径 13、高 36.9 厘米
Bottom diameter 13 cm, Height 36.9 cm

1983 年宁夏回族自治区固原县西郊乡深沟村李贤墓出土
Unearthed from tomb of Li Xian, Shengou Village, in the west suburb of Guyuan County, Ningxia Hui Autonomous Region, 1983
宁夏固原博物馆藏
The Guyuan Museum of Ningxia

　　此银壶造型别致精美，为波斯萨珊王朝手工艺精品，腹部三组画面描绘的是古希腊神话故事：前面是青年帕里斯将金苹果送给爱神阿芙罗狄蒂，左侧是帕里斯在爱神帮助下抢劫美女海伦，转到右侧海伦已经回到了丈夫墨涅拉俄斯身边。此壶出土于中国北周大将军李贤墓中。对研究萨珊与罗马关系，以及与中国的关系都有重要价值。

玻璃碗
Glass Bowl

公元 557 – 581 年（北周）
557 – 581 A.D. (Northern Zhou Dynasty)
高 8、口径 9.5、腹深 6.8、下腹最大径 9.8 厘米
Height 8 cm, Diameter of mouth 9.5 cm, Abdominal depth 6.8 cm, Maximum abdominal diameter 9.8 cm

1983 年宁夏回族自治区固原县西郊乡深沟村李贤墓出土
Unearthed from tomb of Li Xian, Shengou Village, in the west surburb of Guyuan County, Ningxia Hui Autonomous Region, 1983
宁夏固原博物馆藏
The Guyuan Museum of Ningxia

兽首出水口
Gargoyle

公元前 3 世纪
3rd Century B.C.

高 22.5、长 9.5、宽 12.9 厘米
Height 22.5 cm, Length 9.5 cm, Width 12.9 cm

阿富汗阿伊 – 哈努姆
Ai – Khanum, Afghanistan

阿富汗国家博物馆藏
National Museum of Afghanistan

古也门铭文石香炉
An Incense Burner with Musnad Inscription

公元前 4 世纪 – 公元 4 世纪
4th Century B.C. – 4th Century A.D.

高 37、宽 18.5 厘米
Height 37 cm, Width 18.5 cm

沙特阿拉伯法奥
Alfaw, Saudi Arabia

沙特阿拉伯旅游及民族遗产总机构藏
Saudi Commission for Tourism and National Heritage

切割制法玻璃香水瓶
Blown-Cutting-Glass Bottle (Perfume Bottle)

公元 224 – 651 年（萨珊时期）
224 – 651 A.D. (Sassanid Period)

高 6 厘米
Height 6 cm

伊朗吉兰省尼亚瓦市
Niyaval, Gilan Province, Iran

伊朗国家博物馆藏
National Museum of Iran

"田延和" 铭石造像
Stone Statue of Buddha and His Disciples
Sponsored by Tian Yanhe

公元 386 – 534 年（北魏）
386 – 534 A.D. (Northern Wei Dynasty)

高 96、宽 44、厚 10 厘米
Height 96 cm, Width 44 cm, Thickness 10 cm

1973 年河南省淇县城关出土
Unearthed from Qi County, Henan Province, 1973

河南博物院藏
Henan Museum

贴金彩绘石雕菩萨立像
Gilded and Painted Stone Statue of Bodhisattva

公元 550 – 577 年（北齐）
550 – 577 A.D. (Northern Qi Dynasty)

高 115、宽 30 厘米
Height 115 cm, Width 30 cm

1996 年山东省青州市龙兴寺遗址出土
Unearthed from Longxing Temple in Qingzhou,
Shandong Province, 1996

青州博物馆藏
Qingzhou Museum

　　此尊菩萨头戴雕花蔓冠，面相圆润，眉
目清秀，双目低垂，表情庄重。右手施无畏
印，左手残缺。胸、腹平坦，上着僧祇支，
帔帛拖住璎珞自双肩垂下，在腹下交叉上卷。
下身着贴体长裙，裙侧垂璎珞。衣饰华丽，
雕工精细。跣足立于莲台之上，脚趾伸于莲
台外。

贴金彩绘石雕左胁侍菩萨
Gilded Stone Statue of Left Attendant Bodhisattva

公元 534 – 550 年（东魏）
534 – 550 A.D. (Eastern Wei Dynasty)

高 36、宽 35、厚 20 厘米
Height 36 cm, Width 35 cm, Thickness 20 cm

1996 年山东省青州市龙兴寺遗址出土
Unearthed from Longxing Temple in Qingzhou,
Shandong Province, 1996

青州博物馆藏
Qingzhou Museum

石雕大势至菩萨像
Stone Statue of Mahasthamaprapta

公元 618 – 907 年（唐代）
618 – 907 A.D. (Tang Dynasty)

高 86.5、宽 44、厚 45 厘米
Height 86.5 cm, Width 44 cm, Thickness 45 cm

河南省洛阳市龙门唐代奉先寺遗址出土
Unearthed from Fengxian Temple of Tang Dynasty
in Longmen, Luoyang, Henan Province

龙门石窟研究院藏
Longmen Grottoes Research Academy

白石金刚坐像
White Stone Statue of Seated Vajra

公元 618 – 907 年（唐代）
618 – 907 A.D. (Tang Dynasty)

高 75、宽 48、厚 33 厘米
Height 75 cm, Width 48 cm, Thickness 33 cm

1959 年陕西省西安市唐安国寺旧址出土
Unearthed from the original site of Anguo Temple of
Tang Dynasty, Xi'an, Shaanxi Province, 1959

西安碑林博物馆藏
Xi'an Beilin Museum

　　此尊造像为金刚降伏夜叉造型，单尊圆雕，属
密宗造像。金刚盘腿坐于磐石上，头饰火焰纹冠，
怒目圆睁，颈饰璎珞。袒露胸腹，帔帛绕颈随风飘
逸，下着宽裙。右手举金刚剑，左手握拳，有贴金
画彩痕迹。

灰片岩菩萨像
Grey Schist Bodhisattva

公元 2 – 5 世纪
2nd – 5th Century A.D.

高 84 厘米
Height 84 cm

犍陀罗遗址中部
Central Gandhara

巴基斯坦考古与博物馆司藏
Department of Archaeology and Museums,
Government of Pakistan

片岩佛陀及侍者浮雕残像

Fragment of a Frieze in Grey Schist,
Showing Buddha with Attendants

公元 2 – 3 世纪
2ⁿᵈ – 3ʳᵈ Century A.D.

犍陀罗遗址中部
Central Gandhara

巴基斯坦考古与博物馆司藏
Department of Archaeology and Museums,
Government of Pakistan

陶塑毗湿奴坐骑金翅鸟

Garuda

公元 5 – 6 世纪
5ᵗʰ – 6ᵗʰ Century A.D.
高 36、宽 29、深 12 厘米
Height 36 cm, Width 29 cm, Depth 12 cm

印度北部
Northern India
新加坡亚洲文明博物馆藏
Asian Civilisations Museum, Singapore

此件浮雕作品原是一座大型浮雕像的一部分，展现了毗湿奴的半人半鸟坐骑迦楼罗（Garuda）。该作品制作于笈多王朝时期（约公元 320–504 年）。

笈多王朝曾统治印度北部的大部分地区，其艺术风格在王朝灭亡后仍继续蓬勃发展，对东南亚和中国的雕塑艺术都产生了影响。

青铜佛立像
Buddha

公元 4 – 6 世纪（笈多王朝）
4th – 6th Century A.D.
长 26 厘米
Length 26 cm

印度新德里国家博物馆藏
National Museum, New Delhi, India

　　此尊佛像是释迦牟尼佛立像，人物头部略微偏大，表情凝重严肃。佛像身体细长，身披袒右肩式僧衣，左手持僧衣一角，右手施说法印。人物衣饰紧贴身体，显露出内部身形；宽阔的肩膀，纤细的腰部，两腿从上到下逐渐变细，显现出笈多时期造像的典型特征。在中国许多早期金铜佛像，以及一些石窟寺造像上也能看到类似的样式，可见其传播范围之广。

石雕多罗菩萨坐像
Seated Cunda/ Tara

公元 10 世纪
10th Century A.D.

长 30、高 40 厘米
Length 30 cm, Height 40 cm

印度东部帕拉
Pala, Eastern India

印度新德里国家博物馆藏
National Museum, New Delhi, India

此像为佛教中重要的神祇多罗菩萨。造像带有背屏，四臂女性形象的菩萨结跏趺坐在莲花座上，面容安静端详。菩萨的四臂各持不同物件，包括莲花、念珠和圆盘等法器。菩萨除了身上佩戴项链、手镯、臂钏等饰物外，全身赤裸，工匠通过表现丰满的乳房和健壮的身躯以突出女性之美。

石雕观音菩萨像
Lokesvara

公元 11 世纪（波罗王朝）
11th Century A.D.

长 26、宽 9.5、高 44 厘米
Length 26 cm, Width 9.5 cm, Height 44 cm

印度新德里国家博物馆藏
National Museum, New Delhi, India

石雕天女像
Apsara

公元 12 世纪
12th Century A.D.

长 42.5、高 72 厘米
Length 42.5 cm, Height 72 cm

印度中央邦
Madhya Pradesh, India
印度新德里国家博物馆藏
National Museum, New Delhi, India

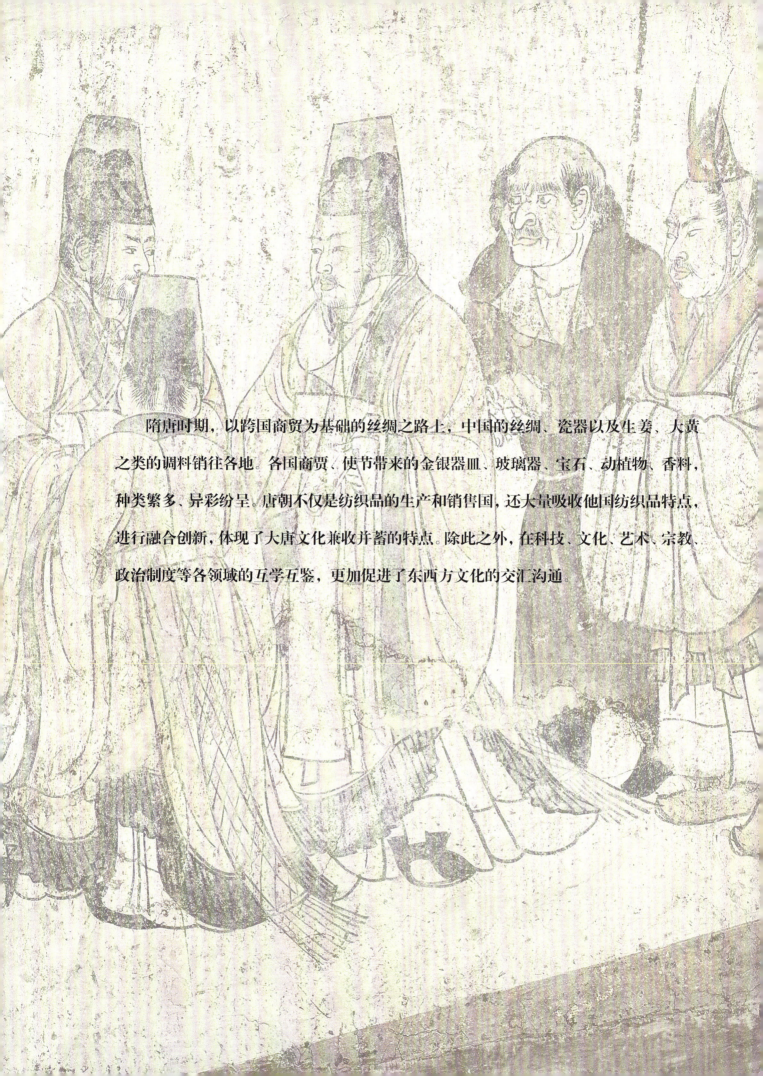

　　隋唐时期，以跨国商贸为基础的丝绸之路上，中国的丝绸、瓷器以及生姜、大黄之类的调料销往各地。各国商贾、使节带来的金银器皿、玻璃器、宝石、动植物、香料，种类繁多、异彩纷呈。唐朝不仅是纺织品的生产和销售国，还大量吸收他国纺织品特点，进行融合创新，体现了大唐文化兼收并蓄的特点。除此之外，在科技、文化、艺术、宗教、政治制度等各领域的互学互鉴，更加促进了东西方文化的交汇沟通。

蓝地对鸟对羊树纹锦

Blue Brocade with Patterns of Pairs of Birds,
Sheep and Lamp-tree

公元 618 – 907 年（唐代）
618 – 907 A.D. (Tang Dynasty)

长 13.8、宽 26.1 厘米
Length 13.8 cm, Width 26.1 cm

1972 年新疆维吾尔自治区吐鲁番市阿斯塔那墓地
出土
Unearthed from Astana Ancient Tombs in Turpan,
Xinjiang Uygur Autonomous Region, 1972

新疆维吾尔自治区博物馆藏
Xinjiang Uygur Autonomous Region Museum

　　此锦以白、蓝，白、绿相间的地色分行，主体
花纹是波斯艺术中常出现的生命树纹样。生命树是
一种古老的植物崇拜图像，图案通常以中心轴对称形
式呈现，以横向排列织出人物头像、禽兽，以及双角
巨兽等图案，吸收了西方特有的图案循环排列方式。

联珠对鸡纹锦

Brocade with Patterns of Pairs of Chickens
Surrounded by Beads

公元 618 – 907 年（唐代）
618 – 907 A.D. (Tang Dynasty)

长 26.8、宽 17.7 厘米
Length 26.8 cm, Width 17.7 cm

1972 年新疆维吾尔自治区吐鲁番市阿斯塔那墓
地出土
Unearthed from Astana Ancient Tombs in Turpan,
Xinjiang Uygur Autonomous Region, 1972

新疆维吾尔自治区博物馆藏
Xinjiang Uygur Autonomous Region Museum

三彩牵驼俑

Tri-colored Glazed Figurine of a Foreign Camel Handler

公元 618 – 907 年（唐代）
618 – 907 A.D. (Tang Dynasty)

高 66 厘米
Height 66 cm

1963 年河南省洛阳市关林唐墓出土
Unearthed from a Tang Dynasty tomb site at Guanlin, Luoyang, Henan Province, 1963

洛阳博物馆藏
Luoyang Museum

三彩载丝骆驼

Tri-colored Glazed Ceramic Camel Carrying Silk

公元 618 – 907 年（唐代）
618 – 907 A.D. (Tang Dynasty)

长 69.7、宽 28.4、高 81.2 厘米
Length 69.7 cm, Width 28.4 cm, Height 81.2 cm

1963 年河南省洛阳市关林唐墓出土
Unearthed from a Tang Dynasty tomb site at Guanlin, Luoyang, Henan Province, 1963

洛阳博物馆藏
Luoyang Museum

　　该骆驼通体主施白釉，头顶、驼峰、颈下、前肢上部及驼尾施褐釉。骆驼呈昂首嘶鸣状，牙齿和舌头的刻画栩栩如生，四肢劲健有力。其周身施淡黄、褐、绿釉，三彩饰釉华丽精美。骆驼背垫彩毯，峰间驮兽囊，载有水壶、食品、丝绸等物，跋涉于丝绸之路，是东西方交流的实物见证。

马球图壁画

Fresco Featuring Polo-playing

公元 618 – 907 年（唐代）
618 – 907 A.D. (Tang Dynasty)

长 305、宽 130 厘米
Length 305 cm, Width 130 cm

2004 年陕西省富平县北吕村李邕墓出土
Unearthed from the tomb of Li Yong at Beilv Village,
Fuping County, Shaanxi Province, 2004

陕西省考古研究院藏
Shaanxi Provincial Institute of Archaeology

此壁画出土时位于墓葬前甬道西壁，画面中有四匹马及手持杖杆的骑手，两端的人和马残缺。中部两人骑马，右侧球手右手肌肉线条鼓张，反手挥杆。两名骑手眼睛皆聚焦在右下方的马球之上，似乎下一瞬间即可抢球成功。马身雄壮浑圆，点状皮毛呈黄褐色，表情充满灵性。该幅壁画线条流畅，人物五官描绘细致精彩，生动记录了当时马上争球的一幕。

仰莲瓣座银罐

Silver Pot with a Lotus Petals-patterned Base

公元 618 – 907 年（唐代）
618 – 907 A.D. (Tang Dynasty)

通高 11.2、腹径 7.2、口径 4 厘米
Height 11.2 cm, Abdominal diameter 7.2 cm, Diameter of mouth 4 cm

1970 年陕西省西安市何家村窖藏出土
Unearthed from Hejia Village Hoard, Xi'an, Shaanxi Province, 1970

陕西历史博物馆藏
Shaanxi History Museum

舞马衔杯纹仿皮囊式银壶

Silver Kettle Featuring Horse Pattern in the Shape of a Leather Bag

公元 618 – 907 年（唐代）
618 – 907 A.D. (Tang Dynasty)

通高 18.5 厘米
Height 18.5 cm

1970 年陕西省西安市何家村窖藏出土
Unearthed from Hejia Village Hoard, Xi'an, Shaanxi Province, 1970

陕西历史博物馆藏
Shaanxi History Museum

此件盛唐时期的银壶，是多元文化交流融合的产物。

造型上，采用了北方游牧民族盛水皮囊的形状；工艺上，表现了丝绸之路开通后中亚、西亚金银器加工技术与中国工艺技法的交融；装饰上，经过特殊训练的骏马口衔酒杯，盛装舞步，反映了西域良马引入中原、马艺表演相互交流的历史。

鎏金鸳鸯纹银羽觞

Silver Double-handle Wine Vessel with Gilded Mandarin Duck Design

公元 618 – 907 年（唐代）
618 – 907 A.D. (Tang Dynasty)

高 3.2、口纵 7.7、口横 10.5 厘米
Height 3.2 cm, Length of mouth 7.7 cm, Width of mouth 10.5 cm

1970 年陕西省西安市何家村窖藏出土
Unearthed from Hejia Village Hoard, Xi'an, Shaanxi Province, 1970

陕西历史博物馆藏
Shaanxi History Museum

此觞侈口，口沿稍向外翻，弧腹，小平底，长云形片状双耳，焊于口沿之下。捶揲成形。器内外满饰珍珠地纹。器底和腹部各刻有宝相花或团花一朵；内壁饰有忍冬纹四株，枝蔓流畅，花繁叶茂。双耳面上各刻小团花一朵。两侧外腹饰有抱合式忍冬、卷草纹一组，覆莲座上立一鸳鸯，一侧为振翅，一侧为合翼，外腹另有振翅鸳鸯一对，下有覆莲座。纹饰均经过鎏金处理，显得端庄华丽。制作工艺则采用了钣金、浇铸、焊接、抛光、捶揲、刻凿等，体现了唐代金银酒器制作的高超技术。

花瓣形凸花银盘
Silver Flower-shaped Plate with Petal Design

公元 618 – 907 年（唐代）
618 – 907 A.D. (Tang Dynasty)
高 1、口径 15.5 厘米
Height 1 cm, Diameter of mouth 15.5 cm

1972 年陕西省西安市曲江池村出土
Unearthed from Qujiangchi Village, Xi'an, Shaanxi Province , 1972
西安博物院藏
Xi'an Museum

高足玻璃杯
High-stem Glass Cup

公元 618 – 907 年（唐代）
618 – 907 A.D. (Tang Dynasty)
高 9.7、口径 12.3、底径 5.5 厘米
Height 9.7 cm, Diameter of mouth 12.3 cm, Bottom diameter 5.5 cm

1989 年新疆维吾尔自治区库车县森木塞姆石窟出土
Unearthed from Senmusaimu Grottos at Kuqa County, Xinjiang Uygur Autonomous Region, 1989
新疆维吾尔自治区博物馆藏
Xinjiang Uygur Autonomous Region Museum

盘口细颈贴塑淡黄色琉璃瓶

Yellow Glass Vase with Dish-shaped Mouth and Thin Neck

公元 618 – 907 年（唐代）
618 – 907 A.D. (Tang Dynasty)

高 21.3、腹深 20、腰径 16、口径 4.7 厘米
Height 21.3 cm, Abdominal depth 20 cm, Waist diameter 16 cm, Diameter of mouth 4.7 cm

1987 年陕西省宝鸡市扶风县法门寺唐代地宫出土
Unearthed from the Tang Dynasty Underground Palace of Famen Temple at Fufeng County, Baoji, Shaanxi Province, 1987

法门寺博物馆藏
Famen Temple Museum

此瓶呈淡黄透明色，无模吹制成形，底部有加工痕迹。肩部与腹部外壁用不同颜色及形状的玻璃丝缠贴装饰，制作精美、纹饰华丽，其制作吸收了古罗马和波斯帝国的玻璃生产工艺，又融入了早期伊斯兰文化风格，为典型萨珊工艺品。

八瓣团花纹蓝色琉璃盘

Blue Glass Plate with Patterns of Eight Petals

公元 618 – 907 年（唐代）
618 – 907 A.D. (Tang Dynasty)

高 3.4、腹深 2.8、口径 19.9 厘米
Height 3.4 cm, Abdominal depth 2.8 cm, Diameter of mouth 19.9 cm

1987 年陕西省宝鸡市扶风县法门寺唐代地宫出土
Unearthed from the Tang Dynasty Underground Palace of Famen Temple at Fufeng County, Baoji, Shaanxi Province, 1987

法门寺博物馆藏
Famen Temple Museum

此盘通体呈蓝色，具透明感，无模吹制成形。内外壁光洁，盘沿外折，腹壁斜收，盘底心凸起。盘内刻满纹饰，装饰有数层金线刻花，中心为八瓣蕉叶围成的团花，蕉叶刻成斜线纹与波浪纹，两两相间。最外层为双线勾出的一圈水波纹，内外相间处以金线描绘填满，并加以果实图案点缀。其多种工艺手法为早期伊斯兰文化及中西方文化交流、中外玻璃发展史研究提供了弥足珍贵的实物资料。

（正面）

（背面）

萨珊银币
Sassanid Empire Silver Coin

公元 386 – 534 年（北魏）
386 – 534 A.D. (Northern Wei Dynasty)

直径 2.7 厘米
Diameter 2.7 cm

1981 年宁夏回族自治区固原县东郊乡雷祖庙村出土
Unearthed from Lei Zu Miao Village, Dongjiao Township, Guyuan County, Ningxia Hui Autonomous Region, 1981

宁夏固原博物馆藏
The Guyuan Museum of Ningxia

拜占庭金币
Byzantium Empire Gold Coins

公元 557 – 581 年（北周）
557 – 581 A.D. (Northern Zhou Dynasty)

直径分别为 1.62、1.54 厘米
Diameter 1.62 cm, Diameter 1.54 cm

1996 年宁夏回族自治区固原县西郊乡大堡村田弘夫妇合葬墓出土
Unearthed from the Joint – Burial Tomb of Tian Hong Couple at Dabao Village, Xijiao Township, Guyuan County, Ningxia Hui Autonomous Region, 1996

宁夏固原博物馆藏
The Guyuan Museum of Ningxia

（正面）

（背面）

　　拜占庭时期的金币较为少见，更多的是银币和铜币，在中国亦然。目前发现的拜占庭金币均采用基本固定的面额和重量标准。正面为国王肖像，国王的名字和称号刻于靠近边缘的地方。每一统治者都戴有自己富有个性的王冠。钱币反面均为圣火祭坛，祭坛两侧各有一祭司。这样的设计主要用来表现君权神授。

（正面）　　　　　　（背面）

笈多银币
Gupta Coin

公元 5 世纪
5th Century A.D.

边长 1 厘米，重 1.6 克
Side Length 1 cm, Weight 1.6 g

印度新德里国家博物馆藏
National Museum, New Delhi, India

釉陶罐
A Small Decorated Glazed Vessel with
Two Missing Handles

公元 7 – 10 世纪
7th – 10th Century A.D.

口径 2.2、腹部直径 5.5、底径 4.4、高 8 厘米
Diameter of mouth 2.2 cm, Abdominal diameter 5.5 cm,
Bottom diameter 4.4 cm, Height 8 cm

沙特阿拉伯拉巴达遗址
Alrabadha site, Saudi Arabia

沙特阿拉伯旅游及民族遗产总机构藏
Saudi Commission for Tourism and National Heritage

釉陶托盘
Tray

公元 12 – 13 世纪　　亚美尼亚德芬遗址
12th – 13th Century A.D. Dvin site, Armenia

直径 30 厘米　　　　　亚美尼亚历史博物馆藏
Diameter 30 cm　　　　History Museum of Armenia

釉陶盘
Dish

公元 11 – 12 世纪　　亚美尼亚德芬遗址
11th – 12th Century A.D. Dvin site, Armenia

直径 23.8 厘米　　　　亚美尼亚历史博物馆藏
Diameter 23.8 cm　　　History Museum of Armenia

云帆远航——海上丝绸之路

　　海上丝绸之路，这条古代海道交通的大动脉经东亚、东南亚、南亚、西亚各国，抵达非洲东部、北部、红海沿岸以及欧洲，是古代世界重要的交通贸易和文化交往的海上通道。因从中国输出的物品多为丝绸、瓷器、茶叶，从海外运至中国的货物以珠宝、香料等为主，所以海上丝绸之路又被称为"陶瓷之路""香料之路"或"茶叶之路"。

The Far Voyage
—— The Silk Road on Sea

　　The Maritime Silk Road, an ancient artery of sea transportation, traversed across East Asia, Southeast Asia, South Asia and West Asia and ended in eastern and northern Africa, the Red Sea coastal areas and Europe. It was an essential maritime route for transportation, trade, and cultural exchange in those days. Silk, as well as porcelain and tea, were the major exports out of China, and jewelry and spices were major exports of other countries. As a result, the Maritime Silk Road is also known as the "Ceramic Road", "Spice Road" or "Tea Road".

公元前 2 世纪，汉武帝派使团分别从徐闻、合浦、日南（今越南中部）等港口出发，远航至东南亚、南亚等地，打开了一条通往海外的贸易通道，促进了汉王朝与周边区域更广泛的交往。

船纹铜提筒

Bronze Wine Vessel with Boat Patterns

公元前 206– 公元 25 年（西汉）
206 B.C. – 25 A.D. (Western Han Dynasty)

口径 34 – 35.5、高 40.7、底径 33 – 33.5、子口高 1、圈足高 1.6 厘米
Diameter of mouth 34 – 35.5 cm, Height 40.7 cm, Bottom diameter 33 – 33.5 cm, Height of mouth 1 cm, Height of ring foot 1.6 cm

1983 年广东省广州市象岗南越文王墓出土
Unearthed from the Tomb of Nanyue King Zhao Mo at Xianggang Mountain, Guangzhou, Guangdong Province, 1983

西汉南越王博物馆藏
The Musuem of the Nanyue King of Western Han Dynasty

　　器身上下绘有 4 组纹饰带，其中腹部的一组船纹为主纹饰——有羽人船 4 条，它们前后相接，首尾高翘，船身修长呈弧形，每船有羽人 5 人，动作各不相同。船上有旌旗装饰、鼓形乐器、高台等，船甲板下分舱，舱内装铜鼓类器物，在船的前后及船下还有水鸟、龟、鱼等动物。

　　提筒是南越文化的代表器形之一，此件提桶为今人了解秦汉时期岭南民俗及造船技术提供了重要的图像参考。

蒜头纹银盒
Silver Box with Garlic Patterns

公元前 206– 公元 25 年（西汉）
206 B.C. – 25 A.D. (Western Han Dynasty)

通高 12.1、口径 13、腹径 14.8、铜圈足高 1.8 厘米
Height 12.1 cm, Diameter of mouth 13 cm, Abdominal
diameter 14.8 cm, Height of copper ring foot 1.8 cm

1983 年广东省广州市象岗南越文王墓出土
Unearthed from the Tomb of Nanyue King Zhao Mo
at Xianggang Mountain, Guangzhou, Guangdong
Province, 1983

西汉南越王博物馆藏
The Musuem of the Nanyue King of Western Han
Dynasty

此银盒盖子和盒身采用捶揲工艺制成对向交
错的蒜头形凸纹。这种纹饰、造型工艺具有古代西
亚波斯银器特点，与中原本土不同。西汉时期，广
州已是重要的港口和商品集散地。该银盒可能是一
件海外舶来品。它进入中国后，工匠根据汉代银器
的特点，在盖子上焊接了盖纽，在盒底加装了圈足，
还在器身上留下了许多铭文。

胡人俑陶座灯
Pottery Servant Figurine Lamp Stand

公元前 206– 公元 25 年（西汉）
206 B.C. – 25 A.D. (Western Han Dynasty)

高 20.5 厘米
Height 20.5 cm

1957 年广东省广州市河南晓港新村刘王殿出土
Unearthed from Liuwangdian, Henan Xiaogangxin Village, Guangzhou, Guangdong Province, 1957

广州博物馆藏
Guangzhou Museum

玛瑙琉璃珊瑚珠饰
Ornamental Beads Made of Agate, Colored Glaze and Coral

公元 25 – 220 年（东汉）
25 – 220 A.D. (Eastern Han Dynasty)

总长 24 厘米
Length 24 cm

1955 年广东省广州市河南晓港新村大元岗出土
Unearthed from Dayuangang, Henan Xiaogang Village, Guangzhou, Guangdong Province, 1955

广州博物馆藏
Guangzhou Museum

广州南越国及两汉墓中出土了大量珠饰，其中品种多为琉璃、玛瑙、珊瑚、水晶、琥珀、石榴石、煤精等，这些原料的输入与当时海上丝绸之路的发展密切相关。

公元 3 至 10 世纪（汉代至唐代），海上丝绸之路持续发展，多条航线开通与延伸，带动了扬州、明州（今宁波）、福州、泉州、广州等港口城市日益繁荣。公元 10 至 14 世纪末（宋代至元代），随着中国经济重心的南移，海上丝绸之路的重要性日益凸显。

公元 8 世纪末开始，中国的陶瓷成为海上丝绸之路的大宗商品，向外输出至东亚、东南亚、南亚、西亚、北非、东非等地。此时海上交通路线主要有两条：一是从扬州或明州（今宁波）出发，经朝鲜抵日本或直达日本的航线；二是从泉州、广州出发前往东南亚各国，再穿马六甲海峡进入印度洋，经斯里兰卡、印度、巴基斯坦到达波斯湾的航线。更多船只继续沿阿拉伯半岛西行至非洲。

《重修天庆观记》碑拓片

Rubbing of Tablet Recording *the Redecoration of the Tianqing Taoist Temple*

公元 960 – 1127 年（北宋）
960 – 1127 A.D. (Northern Song Dynasty)
纵 175、横 127 厘米
Height 175 cm, Width 127 cm

原碑立于广东省广州市天庆观旧址
The original tablet was erected at the former site of Tianqing Taoist Temple, Guang Zhou, Guang Dong Province
广州博物馆藏
Guangzhou Museum

此碑碑文记述了宋时三佛齐国（今印度尼西亚）商人捐资重修广州天庆观的事迹，体现了三佛齐国和宋朝的友好往来。

白釉花口军持

Ding Kiln White Glazed Ewer with Floral-shaped Top

公元 960 – 1279 年（宋代）
960 – 1279 A.D. (Song Dynasty)

高 27.5、口径 8.5、底径 8 厘米
Height 27.5 cm, Diameter of mouth 8.5 cm, Bottom diameter 8 cm

1997 年征集
Collected in 1997

广州博物馆藏
Guangzhou Museum

西村窑青釉彩绘花卉纹盘

Celadon Glazed Plate Painted with Floral Patterns

公元 1127 – 1279 年（南宋）
1127 – 1279 A.D. (Southern Song Dynasty)

高 6.4、口径 24.1、足径 9 厘米
Height 6.4 cm, Diameter of mouth 24.1 cm, Foot diameter 9 cm

菲律宾蒲端出水，Mr. Magbuhos 捐赠
Retrieved from Bu – tuan, Philippines. Donated by Mr. Magbuhos

广州博物馆藏
Guangzhou Museum

青白釉菊瓣纹盏

Bluish White Glazed Flower-patterned Bowl with Unglazed Mouth

公元 960 – 1279 年（宋代）
960 – 1279 A.D. (Song Dynasty)

口径 11.2、足径 3.6、高 4.3 厘米
Diameter of mouth 11.2 cm, Foot diameter 3.6 cm, Height 4.3 cm

2003 年广东省阳江市海域"南海 I 号"出水
Retrieved from Nanhai No.1 shipwreck near Yangjiang, Guangdong Province, 2003

中国国家博物馆藏
National Museum of China

青白釉印花芒口碗

Bluish White Glazed Flower-Patterned Bowl with Unglazed Mouth

公元 960 – 1279 年（宋代）
960 – 1279 A.D. (Song Dynasty)

口径 10.5、足径 4.5、高 5.5 厘米
Diameter of mouth 10.5 cm, Foot diameter 4.5 cm, Height 5.5 cm

2006 年广东省阳江市海域"南海Ⅰ号"出水
Retrieved from Nanhai No.1 shipwreck near Yangjiang, Guangdong Province, 2006

中国国家博物馆藏
National Museum of China

青釉翻口盘

Celadon Glazed Plate with Outward Mouth

公元 960 – 1279 年（宋代）
960 – 1279 A.D. (Song Dynasty)

口径 30.4、足径 9.5、高 9.3 厘米
Diameter of mouth 30.4 cm, Foot diameter 9.5 cm, Height 9.3 cm

2011 年广东省阳江市海域"南海Ⅰ号"出水
Retrieved from Nanhai No.1 shipwreck near Yangjiang, Guangdong Province, 2011

中国国家博物馆藏
National Museum of China

鎏金铜佛坐像
Seated Buddha

公元 6 世纪
6th Century A.D.
高 9.5、长 9.3、宽 6.3 厘米
Height 9.5 cm, Length 9.3 cm, Width 6.3 cm

斯里兰卡
Sri Lanka
新加坡亚洲文明博物馆藏
Asian Civilisations Museum, Singapore

青铜俱毗罗像
Kubura

公元 8 – 9 世纪
8th – 9th Century A.D.
高 11.7、宽 4、长 5 厘米
Height 11.7 cm, Width 4 cm, Length 5 cm

印度尼西亚爪哇中部
Central Java, Indonesia
新加坡亚洲文明博物馆藏
Asian Civilisations Museum, Singapore

进口物资
五金、布匹、胡椒
香料： 龙涎香、安息香、沉香、龙速香等 药材： 乳香、血竭、芦荟、没药、苏合油、 木别子、苏木等
珍宝： 珍珠、宝石、珊瑚等。
珍奇异兽： 狮子、金钱豹、花福鹿(斑马)、 麒麟(长颈鹿)、鸵鸡(鸵鸟)等。
出口物资
绽丝、色绢、青瓷、器皿、 铜钱、麝香、樟脑、烧珠、 茶叶、漆器、铜铁器等。

郑和船队海外贸易进出口物资简表

公元 1405 至 1433 年，郑和七下西洋标志着中国古代航海事业达到极盛。这一伟大的航海活动扩大了中国和亚非国家之间的经济文化交流，使明朝与 30 多个国家建立了友好关系，也堪称是 15 世纪世界范围内"大航海时代"的先驱。

郑和下西洋航海图（拼接）—中国（海南）南海博物馆制

郑和铜钟
Bronze Bell Cast by Zheng He

公元 1368 – 1644 年（明代）
1368 – 1644 A.D. (Ming Dynasty)
高 83.5、口径 49、厚 2 厘米
Height 83.5 cm, Diameter of mouth 49 cm, Thickness 2 cm

1981 年福建省南平市采集
Collected in Nanping, Fujian Province, 1981
中国国家博物馆藏
National Museum of China

　　此钟钟纽为双龙柄，钟肩表面浮印 12 组云气如意纹，腹中部以云水波浪纹为母题；主纹饰上部环绕一周八卦纹，共 5 组，其中第二、四组各铸有"国泰民安"和"风调雨顺"铭文。铜钟下部的铭文为"大明宣德六年岁次辛亥仲夏吉日，太监郑和、王景弘等同官军人等，发心铸造铜钟一口，永远长生供养，祈保西洋回往平安吉祥如意者"。此钟是明代海上丝绸之路繁荣的见证。

金镶宝帽顶
Crown with Pattern of Peony in Gold and Jade

公元 1368 – 1644 年（明代）
1368 – 1644 A.D. (Ming Dynasty)
通高 3.9、底径 5.1 厘米
Height 3.9 cm, Bottom diameter 5.1 cm

2001 年湖北省钟祥市梁庄王墓出土
Unearthed from Tomb of Prince Zhu Zhanji of Ming in Zhongxiang, Hubei Province, 2001
湖北省博物馆藏
Hubei Provincial Museum

　　此帽顶由金质椭圆形喇叭状底座和白玉镂空龙纹顶饰组成，覆莲瓣面上现存宝石 7 颗，采用了捶揲、镶嵌、焊接、抛光、刻凿等工艺制成，为明代亲王墓中首次发现。梁庄王墓出土文物中的各色宝石产地均为东南亚各国，见证了海上丝绸之路的繁荣。

镶宝石金镯
Gold Bracelet Inlaid with Precious Stones

公元 1368 – 1644 年（明代）
1368 – 1644 A.D. (Ming Dynasty)

高 2.6、直径 6.2 – 5.7 厘米
Height 2.6 cm, Diameter 6.2 – 5.7 cm

2001 年湖北省钟祥市梁庄王墓出土
Unearthed from Tomb of Prince Zhu Zhanji of Ming
in Zhongxiang, Hubei Province, 2001

湖北省博物馆藏
Hubei Provincial Museum

嵌宝石金戒指
Gold Cocktail Ring

公元 1368 – 1644 年（明代）
1368 – 1644 A.D. (Ming Dynasty)

直径 1.9 厘米
Diameter 1.9 cm

2001 年湖北省钟祥市梁庄王墓出土
Unearthed from Tomb of Prince Zhu Zhanji of Ming
in Zhongxiang, Hubei Province, 2001

湖北省博物馆藏
Hubei Provincial Museum

青花凤纹盘
Blue-and-white Phoenix-patterned Plate

公元 1368 – 1644 年（明代）
1368 – 1644 A.D. (Ming Dynasty)

口径 19.7、底径 10.5、高 3.5 厘米
Diameter of mouth 19.7 cm, Bottom diameter 10.5
cm, Height 3.5 cm

2009 年广东省汕头市"南澳Ⅰ号"沉船遗址出水
Retrieved from Nan'ao No. 1 shipwreck in Shantou,
Guangdong Province, 2009

广东省博物馆藏
Guangdong Museum

青花带盖钵
Blue-and-white Lidded Bowl

公元 1368 – 1644 年（明代）
1368 – 1644 A.D. (Ming Dynasty)

口径 19.2、腹径 20.5、底径 10.8、高 15 厘米
Diameter of mouth 19.2 cm, Abdominal diameter
20.5 cm, Bottom diameter 10.8 cm, Height 15 cm

2009 年广东省汕头市"南澳 I 号"沉船遗址出水
Retrieved from Nan'ao No.1 shipwreck in Shantou,
Guangdong Province, 2009

广东省博物馆藏
Guangdong Museum

　　此器物由钵盖、钵身组成。钵盖为子口，圆纽。外壁饰青花花卉纹，纹饰呈色泛灰，浓重处呈色发黑。钵身外壁饰缠枝花卉纹。瓷钵出水时多与小瓷罐、小杯等成套出水，再现了明代海上丝绸之路贸易交流的盛景。

元青花梅瓶
Blue and White Porcelain Jar

公元 16 世纪（萨菲王朝时期）
16th Century A.D. (Safavid Dynasty)

直径 7、高 54 厘米
Diameter 7 cm, Height 54 cm

伊朗阿尔达比勒省谢赫萨菲阿德丁墓出土
Sheikh Safi al – Din Khānegāh and Shrine Ensemble,
Ardabil Province, Iran

伊朗国家博物馆藏
National Museum of Iran

　　此瓶为中国江西景德镇出品，是元代青花瓷中的精美之作。瓶肩部绘有瑞兽，四周由缠枝莲环绕其间。腹部的纹饰为缠枝牡丹纹，栩栩如生。牡丹有富贵吉祥的美好寓意。主体纹饰上下方均由带状卷草纹装饰。腹下至近足部为仰莲垂珠纹装饰，层次分明。该瓶的肩部和足部均刻有卡塔查盖（Qarachaghay）的字样，表明此青花梅瓶与另两件青花盘均出自萨法维时期苏菲派主要领袖萨菲阿德丁族长的陵墓，是萨法维国王阿拔斯一世从中国购买并放在祖先陵墓里作为圣礼器具，这是当时中伊之间文化与商贸交流的见证。

黄铜星象仪
Bronze Globe/Astrological Object with Two Date Inscriptions

公元 1141 年和 1887 年（塞尔柱王朝和恺加王朝）
1141/1887 A.D. (Seljuq Dynasty/ Qajar Dynasty)
直径 14、17.5 厘米
Diameter 14 cm, 17.5 cm

伊朗伊斯法罕省
Isfahan Province, Iran
伊朗国家博物馆藏
National Museum of Iran

　　在古代伊斯兰世界，星象仪被用来确定日出和恒星升起的时间，帮助安排晨祷。在指南针和六分仪发明之前，它一直是主要的航海仪器。其用途包括定位和预测太阳、月亮、行星和恒星的位置，还可确定指定地点的经度，或用于测量和三角校准。

砂岩浮雕狮子建筑构件
Architectural Relief of a Lion

公元 10 世纪
10th Century A.D.
高 47 、长 36、宽 19 厘米
Height 47 cm, Length 36 cm, Width 19 cm

越南中部
Central Vietnam
新加坡亚洲文明博物馆藏
Asian Civilisations Museum, Singapore

片岩浮雕恰门达神像
Chamunda

公元 11 世纪
11th Century A.D.
长 26.5、宽 4.5、高 63 厘米
Length 26.5 cm, Width 4.5 cm, Height 63 cm

印度东北部
North – eastern India
新加坡亚洲文明博物馆藏
Asian Civilisations Museum, Singapore

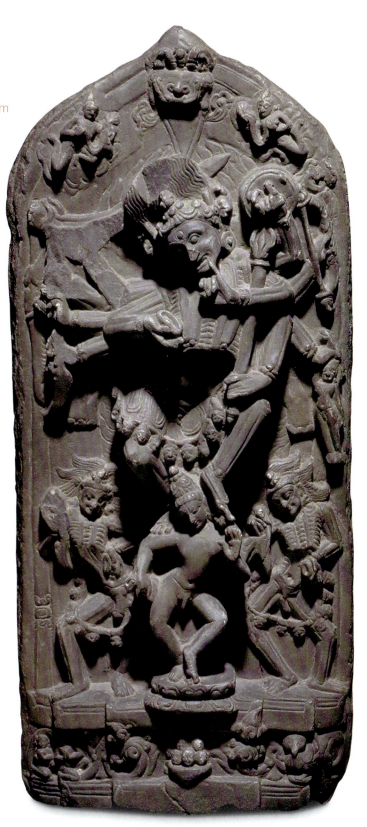

青铜佛坐像
Seated Buddha

公元 15 – 16 世纪
15th – 16th Century A.D.

高 45.5、长 25 厘米
Height 45.5 cm, Length 25 cm

泰国北部
Northern Thailand

新加坡亚洲文明博物馆藏
Asian Civilisations Museum, Singapore

瓷盘
Plate

公元 1752 年
1752 A.D.

高 2.8、直径 22.8 厘米
Width 2.8 cm, Diameter 22.8 cm

中国
China

新加坡亚洲文明博物馆藏
Asian Civilisations Museum, Singapore

　　此盘由荷兰东印度公司的格尔德马尔森号（Geldermalsen）沉船打捞而得。这艘船于 1752 年 1 月 3 日在中国南海触礁沉没，当时该船正从广州返航，船上载有大量货物，包括茶叶、黄金和逾 15 万件中国瓷器。打捞回的瓷器大多有钴蓝色釉底装饰，多半用作餐盘。此外，还打捞出了大量碗具、茶壶、牛奶壶，以及茶杯和茶托、咖啡和巧克力。这艘船的货物进一步展示了东西方之间的贸易交往和 18 世纪中叶荷兰对中国瓷器的欣赏品位。

龙形喷水口
Water spout

公元 1910 年之前
Before 1910 A.D.

长 28、高 41 厘米
Length 28 cm, Height 41 cm

印度尼西亚爪哇省东部港口井里汶
Cirebon, Java, Indonesia

印度尼西亚国家博物馆藏
National Museum of Indonesia

　　龙的形象在古代印度尼西亚艺术中随处可见，其受到印度佛教及印度教文化的影响，被称之为那迦。

　　此件水口通身为青铜铸造。龙细长的脖颈被设计成通水管，龙嘴作为出水口。龙头的整体造型特点与中国龙的形象近似，长有分叉的龙角和耳朵，头顶似戴有宝冠，两侧有下垂的尖头状垂饰。龙嘴鼻的上部较为饱满，口中长满尖牙，周身布满细密的鳞片，具有鲜明的地域特色。

石雕亚历山大大帝头像
Bust of Alexander the Great

公元前 340 – 前 330 年
340 – 330 B.C.
高 35、宽 24 厘米
Height 35 cm, Width 24 cm

希腊雅典卫城博物馆藏
Acropolis Museum

　　此件雕塑，雕刻的是公元前 4 世纪马其顿国王亚历山大。他建立了地跨欧、亚、非三大洲的大帝国，推动了东西方经济文化交往。

　　雕塑英雄是古希腊艺术的重要传统。公元前 4 世纪至公元 1 世纪（亚历山大及其之后的几百年），是古希腊文化繁荣发展并广泛传播的时期，史称"希腊化时代"。希腊文化在地中海沿岸、西亚、中亚、南亚地区传播，并与东方文化对话交流。亚洲的城市里出现了希腊式雕塑和建筑，东方的天文学和数学知识也传入了西方。早期佛教中没有明确的"佛"的形象，受古希腊雕塑艺术的影响，在位于南亚次大陆西北部的犍陀罗地区出现了最早的佛像，被称为"犍陀罗造像"，对于中国早期佛教造像艺术也产生了重要影响。

 在亚洲文明对话大会开幕式的"亚洲文物精品展"展出

古埃及圆拱形石碑（复制品）

Ancient Egyptian Stele With an Arch (Replica)

原件：公元前 332 – 前 30 年（希腊化时期）
Date of Original piece: 332 – 30 B.C. (Hellenistic Period)

长 98、宽 40、厚 4.8 厘米
Height 98 cm, Width 40 cm, Thickness 4.8 cm

原为清末端方收藏
Date of Original piece collected by Duanfang in the late Qing Dynasty

中国国家博物馆藏
National Museum of China

古埃及长方形石碑（复制品）
Rectangular Ancient Egyptian Stele (Replica)

原件：公元前 332 – 前 30 年（希腊化时期）
Date of Original piece: 332 – 30 B.C. (Hellenistic Period)

原为清末端方收藏
Date of Original piece collected by Duanfang in the late Qing Dynasty
中国国家博物馆藏
National Museum of China

此墓碑上的图像表现了一男子向四位神祇祈求的情景。坐在中间的是太阳神阿蒙，后面是秃鹫女神穆特，她是阿蒙的配偶。二者之后是他们的儿子洪苏，再后面是羊头的繁殖之神赫努姆，其配偶萨提斯头戴羽冠，站在最后。神祇左手都持象征统一的权杖，右手拿着象征生命的符号。在众神面前摆满供品的桌子上，有面包、禽类、莴苣、水果等，桌子下面是两个油罐。下面的铭文内容是死者向神祇祈求面包、酒、肉类、禽类、牛奶等供品。

美美与共
天下大同

EMBRACE DIFFERENCES
STRENGTHEN COOPERATION

人类只有一个地球，各国共处一个世界。世界好，亚洲才能好；亚洲好，世界才能好。亚洲各国一直致力于共同保护人类文化遗产，在跨国联合申报世界文化遗产、考古发掘、文化遗产保护、文物展览、专业人员培训、水下文化遗产保护等领域开展全方位的交流与合作，增进了各国人民友谊，为维护世界和平发展作出了重要贡献。

Mankind has only one earth, and each nation must co-exist in this one world. To do well, Asia and the world could not do without each other. Asian countries are committed to jointly protecting mankind's cultural heritage. Many countries have carried out exchanges and cooperations in the fields of world cultural heritage nomination, archaeological excavation, cultural heritage protection, cultural relic exhibition, professional training, underwater cultural heritage protection, etc., which enhanced the friendship between countries and made important contributions to the maintenance of world peace and development.

联合考古与文化遗产保护

Archaeological Collaboration and
Conservation of Cultural Heritage

中国－乌兹别克斯坦

联合考古和文化遗产保护项目

China - Uzbekistan Joint Archaeological Efforts and Cultural Heritage Protection Project

2009年开始，中乌两国陆续展开各项考古合作，先后对一系列古代遗存进行了考古调查，并联合发掘了安集延州的明铁佩（Mingtape）遗址、撒马尔罕市西南部撒扎干遗址、苏尔汉河州拜松区南部拉巴特等遗址。

2013年9月，中国和乌兹别克斯坦签署了联合宣言，进一步加强和拓宽科技、文化、人文领域的合作。中国国家文物局等单位积极同乌方开展联合考古和文物保护修复工作，为恢复丝绸之路历史风貌作出不懈努力。

2016年3月，中乌双方组成联合技术组，开展对乌兹别克斯坦花剌子模州阿米尔·图拉经学院与哈桑·穆拉德库什别吉清真寺的建筑本体修缮及环境整治工程。

拉巴特遗址出土的串饰和斯芬克斯吊坠
Strings of beads and a pendant in the shape of a sphinx, both
excavated at the Rabat Site

经学院修复前后对比
The Mosque before and after restoration

中国－柬埔寨

吴哥古迹保护和联合考古项目

China - Cambodia Protection Plan for Angkor Relics and Joint Archaeological Project

1993 年，由联合国教科文组织倡导，法国、日本、中国、德国、印度等 30 多个国家和国际组织参与的联合拯救吴哥古迹国际保护行动，是全球范围内文化遗产保护的典范。中国政府参与吴哥古迹保护修复与研究至今已 20 余年。

周萨神庙建筑主体归安
The main section of the Chau Say Thevoda being reinstated

1998 年 2 月，中方开始承担周萨神庙保护修复工作，这是中国首次参与大规模文物保护国际合作项目。工程于 2000 年 3 月正式开工，2008 年 12 月竣工验收。对周萨神庙的 8 座建筑进行了整体维修，整治了周边环境，重建了排水系统。

2009 年 12 月，中柬双方启动茶胶寺保护修复工程，2018 年竣工验收。通过修复，茶胶寺整体安全状况得到了改善，文物险情被排除，原有历史风貌得以展现。

茶胶寺东南台须弥角修复前后对比
Southeastern corner of the Sumeru Throne at Ta Keo before and after restoration

2011 年，中柬两国组成联合考古队，对与茶胶寺庙山主体结合紧密的外围基础等重点区域实施考古勘探和发掘，为茶胶寺遗址保护规划提供了更准确的考古学依据。联合考古也为柬方培养了文化遗产保护和考古专业人才，有效推进了茶胶寺考古工作的整体进展和国际间的学术交流。

考古发掘团队清理发掘石造像
The excavation team cleaning a stone statue

中国－日本

联合考古与文化遗产保护项目

China - Japan Joint Archaeological Efforts and Cultural Heritage Protection Project

敦煌石窟文物保护研究陈列中心外景
Outside view of the Exhibition Center for the Conservation and Research of Dunhuang Grottoes

1992–1994 年，日本政府无偿援助建设"敦煌石窟文物保护研究陈列中心"，集敦煌石窟文物保护、研究、陈列等功能为一体，为保护和展示敦煌石窟发挥了积极作用。

1992 年，中国政府与联合国教科文组织及日本政府商定，共同保护新疆维吾尔自治区交河故城，投资 100 万美元，对交河故城进行保护、维修和局部复原工程。

1995 年 7 月，在西安举行的项目签字仪式
A project signing ceremony held in July, 1995 in Xi'an

联合国教科文组织保护世界文化遗产日本信托基金为唐大明宫含元殿遗址保护项目提供资金，主要用于对考古发掘、地质调查、方案设计及遗址本体的保护。

　　1995 年，中日尼雅遗址考察队首次发现并发掘尼雅王族墓地，首次发掘官署、佛寺遗迹，出土西晋时期汉文木简等珍贵文物。

尼雅王族墓地
Niya Ruins

　　2002–2008 年，联合国教科文组织、中国国家文物局、新疆维吾尔自治区文物局和新疆维吾尔自治区龟兹石窟研究所联合组织中日专家开展了新疆维吾尔自治区库木吐喇千佛洞保护工程。

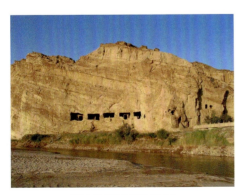

库木吐喇千佛洞外景
Outside view of the Kumtura Caves

库木吐喇千佛洞沟口区第 20 窟坐佛
A seated Buddha in the 20th cave of the Kumtura Caves in
Goukou District

291

中国－蒙古国

文物保护修复工程及联合考古

China - Mongolia Cultural Heritage Protection and Restoration Project and Joint Archaeological Efforts

博格达汗宫位于蒙古国首都乌兰巴托南郊，始建于1893年，是蒙古国重要历史古迹之一。

2006年5月至2007年10月，中国同蒙古国合作开展蒙古国博格达汗宫博物馆门前区维修工程。这是中蒙两国在文物保护修复领域的首次重要合作。通过一年半的修复工程，消除了博格达汗宫的安全隐患，使古建筑恢复了原貌，周边环境也得到改观。

中牌楼修复前后对比图
A pailou (traditional Chinese architectural gateway) before and after restoration

2007年11月至2008年1月，蒙方派出4名学员赴中国进行文物保护修复理念和技术交流培训，为促进中蒙文物保护交流储备了人才力量。

2014—2018年，中蒙两国组成联合考古队，开展"匈奴城址与聚落的调查与发掘"项目，对蒙古国后杭盖省乌贵诺尔苏木境内的匈奴时期和日门塔拉城址进行考古发掘，同时对蒙古国中北部地区的匈奴城址进行系统调查，取得了一系列重要成果。

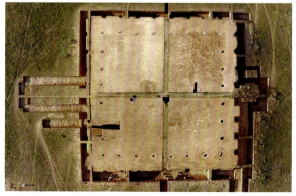

和日门塔拉城址发掘后，结合航拍复原的中城中心建筑台基平面图
The floor plan of the foundation at the center of the Khermen Tal City Site, restored according to the aerial photos after excavation

中国 – 尼泊尔

加德满都杜巴广场九层神庙修复项目

China - Nepal Joint Restoration of the Nine-Storey Basantapur Tower at Kathmandu Durbar Square

2015年10月，中方组织专家赴尼泊尔，对因地震受损的九层神庙进行现场考察和项目可行性研究。2017年8月，九层神庙修复项目开工，工期5年。截至2018年底，已陆续完成Lalitpur塔（东南角）的落架维修和Kirtipur塔（西北角）的整体维修工作，排除了文物本体的险情和安全隐患。

九层神庙建筑群（震前）
The architectural complex built around the nine-storey Basantapur Tower (before the earthquake)

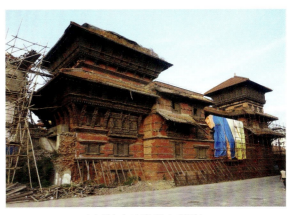

九层神庙建筑群（震后）
The architectural complex of the nine-storey Basantapur Tower (after the earthquake)

尼泊尔国家博物馆施工现场
Construction site of the National Museum of Nepal

修复完成后鸟瞰效果图
Aerial rendering of the restored Tower

中尼双方工作人员在九层神庙修复工地合影
Group photo of Chinese and Nepali staff working on the restoration of the nine-storey Basantapur Tower

中国－印度

奎隆港口遗址联合调查发掘

China - India Joint Investigation and Excavation of the Kollam Port Site

2016 年 12 月，中印两国组成联合考古队，在奎隆港口进行考古勘察工作。通过考古发掘，出土了中国瓷器残片、中国铜钱、印度本地红陶残片及朱罗王朝时期的银币、铜币等遗存。这次联合调查发掘为深入研究中国手工业产品海上贸易等情况提供了珍贵资料。

专家整理奎隆港口遗址出土的中国铜钱
An expert sorting out the Chinese copper coins unearthed at the Kollam Port Site

奎隆港口遗址出土的元丰通宝铜钱
The Yuanfeng Tongbao copper coins unearthed at the Kollam Port Site

奎隆港口遗址出土的中国青瓷及褐色釉瓷残片
Chinese Celadon and brownish-glazed porcelain fragments unearthed at the Kollam Port Site

中印双方开展学术交流活动
Chinese and Indian professionals engaged in academic exchanges

中国－孟加拉国

毗诃罗普尔古城纳提什瓦遗址联合考古发掘

China - Bangladesh Joint Archaeological Excavation
of the Nateshwar Site in Vikrampura

　　2014年12月至2019年1月，中孟两国组成联合考古队，对毗诃罗普尔古城的纳提什瓦遗址开展4次大规模的考古发掘工作，发掘面积达6000余平方米，基本完成了遗址全域的发掘，取得重要成果。

第一期寺院建筑局部（约公元8–10世纪）
Example of monastic architecture, phase I (circa 8th-10th century A.D.)

第二期寺院遗迹局部（约公元10–13世纪）
Example of monastic architecture, phase II (circa 10th-13th century A.D.)

古城出土的佛造像（约公元11世纪）
Buddhist statue excavated at the Nateshwar Site (circa 11th century A.D.)

纳提什瓦遗址鸟瞰
A bird's view of the Nateshwar Site

遗址发掘和保护国际研讨会
International seminar on site excavation and conservation

中国－哈萨克斯坦

拉哈特古城遗址联合考古发掘与合作研究

China - Kazakhstan Joint Archaeological Excavation and Study on the Ancient City of Rahat

2017–2018 年，中哈两国联合考古工作队先后调查、发掘了拉哈特古城 13 处遗迹，清理 15 座墓葬，通过现场勘查发掘与多种现代技术相结合，判明拉哈特遗址整体结构，推测其主体时代在公元前 3 世纪前后。此次联合考古工作为进一步深入探讨古代哈萨克游牧文化积累了宝贵资料和经验。

拉哈特遗址发掘探方位置航拍
Aerial photo of the excavation unit of the Rahat Site

考古工作中发现的马坑遗迹
Remains of a sacrificial horse pit discovered during the excavation

部分出土文物
Excavated Cultural Relics

考古队员清理遗址
Member of the archaeological team cleaning the site

中国－吉尔吉斯斯坦

红河古城佛寺遗址联合考古发掘

China - Kyrgyzstan Joint Archaeological Excavation of Temple Ruins in the Ancient City of Navekat (Krasnaya Rechka)

　　2018 年 6 月，中吉两国组成的联合考古队在红河古城西侧佛寺遗址，综合运用多种技术手段进行考古发掘，并全方位记录古城情况。发掘结束后，对发掘区进行了覆盖保护。考古工作初步探明了西侧佛寺遗址的围墙范围，第一次对整个红河古城遗址进行了比较精确的测绘，同时也积累了在中亚地区发掘土坯类遗迹的相关经验。

红河古城遗址
Remains of the ancient city of Navekat (Krasnaya Rechka)

西侧佛寺遗址发掘前（左下为发掘点）
Ruins of a Buddhist temple on the west side before the excavation (the excavation took place in the lower left corner of the image)

出土陶罐
Unearthed clay pot

遗址覆盖保护
Covering the site for protective purposes

中国－沙特阿拉伯

塞林港遗址联合考古调查与发掘

China - Saudi Arabia Joint Archaeological Investigation and Excavation of the Al-Serrian Site

2018 年 3 月至 2019 年 1 月，中沙联合考古队对红海之滨的港口遗址——沙特阿拉伯塞林港遗址先后进行两次考古工作，完成塞林港遗址周边环境遥感考古与测绘，并对重点遗址进行调查、测绘和发掘。为海上丝绸之路考古研究提供了十分珍贵的资料。

塞林港遗址面积超过 100 万平方米，出土了青铜砝码、波斯釉陶、阿拉伯陶器和中国瓷器，结合文献记载，可以确认此处为红海之滨的重要朝圣贸易港。

遗址周边海域海底泥沙采样
Sampling seabed sediments from waters surrounding the site

遗址周边海域水下地质探查
Underwater geological survey of waters surrounding the site

中沙联合考古队员工地合影
Group photo of members of the Sino-Saudi joint archaeological team

发掘现场研讨
Investigation and discussion of the excavation site

讨论拓片碑文
Discussing inscriptions on the tablet rubbings

遗址发现墓碑拓片
Rubbing of an epitaph discovered at the Site

联合申报世界文化遗产

Joint Application for World Cultural Heritage

2014 年 6 月，中国、哈萨克斯坦、吉尔吉斯斯坦联合申报的"丝绸之路：长安 – 天山廊道的路网"项目列入《世界遗产名录》，成为首例跨国合作成功申遗的项目。

"丝绸之路：长安 – 天山廊道的路网"
路线及沿途文化遗产
Silk Road: the Routes Network of Chang'an-
Tianshan Corridor and Heritage along the
Routes

观众参观"绵亘万里：世界遗产丝绸之路展"
Visitor at the exhibition "Miles upon Miles: World Heritage along
the Silk Road"

克孜尔石窟壁画
Mural from the Kizil Grottoes

文化遗产保护人才培训合作

Collaboration on Training Cultural Industry
and Museum Professionals

亚非国家文物保护和管理培训项目

Training Program of Cultural Heritage Protection and Management for Asian and African Countries

　　亚非国家文物保护和管理培训项目是中国文博系统开展的首个对外培训项目。从 2004 年开始，先后有来自 50 个亚、非、阿国家的 83 名文化遗产保护官员和技术专家参加培训。通过该项目，向各国介绍了中国文化遗产保护理念和经验，构建了文明交流互鉴的渠道与平台，为文化遗产保护领域进一步开展国际合作起到了积极的推动作用。

开学典礼
Opening ceremony of the class

学员参观实验室
Students visiting the laboratory

学员学习理论课程
Students taking theoretical courses

中日韩合作"丝绸之路沿线文物保护修复人员培养计划"

The "China - Japan - Korea Training Program for Professionals of Cultural Heritage Protection and Restoration Along the Silk Road"

中日韩合作"丝绸之路沿线文物保护修复人员培养计划"始于 2006 年春，通过中日韩三方的共同努力，用时 5 年，共培养 102 名专业技术人员。在实现人才培养目标的基础上，搭建了东亚三国在文物保护修复领域交流合作的新平台，开创了政府机构、慈善机构、企业机构和科研机构联合开展文化遗产保护人才培养国际合作的成功范例。

考古现场保护班梁带村墓地青铜片加固提取
The archaeological fieldwork preservation class
consolidating and picking up bronze pieces at the Cemetery
in Liangdai Village

陶瓷金属文物保护修复培训班中日专家执教实习
Chinese and Japanese experts teaching students the
preservation and repairing of ceramic and metal artifacts

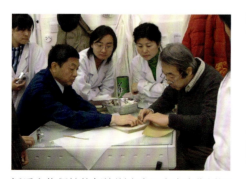

纸质文物保护修复培训班中日专家合作授课
Chinese and Japanese experts jointly giving
lectures on the preservation and repairing of
paper-based artifacts

中日韩三方代表参加培养计划总结研讨会
Chinese, Japanese and Korean representatives participating in the training
program review seminar

"一带一路"沿线国家水下考古培训

Training Courses in Underwater Archaeology for the Belt and Road Countries

2016 年，中国应柬埔寨、泰国、印度尼西亚、印度、斯里兰卡、伊朗和沙特阿拉伯等海上丝绸之路沿线国家邀请，举办了"'一带一路'沿线国家水下考古培训班"。经过两个年度共计 4 个月的潜水培训与实习，所有学员顺利结业。水下考古培训工作为今后"一带一路"沿线国家开展联合考古打下了学术基础，建立了良好关系。

潜水技术练习
Practicing diving skills

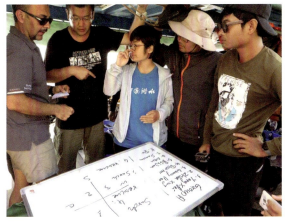

讨论水下工作计划
Discussing the underwater operations

完成水下绘图任务
Underwater drawing

文物展览交流

Exchanges of Exhibitions
of Cultural Relics

中国－日本文物展览交流

China - Japan Cultural Heritage Exhibitions

　　中日两国文物展览交流频繁，自20世纪50年代始，中国赴日举办文物展览不胜枚举。著名展览包括"中华人民共和国出土文物展览""兵马俑展""黄河文明展""曾侯乙墓出土文物特别展""中国国宝展""大三国志展""中国西藏秘宝展""故宫博物院文物精华展""中华大文明展""汉字的历史与美学"等，深受日本民众欢迎。日本也先后来华举办过"鉴真与空海——中日文化交流的见证""日本考古展——古都奈良考古文物精华展""醍醐寺艺术珍宝展""伊万里瓷器展"等展览。文物展览交流增进了中日两国人民之间的相互理解和友谊。

1986年，赴日本"黄河文明展"海报
Poster for the exhibition "Yellow River Valley Civilization" held in Japan in 1986

1992年5月，日本明仁天皇夫妇参观"曾侯乙墓出土文物特别展"
Japanese Emperor Akihito and Empress Michiko at the "Special Exhibition: Cultural Relics Unearthed from the Tomb of Marquis Yi of Zeng" in May, 1992

2008年5月，"大三国志展"在日本东京富士美术馆等7地巡展
In May 2008, the "Great Romance of the Three Kingdoms" exhibition was held in seven venues, including the Tokyo Fuji Art Museum

2012年10月，"中华大文明展"在东京国立博物馆等地展出
In October 2012, "China: Grandeur of the Dynasties" was held at Tokyo National Museum and other venues

2016 年，日本"醍醐寺艺术珍宝展"在上海博物馆、陕西历史博物馆展出
In 2016, the exhibition "The Beauty of Mantra: Arts in the Collection of Daigo-ji Temple" was held at Shanghai Museum and Shaanxi History Museum respectively

2017 年 12 月，"汉字的历史与美学展"在东京富士美术馆等地展出
In December 2017, "Chinese Characters: A Legacy and Marvel Perfected over Three Millennia" toured several Japanese museums, including the Tokyo Fuji Art Museum

中国－韩国文物展览交流

China - Korea Cultural Heritage Exhibitions

  2015 年 9 月，中韩两国合作举办的"古代佛教艺术展"在韩国国立中央博物馆开幕。展览汇集来自中国、韩国、印度、日本等 8 个国家的 210 余件展品，通过展示不同国家、不同时期的古代佛教艺术作品，阐释了佛教文化的丰富内涵及其在亚洲地区的传播和影响。

参展各国嘉宾庆祝展览开幕
Guests from participating
countries celebrating the
opening of the exhibition

观察研究展品
Examining and studying the exhibits

嘉宾参观展览
Guests visiting the exhibition

阿富汗古代珍宝在华巡展

Ancient Treasures of Afghanistan Exhibited in China

代表着 20 世纪阿富汗考古发掘成果的 231 件（组）文物，自 2006 年开始在全球巡展。展览自 2017 年 3 月开始，先后在故宫博物院、敦煌研究院、成都博物馆、深圳南山博物馆、湖南省博物馆、清华大学艺术博物馆展出，引起中国观众的热烈反响。

2017 年 3 月，"浴火重光——来自阿富汗国家博物馆的宝藏"展在故宫开幕
The exhibition "Afghanistan: Hidden Treasures from the National Museum, Kabul" opened at the Palace Museum in March, 2017

阿富汗国家博物馆馆长在湖南省博物馆的讲座
Director of the National Museum of Afghanistan at a lecture held at Hunan Museum

阿富汗国家博物馆馆长为嘉宾介绍金冠
Director of the National Museum of Afghanistan introducing the gold crown to the guests

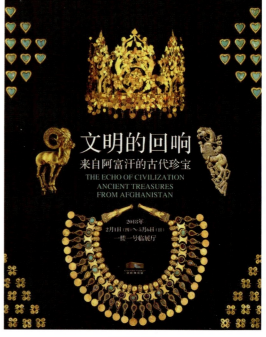

展览海报
Exhibition Poster

中国－沙特阿拉伯文物展览交流

China - Saudi Arabia Cultural Heritage Exhibitions

　　2016年12月至2017年3月，"阿拉伯之路——沙特阿拉伯出土文物"展在中国国家博物馆举办，展品共计466件（组）沙特阿拉伯出土文物，均为首次来华展出，反映了过去40年间沙特阿拉伯考古发掘研究工作的重要成果。2017年3月16日，中国国家主席习近平同沙特阿拉伯国王萨勒曼共同出席了展览闭幕式。习近平主席在闭幕式致辞中指出，此次展览是双方推动文化对话、加强文化交流互鉴的一项成果，也是中沙全面战略伙伴关系的重要体现。

中国文化部领导陪同沙方嘉宾参观"阿拉伯之路——沙特阿拉伯出土文物"展
Leaders of the Ministry of Culture, PRC accompanying Saudi Arabian guests at the exhibition "Roads of Arabia: Archaeological Treasures of Saudi Arabia"

　　2018年9月，"华夏瑰宝展"在沙特阿拉伯利雅得国家博物馆举办，这是中国文物首次赴沙特阿拉伯展出。展览通过200余件展品展示了中华文明的发轫、成长与传承，还首次展示了中沙联合考古队在沙特阿拉伯塞林港遗址发现的中国古代瓷器残片、青铜砝码和石墓碑等最新考古成果，再次证明古代中国与红海地区有着密切的海上交往。

中外嘉宾出席"华夏瑰宝展"开幕式
Guests from China, Saudi Arabia and other countries attending the opening ceremony of the exhibition "Treasures of China" in Saudi Arabia

4

第四部分

美人之美
礼尚往来

RESPECT DIVERSITY ENHANCE FRIENDSHIP

"国之交在于民相亲"，而文化渊源构成亚洲国家的精神纽带。在"一带一路"倡议的推动下，文明融通将成为人类文明不可阻挡的历史命运，"各美其美，美人之美，美美与共，天下大同"的文明愿景正逐渐变为现实。

自 1949 年中华人民共和国成立以来，中国政府一直坚定不移地奉行独立自主的外交政策，积极加强同世界各国的合作与交往，努力增进同周边国家的睦邻友好关系。在国际交往中，礼品凝结着中国人民和世界各国人民的友好情谊，也反映了不同国家别具特色的文化传统和多姿多彩的艺术风格，具有珍贵的历史价值、艺术价值和纪念意义。

亚洲地域广袤，国家、民族众多，历史悠久，文化习俗不尽相同，礼品风格迥异，不乏立意独到、构思新颖、造型精巧、工艺精湛的佳作，为我们带来了丰富多彩的异域风情和积淀深厚的文化底蕴，也展示了亚洲各国人民的聪明才智和亚洲文化的魅力。

"A country's diplomatic relationships depend on its people." The common cultural origin of Asian countries establishes a spiritual bond among them. With the implementation of "the Belt and Road Initiative", the integration of civilizations will become an unstoppable part of human civilization's future history. The goal that countries should respect each other's interests while pursing their own and advance the common interests of all is gradually becoming a reality.

Since the founding of the People's Republic of China in 1949, the Chinese government has unswervingly pursued an independent and peaceful coexistent foreign policy, actively strengthened cooperation and exchanges with countries in the world, and strove to enhance friendly relations with neighboring countries. The diplomatic gifts convey the friendship between Chinese people and people in other countries and reflect unique cultural traditions and various artistic styles. Gifts also have invaluable historical worth, artistic value, and commemorative significance.

The vast territory and the long history of Asia created a large number of countries and nationalities with different cultural customs and interesting artefacts made from unique and novel ideas, formed into delicate shapes or exquisitely crafted, demonstrate colorful exotic customs and profound cultural heritage, while also displaying the ingenuity and charm of Asian culture.

青金石嵌花纹桌
Lapis Lazuli Mosaic Table

1957 年 10 月阿富汗首相赠中国国家领导人
A diplomatic gift from the then-Prime Minister of Afghanistan to Chinese leader, presented in October, 1957

桌面直径 60、高 46 厘米
Table : Diameter 60 cm, Height 46 cm

中国国家博物馆藏
National Museum of China

玉石镶金摆件
Jade Ornament Inlaid with Gold

2000 年 12 月亚美尼亚总理赠中国国家领导人
A diplomatic gift from the then-Prime Minister of Armenia to Chinese leader, presented in December, 2000

底座直径 9.3、高 15.2 厘米
Bottom diameter 9.3 cm, Height 15.2 cm

中国国家博物馆藏
National Museum of China

银镀金酒具
Silver-Gilt Wine Set

2000 年 6 月阿塞拜疆总统赠中国国家领导人
A diplomatic gift from the then-President of Azerbaijan to Chinese leader, presented in June, 2000

盘长 28、宽 23.5、高 1.5 厘米
Plate: Length 28 cm, Width 23.5 cm, Height 1.5 cm

壶长 19.5、宽 20、高 34 厘米
Pot: Length 19.5 cm, Width 20 cm, Height 34 cm

中国国家博物馆藏
National Museum of China

银镀金城堡模型
Silver-Gilt Miniature Castle

2002 年 5 月巴林首相赠中国国家领导人
A diplomatic gift from the Prime Minister of Bahrain to Chinese leader, presented in May, 2002

长 39、宽 21、高 20 厘米
Length 39 cm, Width 21 cm, Height 20 cm

中国国家博物馆藏
National Museum of China

油画《夕阳帆船》
Oil Painting *Sailing Boat at Sunset*

2014 年 6 月孟加拉国总理赠中国国家领导人
A diplomatic gift from the Prime Minister of Bangladesh to Chinese leader, presented in June, 2014

长 122、宽 76 厘米
Length 122 cm, Width 76 cm

中央礼品文物管理中心藏

银雕花长方烟盒
Silver Embossed Cigarette Case

1988 年 5 月不丹国王赠中国国家领导人
A diplomatic gift from the then-King of Bhutan to Chinese leader, presented in May, 1988

长 13、宽 8、高 5 厘米
Length 13 cm, Width 8 cm, Height 5cm

中国国家博物馆藏
National Museum of China

雕花银盒
Embossed Silver Box

2004 年 9 月文莱苏丹赠中国国家领导人
A diplomatic gift from the Sultan of Brunei to Chinese leader, presented in September, 2004

长 23.5、宽 24、高 16.3 厘米
Length 23.5 cm, Width 24 cm, Height 16.3 cm

中国国家博物馆藏
National Museum of China

石雕四面菩萨头像
Stone Head of a Four-Faced Bodhisattva

1966 年 7 月柬埔寨国家元首赠中国国家领导人
A diplomatic gift from the then-Head of State of Cambodia to Chinese leader, presented in July, 1966

直径 10.2、高 31 厘米
Diameter 10.2 cm, Height 31 cm

中国国家博物馆藏
National Museum of China

瓷花瓶
Porcelain Vase

1991 年 10 月朝鲜国家主席赠中国国家领导人
A diplomatic gift from the then-President of the Democratic People's Republic of Korea to Chinese leader, presented in October, 1991

直径 35、高 74.5 厘米
Diameter 35 cm, Height 74.5 cm

中国国家博物馆藏
National Museum of China

铜錾刻画
Embossed Copper Picture

1993 年 6 月格鲁吉亚国家元首、议会主席赠中国国家领导人

A diplomatic gift from the then–Head of State and Chairman of Parliament of Georgia to Chinese leader, presented in June, 1993

边长 46、厚 3.5 厘米
Side length 46 cm, Thickness 3.5 cm

中国国家博物馆藏
National Museum of China

檀香木雕象盒
Sandalwood Box with Engraved Elephant Design

1956 年 9 月印度国会代表团赠中国国家领导人
A diplomatic gift from the Indian Parliamentary Delegation to Chinese leader, presented in September, 1956

长 44、宽 29，高 34 厘米
Length 44 cm, Width 29 cm, Height 34 cm

中国国家博物馆藏
National Museum of China

哇扬皮影木偶

Wayang Kulit

2015 年 4 月印度尼西亚总统夫妇赠中国国家领导人

A diplomatic gift from the Presidential Couple of Indonesia to Chinese leader, presented in April, 2015

长 14、宽 10、高 54 厘米

Length 14 cm, Width 10 cm, Height 54 cm

中央礼品文物管理中心藏

波斯地毯

Persian Carpet

2008 年 9 月伊朗总统赠中国国家领导人

A diplomatic gift from the then-President of Iran to Chinese leader, presented in September, 2008

毯长 177、宽 108 厘米

Carpet: Length 177 cm, Width 108 cm

中国国家博物馆藏

National Museum of China

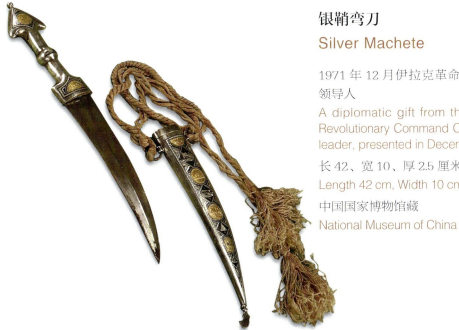

银鞘弯刀

Silver Machete

1971 年 12 月伊拉克革命执委会委员赠中国国家
领导人

A diplomatic gift from the then-member of the
Revolutionary Command Council of Iraq to Chinese
leader, presented in December, 1971

长 42、宽 10、厚 2.5 厘米

Length 42 cm, Width 10 cm, Thickness 2.5 cm

中国国家博物馆藏

National Museum of China

仿古陶瓶

Antique Pottery Vase

2013 年 5 月以色列总理赠中国国家领导人

A diplomatic gift from the Prime Minister of Israel to
Chinese leader, presented in May, 2013

壶长 21.5、宽 28、厚 7 厘米

Pot: Length 21.5 cm, Width 28 cm, Thickness 7 cm

中国国家博物馆藏

National Museum of China

瓷绘鸢尾花镜框画
Framed Porcelain Painting of Irises

1986 年 11 月日本首相赠中国国家领导人
A diplomatic gift from the then-Prime Minister of Japan to Chinese leader, presented in November, 1986

长 70.7、宽 42.4 厘米
Length 70.7 cm, Width 42.4 cm
中国国家博物馆藏
National Museum of China

蓝玻璃水具
Blue Glassware

1999 年 12 月约旦国王赠中国国家领导人
A diplomatic gift from the King of Jordan to Chinese leader, presented in December, 1999
玻璃杯（4 件）长 8、高 9 厘米
Glass (4 pieces): Length 8 cm, Height 9 cm

玻璃壶（1 件）直径 13.5、高 20.3 厘米
Glass kettle (1 piece): Diameter 13.5 cm, Height 20.3 cm
中国国家博物馆藏
National Museum of China

镀金孔雀形杯
Gilded Peacock-Shaped Cups

2012 年 6 月哈萨克斯坦总统赠中国国家
领导人
A diplomatic gift from the then–President
of Kazakhstan to Chinese leader, presented
in June, 2012
长 13、宽 8.5、高 18 厘米
Length 13 cm, Width 8.5 cm, Height 18 cm
中国国家博物馆藏
National Museum of China

木船模型
Wooden Boat Model

2017 年科威特驻华大使赠中国国家领导人
A diplomatic gift from the ambassador of
Kuwait to Chinese leader, presented in 2017
长 48、宽 10、高 45 厘米
Length 48 cm, Width 10 cm, Height 45 cm
中央礼品文物管理中心藏

骑士雕像

Knight Statue

2017 年 5 月吉尔吉斯斯坦总统赠中国国家
领导人

A diplomatic gift from the then-President of
Kyrgyzstan to Chinese leader, presented in
May, 2017

长 16、宽 8、高 21 厘米

Length 16 cm, Width 8 cm, Height 21 cm

中央礼品文物管理中心藏

红木雕刻画

Mahogany Carvings

2016 年 5 月老挝人民革命党总书记、国家主席赠
中国国家领导人

A diplomatic gift from the General Secretary of Lao
People's Revolutionary Party and President of Laos
to Chinese leader, presented in May, 2016

长 92、宽 34、厚 5 厘米

Length 92 cm, Width 34 cm, Height 5 cm

中央礼品文物管理中心藏

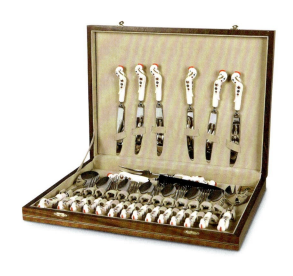

象牙柄不锈钢餐具
Stainless Steel Tableware with Ivory Handles

2001 年 4 月黎巴嫩议长赠中国国家领导人
A diplomatic gift from the Speaker of Lebanese Parliament to Chinese leader, presented in April, 2001

盒长 48.5、宽 36、高 6 厘米
Box: Length 48.5 cm, Width 36 cm, Height 6 cm

刀长 31.5、宽 4.5 厘米
Knife: Length 31.5 cm, Width 4.5 cm

中国国家博物馆藏
National Museum of China

鎏金银花瓶
Silver-Gilt Vase

2005 年 3 月马来西亚最高元首赠中国国家领导人
A diplomatic gift from the then-Supreme Head of Malaysia to Chinese leader, presented in March, 2005

直径 16、高 27 厘米
Diameter 16 cm, Height 27 cm

中国国家博物馆藏
National Museum of China

手工木刻船
Dhoni Sailboat Model

2014 年 8 月马尔代夫总统赠中国国家领导人
A diplomatic gift from the then-President of the Maldives to Chinese leader, presented in August, 2014

长 62、宽 18、高 43 厘米
Length 62 cm, Width 18 cm, Height 43 cm

中央礼品文物管理中心藏

钢刀
Mongol Sword

2017 年 5 月蒙古国总理赠中国国家领导人

A diplomatic gift from the then-Prime Minister of Mongolia to Chinese leader, presented in May, 2017

长 102、宽 13 厘米

Length 102 cm, Width 13 cm

中央礼品文物管理中心藏

象牙雕刻烟盒
Ivory Engraved Cigarette Case

20 世纪 50 年代缅甸总理赠中国国家领导人

A diplomatic gift from the then-Prime Minister of Burma to Chinese leader, presented in the 1950s

长 15.5、宽 12、高 6 厘米

Length 15.5 cm, Width 12 cm, Height 6 cm

中国国家博物馆藏

National Museum of China

木雕孔雀
Wood Carved Peacock

1992 年 3 月尼泊尔首相赠中国国家领导人

A diplomatic gift from the then-Prime Minister of Nepal to Chinese leader, presented in March, 1992

长 38.6、宽 21.5、高 56 厘米

Length 38.6 cm, Width 21.5 cm, Height 56 cm

中国国家博物馆藏

National Museum of China

银錾花咖啡壶

Silver Repoussé Coffeepot

1999 年 12 月阿曼国家委员会主席赠中国
国家领导人

A diplomatic gift from the Chairman of the
Council of State of Oman to Chinese leader,
presented in December, 1999

长 26、宽 13、高 32.2 厘米
Length 26 cm, Width 13 cm, Height 32.2 cm

中国国家博物馆藏
National Museum of China

木雕花箱

Wood Engraved Box

2002 年 6 月巴基斯坦总统赠中国国家领导人

A diplomatic gift from the then–President of Pakistan
to Chinese leader, presented in June, 2002

长 92.5、宽 46、高 47.5 厘米
Length 92.5 cm, Width 46 cm, Height 47.5 cm

中国国家博物馆藏
National Museum of China

贝雕清真寺长方盒
Shell-Encrusted Jewelry Box

1981 年 10 月巴勒斯坦解放组织执行委员会主席赠
中国国家领导人

A diplomatic gift from the then–President of Palestine Liberation Organization Executive Committee to Chinese leader, presented in October, 1981

长 39、宽 29、高 12 厘米
Length 39 cm, Width 29 cm, Height 12 cm

中国国家博物馆藏
National Museum of China

银羚羊摆件
Silver Antelope Ornament

2008 年卡塔尔王储赠中国国家领导人

A diplomatic gift from the then–Crown Prince of Qatar to Chinese leader, presented in 2008

长 23、宽 12、高 21.5 厘米
Length 23 cm, Width 12 cm, Height 21.5 cm

中国国家博物馆藏
National Museum of China

嵌螺钿漆盒

Lacquered Box Inlaid with Mother-of-pearl Design

1994 年 3 月韩国总统赠中国国家领导人

A diplomatic gift from the then-President of the Republic of Korea to Chinese leader, presented in March, 1994

长 35、宽 27.5、高 14 厘米

Length 35 cm, Width 27.5 cm, Height 14 cm

中国国家博物馆藏

National Museum of China

四方宫模型

Miniature of the Murabba Palace

2016 年 1 月沙特阿拉伯国王赠中国国家领导人

A diplomatic gift from the King of Saudi Arabia to Chinese leader, presented in January, 2016

长 62、宽 52、高 40 厘米

Length 62 cm, Width 52 cm, Height 40 cm

中央礼品文物管理中心藏

陶艺品

Ceramic Ware

2016 年 9 月新加坡总理赠中国国家领导人

A diplomatic gift from the Prime Minister of Singapore to Chinese leader, presented in September, 2016

长 30、宽 18、高 45 厘米

Length 30 cm, Width 18 cm, Height 45 cm

中央礼品文物管理中心藏

郑和《布施锡兰山佛寺碑》拓片
Rubbing of the Galle Trilingual Inscription Installed by Zheng He

2014 年 9 月斯里兰卡总统赠中国国家领导人
A diplomatic gift from the then-President of Sri Lanka to Chinese leader, presented in September, 2014

长 210、宽 98 厘米
Length 210 cm, Width 98 cm

中央礼品文物管理中心藏

铜錾花罐
Copper Repoussé Pot

1987 年 1 月叙利亚副总统赠中国国家领导人
A diplomatic gift from the then-Vice President of Syria to Chinese leader, presented in January, 1987

直径 23、高 42 厘米
Diameter 23 cm, Height 42 cm

中国国家博物馆藏
National Museum of China

帽子

腰带

塔袍（三件套）
Tajik Robe (Three-piece Suit)

2014 年 9 月塔吉克斯坦总统赠中国国家领导人
A diplomatic gift from the President of Tajikistan to Chinese leader, presented in September, 2014

长 140 厘米
Length 140 cm

中央礼品文物管理中心藏

人偶
Figurines

2015 年泰国总理赠中国国家领导人
A diplomatic gift from the Prime Minister of Thailand to Chinese leader, presented in 2015

长 18、宽 10、高 61 厘米
Length 18 cm, Width 10 cm, Height 61 cm

中央礼品文物管理中心藏

硬木雕人物屏风
Carved Hardwood Screen with Human Figures

1975 年 6 月菲律宾总统赠中国国家领导人
A diplomatic gift from the then-President of the Philippines to Chinese leader, presented in June, 1975

长 268、高 163、厚 5.7 厘米
Length 268 cm, Height 163 cm, Thickness 5.7 cm

中国国家博物馆藏
National Museum of China

银掐丝传统民居模型
Cloisonné Silver-Wire Miniature of a Traditional House

2014 年 4 月东帝汶总理赠中国国家领导人
A diplomatic gift from the then–Prime Minister of East Timor to Chinese leader, presented in April, 2014

长 13、宽 13、高 35 厘米
Length 13 cm, Width 13 cm, Height 35 cm

中央礼品文物管理中心藏

银茶具
Silver Tea Set

2012 年土耳其总理赠中国国家领导人
A diplomatic gift from the then–Prime Minister of Turkey to Chinese leader, presented in 2012

壶长 21、宽 12、高 31 厘米
Pot: Length 21 cm, Width 12 cm, Height 31 cm

盘直径 33.5、高 7.5 厘米
Plate: Length 33.5 cm, Height 7.5 cm

中国国家博物馆藏
National Museum of China

地毯
Carpet

2014 年土库曼斯坦总统赠中国国家领导人
A diplomatic gift from the President of Turkmenistan to Chinese leader, presented in 2014

长 150、宽 100 厘米
Length 150 cm, Width 100 cm

中央礼品文物管理中心藏

抽象水彩画《中国，阿拉伯联合酋长国》
Abstract Watercolor Painting *China and United Arab Emirates*

2018 年 7 月阿拉伯联合酋长国阿布扎比王储赠中国国家领导人
A diplomatic gift from the Crown Prince of Abu Dhabi to Chinese leader, presented in July, 2018

长 183、宽 135 厘米
Length 183 cm, Width 135 cm

中央礼品文物管理中心藏

镜框画《丝绸之路》
Framed Painting *Silk Road*

2012 年 6 月乌兹别克斯坦总统赠中国国家领导人
A diplomatic gift from the then-President of Uzbekistan to Chinese leader, presented in June, 2012

长 67、宽 47 厘米
Length 67 cm, Width 47 cm

中国国家博物馆藏
National Museum of China

传统图腾陶像
Clay Sculpture of Traditional Totem

2016 年 11 月越南国家主席赠中国国家领导人
A diplomatic gift from the then President of Vietnam to Chinese leader, presented in November, 2016
长 19、宽 12、高 29 厘米
Length 19 cm, Width 12 cm, Height 29 cm
中央礼品文物管理中心藏

银镶宝石腰刀
Silver Jambiya Inlaid with Gemstones

2013 年 11 月也门总统赠中国国家领导人
A diplomatic gift from the President of Yemen to Chinese leader, presented in November, 2013

长 61、宽 8、厚 4 厘米
Length 61 cm, Width 8 cm, Thickness 4 cm
中国国家博物馆藏
National Museum of China

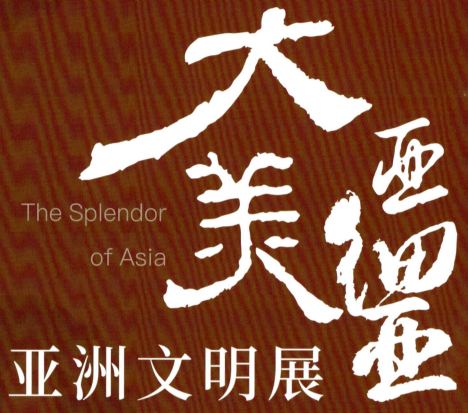

Joint Exhibition of Asian Civilizations

亚洲文明联展 之

The Splendor
of Asia

亚洲文明展

An Exhibition of Asian Civilizations

结 束 语

　　亚洲文明，灿若星河，在人类数千年的文明史中占有举足轻重的地位。悠久的历史文化是亚洲文明的重要内涵，时至今日，我们仍然从中不断汲取着有益的营养。珍视历史、交流互鉴，面向未来，已经成为亚洲各国发展前进的共识。亚洲人民比以往任何时候都更有能力、有信心携手创造共同的繁荣与幸福，为推动构建人类命运共同体而贡献亚洲智慧与力量。

CONCLUSION

　　Asia's grand civilization has played a decisive role in the history of human civilization for thousands of years. The long history and well-established culture have formed an important feature of Asian civilization, which continues to benefit Asian countries even now. Cherishing history, creating mutual exchanges, and facing the future have already become the accepted path of development and progress in Asia. More than ever before, Asian people are both able and confident about working together in order to prosper together. Asians are dedicated to contributing their wisdom and strength to build a better tomorrow for mankind.

美美与共　有容乃大

——"亚洲文明展"述记

　　亚洲是世界上面积最广袤、人口与民族最多的大陆。亚细亚洲是亚洲的全称，意为"太阳升起的地方"。诚如其名，人类文明的火种最早在这里点燃，作为世界文明的重要发祥地，亚洲照亮了人类历史的天空。历经漫长的历史积淀，亚洲多姿多彩的文明交相辉映，为人类保存着最久远的文明记忆和波澜壮阔的文明图谱。

　　2019 年 5 月 15 日，在习近平主席的倡议下，亚洲文明对话大会在北京开幕。这次大会是汇聚亚洲文明、凝聚亚洲共识的宽广平台，也是亚洲文化大交流、人民大联欢的人文盛事，是激发文化共鸣点、维护文明多样性的文明盛会。"大美亚细亚——亚洲文明展"是配合亚洲文明对话大会举办的"亚洲文明联展"系列文物展之主展览，由中华人民共和国文化和旅游部、国家文物局主办，中国国家博物馆和中国文物交流中心承办。展览汇集亚洲全部 47 国及希腊、埃及两个文明古国伙伴的 451 件（组）文物，以精美丰富的展品和多样化的展陈方式，生动展示了亚洲先辈们共同创造的璀璨文明成果与今日亚洲文明交流互鉴的瑰丽图景。展览的成功举办激发了亚洲人民对自己多彩文化的自豪，更推动不同民族、不同国家、不同文明之间的平等对话，让亚洲和世界文明在新时代熠熠生辉。

　　展览以"大美亚细亚"为题，大美者，海纳百川，有容乃大，美美与共，天下大同。这一主题呼应习近平主席倡导的文明交流互鉴和构建亚洲命运共同体、构建人类命运共同体等重要理念，旨在通过文化遗产讲述各国文明故事，呈现各国文明之美，为亚洲各国相互交流、展示、沟通、了解搭建重要平台。为更好地表达亚洲悠久灿烂、多元共生的文明特征，展览以"多元文明并置，古今文明相通"为主线，既回顾历史，也聚焦当下。借由文物资料的佐证，我们追溯亚洲文明的源流，思考各文明在交流互鉴的进程中不断认知自我、改变世界的深刻意义；我们关注亚洲文明在当今大发展大变革大调整时期的发展方向，领悟开拓创新与合作共赢带给亚洲文明薪火相传、生生不息的前行动力。

　　在此基础上建构起展览的四个部分。第一部分"美成在久，日出东方"，以文物为载体，凸显各国历史文化特色，回溯两河流域文明、印度河文明和中华文明的起源与发展，诠释亚洲作为文明之源对于全人类的重大贡献。展出的文物精品荟萃，新石器时代中国良渚文化玉琮、距今 3000 年的老挝铜鼓、公元前 8– 前 7 世纪亚美尼亚陶鸟形来通、公元前 4 世纪沙特阿拉伯塔布克地区的石雕人像，见证着在遥远的史前时期，亚洲大地上就留下了各族文明的瑰丽遗存。第二部分"美在通途，行久致远"，集中展示陆上及海上丝绸之路的繁盛景象，盛唐三彩载丝骆驼、《张骞出使西域图》敦煌莫高窟唐初壁画摹本、南宋"南海Ⅰ号"沉船出水瓷器等文物，直接或间接地反映了丝绸之路不仅是经济交流之路，也是文明互鉴之路。第三部分"美美与共，天下大同"，由历史转入现实，从文物本身转向考古发掘保护的现场，向公众讲述中国与亚洲各国在文化遗产领域交流合作的研究成果。从中国参与吴哥古迹保护修复到中印联合调查发掘奎隆港口遗址，从中哈吉三国联合申报世界文化遗产到"一带一路"沿线国家水下考古培训，亚洲各国合作的范围更广、形式更多样，向世界表明了文明对话、携手合作的亚洲，为传承文明付出的努力和坚定决心。第四部分"美人之美，礼尚往来"，展示中国国家领导人在与亚洲各国领导人外交活动中受赠的 46 件（组）礼品。这些礼品是和平与友谊的象征、亚洲文明的瑰宝，具有特殊的历史意义和很高的艺术价值。它们反映了不同国家各具特色的文化艺术，凝结着中国人民和亚洲各国人民的友好情谊。

此次参展国家数量、文物数量和精致程度前所未有，堪称"文物领域的奥林匹克盛会"。展品的遴选主要考虑两个因素：一是能够代表本国文明的独特风貌。例如，中国展区文物就以突出中华文明这一人类历史上唯一从未间断过的古老文明为核心，反映中华文明在礼制与思想、科学与技术、文化与艺术、经济与生活等领域辉煌成就的代表性文物。红山文化青玉猪龙、二里头文化嵌绿松石青铜牌饰、殷墟刻辞卜甲、西周青铜何尊等文物，诉说"中国"从何而来，展示中国早期文明起源的多元性；战国曾侯乙铜尊盘、西汉鎏金铜长信宫灯、唐代舞马衔杯仿皮囊式银壶等集科学、艺术、技术于一体的实用器，尽显古人高超的技艺和独特的匠心；元青花四爱图梅瓶、赵孟頫行书《为隆教禅寺石室长老疏卷》、明《永乐大典》副写本、清《耕织图》册页等文物，展示中华传统文化的人文意蕴与美学精髓。凡此种种，多为国家一级文物，全方位展示中华文明的源远流长与博大精深。不仅中国文物如此，阿富汗国家博物馆策展人纳斯林·贝拉利这样评价，"这个展览走一圈，就像从几十个国家走过一遍，能够领略亚洲各国的历史文化风貌"。二是能够反映亚洲文明交往的悠久历史。古老的亚洲，从很早时候开始就已是一个休戚与共的命运共同体。"你中有我、我中有你"，是亚洲各文明的共同特征。丝绸之路、茶叶之路、香料之路等古老商路上交往交流、互通有无的动人故事，在展览中通过文物的载体向公众娓娓道来。展厅入口处的郑和布施锡兰山佛寺碑复制品是明代航海家郑和第二次下西洋时所立，碑文以中文、泰米尔文和波斯文表达了对佛教、印度教和伊斯兰教的敬仰，体现出中国自古以来对不同文明的尊重，它是海上丝绸之路与中斯友谊的重要见证，也是中华文明亲仁善邻、协和万邦的最好讲述者。来自新加坡亚洲文明博物馆的清光绪粉彩盖盅，是"峇峇娘惹"瓷器的代表，这件融合中式装饰风格与马来文化使用方式的外销瓷，见证了中华民族与马来民族悠远的人文交流史。来自亚美尼亚历史博物馆的比尼遗址陶鸟形来通杯与来自伊朗国家博物馆的波斯时期来通杯，不禁让人联想起中国西安发现的镶金兽首玛瑙来通杯，具有典型的西方古代玉雕特点。这些产地与形象各异，但形制相近的来通杯，勾画出一幅清晰的文明交流路线图。

多样的展陈手段与独特的展览空间设计也为本次展览锦上添花。展览开篇的弧幕影片《大美亚细亚》，以现代影视艺术手段展现了恢弘壮美的亚洲世界文化遗产和著名文化景观，铺陈了孕育亚洲文明的自然地理和人文环境。展览主色调选用了在亚洲文化中象征幸福与庆祝的绛红色，热情而不失沉稳。根据展区主题的不同，在红色背景中辅以丝绸之路、文化遗产、城市剪影等抽象的主题创作，烘托氛围又不喧宾夺主。展柜侧面以中英文双语标示出参展国家名称与概况，星罗棋布的陈列岛展开了亚洲各国跨越时空的文明对话：巴基斯坦犍陀罗佛像、印度石雕象头神像、柬埔寨吴哥神像、约旦亚历山大里亚图景马赛克……比邻而望，相互凝视，观众能直观地从艺术形象的嬗变中窥探到亚洲各民族多元的文化传统。隔而不断、相互联系的空间布局正如同亚洲多种文明分别兴起、独立发展的同时，在交流互鉴中守望相助、共同发展的形态。贴于展柜玻璃上的文物说明配合展签，以及地图、照片、图表、文物局部详图等内容的辅助展板，为公众了解文物背后的故事提供了全面详实的信息。展览中亮相的"文物带你看亚洲"多媒体互动展示系统，采用三维还原技术，观众能够在屏幕上自由地翻转、全方位地查看亚洲 13 个国家近 60 件文物的细节，亲身感受数字文物展示的精彩与震撼。

　　本次展览的成功举办离不开亚洲各国的高度重视和大力支持，展览筹备过程本身就是一次亚洲各国文化交往的良好实践。展示是文明互鉴的最好开篇，亚洲国家将以此次展览为契机，在文化领域开启更加广泛、深入的交流合作。

　　"一花独放不是春，百花齐放春满园。"亚洲文明从来都是在对话中前进，在互鉴中发展。亚洲文明展览丰富了文明对话的形式，不同文明的展示与呈现，让各国增进和深化对各自文明的认识，推动为构建人类命运共同体理念凝聚更多共识。人类文明发展的道路在共同的前方，面向未来，让我们一道拥抱世界之美，各美其美，美美与共。

姚安

INCLUSIVE CIVILIZATIONS

—— Overview on "An Exhibition of Asian Civilizations"

As the largest continent in the world, Asia has been home to the largest population and ethnic groups. Asia means "the land of the rising sun". The name implies that human civilization originates from here. As an important cradle of world civilization, Asia has been a pearl in human history. The long historical accumulation has created the wonderful civilization, preserving the oldest and magnificent civilization records for mankind.

On May 15, 2019, the Conference on Dialogue of Asian Civilizations was held under the initiative of President Xi Jinping. The conference aims to bring together Asian civilizations, unite Asian consensus, promote Asian cultural exchanges and people-to-people communications, inspire cultural resonance and promote cultural diversity. As the main exhibition of the series of "Joint Exhibition of Asian Civilizations" for the Conference on Dialogue of Asian Civilizations, "The Splendor of Asia–An Exhibition of Asian Civilizations" is hosted by the Ministry of Culture and Tourism of the People's Republic of China and National Cultural Heritage Administration and organized by National Museum of China and Art Exhibitions China. The exhibition displays 451 pieces of the cultural relics from all 47 Asian countries and two great ancient civilizations—— Greece and Egypt. With exquisite and rich exhibits and diverse exhibition methods, it vividly shows the splendid civilization achievements jointly created by Asian ancestors and the magnificent exchanges and mutual learning among Asian civilizations nowadays. The exhibition has inspired Asian people to take pride in their wonderful cultures, and has promoted equal dialogue among different nations, countries and civilizations. In such a way, Asian civilizations, or even world civilizations, shines in the new era.

The theme of the exhibition is "The Splendor of Asia". "Splendor" civilizations, or refers to the inclusiveness of civilizations. The theme reflects the important concepts initiated by President Xi Jinping, such as civilization exchange, Asia community of shared future and community of shared future for all mankind. The aim is to develop an important platform for mutual exchange, displaying, communication and understanding for Asian countries through civilization stories and beauties of various countries reflected in cultural relics. To better present such civilization characteristics as long history, glory and multiplex symbiosis, the exhibition focuses on the theme of "civilizations of all times and various nations" to show the past and present civilizations. With such cultural relics, we trace back to the origins of Asian civilizations to think about the profound significance of each civilization's continuous recognition of itself and changing the world in the process of mutual exchanges. Focusing on the development direction of Asian civilizations in the undergoing major development, changes and adjustments, we understand the lasting imspetus of innovation and win-win cooperation.

Based on these aspects, the exhibition is divided into four parts: The first part is "Cradles of Civilization Witness to History". It takes cultural relics as a carrier to highlight the historical and cultural characteristics of various countries, trace back the origin and development of Mesopotamian civilization, Indus civilization and Chinese civilization, and interprets Asia's great contribution to the mankind as the source of civilization. The cultural relics on display has witnessed the various ethnic civilizations in Asia in the distant prehistoric period, ranging from Jade Cong of Liangzhu culture in the Neolithic Age, the 3,000-year-old Laotian bronze drum, to Armenian Rython Bird-Shaped in the 8th–7th century B.C., stone carvings in Tabuk, Saudi Arabia in the 4th century B.C. The second part is "Voyage of Discovery Bridge of Communication". It shows the prosperity along the Silk Road on land and sea. Cultural relics directly or indirectly reflect that the Silk Road is not only a road of economic exchange, but also a road of mutual learning for civilizations, such as the Tang Tri-colored Glazed Ceramic Camel Carrying Silk, the copy of cave painting *Zhang Qian's Travel to the Western Regions* from Early Tang Dynasty in Mogao Caves,Dunhuang, and the porcelains from Nanhai No.1 shipwreck in the Southern Song Dynasty. The third part is "Embrace Differences Strengthen Cooperation". This part focuses on reality instead of history–the archaeological, excavation protection sites rather than the cultural relics. It shows the research results of exchanges and cooperation between China and Asian countries in cultural heritage. Asian countries had broad and diverse cooperation, ranging from China's participation in the protection and restoration of the historical site of Angkor to the joint investigation and excavation of the Kollam Port Site by China and India, from the joint declaration of world cultural heritage by China, Kazakhstan and Kyrgyzstan to the underwater archaeological training of countries along the "the Belt and Road". This part shows Asia's great efforts and firm determination to inherit civilization through dialogue and cooperation among civilizations. The fourth part is "Respect Diversity Enhance Friendship". This part shows 46 gifts/sets received by Chinese leaders in diplomatic activitie's with other Asian leaders. As symbols of peace and friendship, treasures of Asian civilizations, these gifts show special historical significance and high artistic value. Reflecting various cultures and arts of various countries, these gifts symbolize the friendship between the Chinese and other Asian peoples.

With so many participating countries and delicate cultural relics, the exhibition can be called "Olympics of cultural relics". The selection of exhibits mainly depends on two factors: first, the exhibit shall represent the unique features of the country's civilization. For example, the cultural relics in the Chinese exhibition area shall highlight the Chinese civilization, the only uninterrupted ancient civilization in human history, and reflect the brilliant achievements of Chinese civilization in the fields of etiquette and ideology, science and technology, culture and art, economy and life. The cultural relics show the diversity of the origin of early Chinese civilization, such as the Jade Animal of Hongshan culture, the Bronze Turquoise-inlaid Plaque with an Animal Face of Erlitou culture, Oracular Turtle Shell and Bronze He Zun of Western Zhou Dynasty. Integrating science, art and technology, the practical devices show the ancients' superb skills and unique ingenuity, including the "most beautiful bronze ware" of the Bronze Zun (Ritual Wine Vessel) and Pan (Plate) of Marquis Yi of State Zeng, the Gilt Bronze Human-Shaped Lamp of the Western Han Dynasty, and the Silver kettle Featuring Horse Pattern in the Shape of Leather Bag of Tang Dynasty. The following cultural relics show the humanistic implication and aesthetic essence of Chinese traditional culture, including the Blue-and-white "four Predilections" Meiping (Plum Bottle) of the Yuan Dynasty, Zhao Mengfu's

Semi-cursive Calligraphic Work: *For the Abbot of LongJiao Temple*, the copy of *Yongle* Dadian of the Ming Dynasty, and *Picture of Farming and Weaving* by jiao Bingzheng of the Qing Dynasty. All these are mostly national first-class cultural relics, showing the long history and profound Chinese civilization in an all-round way. These features are not unique to Chinese cultural relics. Nasrin Beilali, the curator of the National Museum of Afghanistan, said, "Viewing the exhibition is like walking through dozens of countries: viewers may appreciate the historical and cultural features of Asian countries." Second, the exhibit shall reflect the long exchanges of Asian civilizations. The ancient Asia has been a community of shared future since a very early time. "Integration" is a common feature of Asian civilizations. In the exhibition, the moving stories of exchanges on the ancient commercial roads, such as the Silk Road, the Tea Road, and the Spice Road, are shown to the public through the cultural relics on display. The Galle Trilingual Inscription Installed by Zheng He (Replica) is displayed at the entrance to the exhibition hall. The stele was erected by Zheng He, the navigator of the Ming Dynasty, on his second voyage to the west. The inscription is in Chinese, Tamil and Persian, expressing admiration for Buddhism, Hinduism and Islam and China's respect for different civilizations since ancient times. It serves as an important witness to the Maritime Silk Road and the friendship between China and Sri Lanka, and the best narrator of the Chinese civilization's neighborliness and harmony with other nations. As an antique in Singapore's Asian Civilizations Museum, the *Kamcheng* of Emperor Guangxu of the Qing Dynasty is a representative of "Peranakan" porcelain. Integrating Chinese decorative style with Malay culture, the export porcelain has witnessed the long cultural exchange between the Chinese and the Malay. The Rython Bird in the History Museum of Armenia and the rhyton of the Persian era in the National Museum of Iran may remind viewers of the gold-inlaid beast head-shaped agate rhyton found in Xi'an, China, since it shows typical characteristics of ancient western jade carvings. Though from different origins, these rhytons are in similar appearance but different shapes, showing a clear road map for civilization exchanges.

Various ways of presentation and unique exhibition space make the exhibition even better. With the introductory arc-screen film, The Splendor of Asia shows the magnificent Asian world cultural heritage and famous cultural landscape by modern film and television art, laying out the natural geography and human environment that nurtured Asian civilizations. The main color of the exhibition is crimson, which symbolizes happiness and celebration in Asian culsture-showing enthusiasm and calmness. According to the various themes of the exhibition area, abstract theme exhibitions are on display against the red background, including the Silk Road, cultural heritage, and urban silhouette. Thus, the layout shows the atmosphere without overwhelming the themes. The sides of the display cabinet show the names and general situation of participating countries in both Chinese and English. The scattered display islands present a civilization dialogue across time and space among Asian countries: Pakistan Gandhara Buddha, Indian Ganesha, Cambodian Angkor statues of God, Mosaic with the Representation of Alexandria... These cultural relics echo each other in the exhibition, so the audience may intuitively appreciate the diverse cultural traditions of Asian nations from the development of artistic images. The continuous and interrelated space layout shows the mutual help and common development in mutual exchanges during the emergence and independent development of various Asian civilizations. The description of the cultural relics pasted on the glass of the display cabinets, together with the exhibition signs and the auxiliary display boards (maps, photos, charts, local details of the cultural relics, etc.), provide comprehensive and detailed information for the public to understand the story beyond the cultural relics. In the exhibition, the multimedia interactive display system "Cultural relics show you Asia" uses three–dimensional restoration technology. The audience can freely turn over and thoroughly view the details of nearly 60 cultural relics from 13 countries in Asia on the screen, to feel the wonderful and spectacular display of digital cultural relics.

The success of this exhibition owes to the high attention and strong support of Asian countries. The exhibition preparation is a process of cultural exchanges among Asian countries. As the best opening for civilization exchanges, the exhibition serves as a platform for wider and deeper cultural exchanges and cooperation of Asian countries.

"A single flower does not make spring, while one hundred flowers in full blossom bring spring to the garden." Asian civilizations have always advanced through dialogue and mutual learning. The exhibition of Asian civilizations enriches the communication forms among civilizations. Through the exhibition and presentation of different civilizations, various countries may enhance and deepen their understanding of their respective civilizations and promote the formation of more consensuses on building a community of shared future for mankind. The development of human civilization lies in joint efforts. In the future, we shall embrace various civilizations in the world.

Yao An

多彩文明的熠熠印记

——亚洲的文物交流与文化互鉴

"亚洲"概念传说是被古代地中海活跃的腓尼基人赠送了一个"亚细亚"的美名，意思是"太阳升起的地方"，从而名扬世界历经数千年不衰。亚洲是世界上面积最大的洲，广袤地理环境上的"世界之最"比比皆是，而且是人类最早的定居地之一，历史悠久积淀出深厚的文明。

放眼世界壮阔的版图，数十条廊道和穿行在绿洲平原、褐色高原、黄色沙漠之间的路网，不仅将亚洲有机地串联在一起，而且连系的两河流域，印度河流域、中国黄河－长江流域是三个重要的人类文明的发祥地，仅在亚洲土地上就有一千多个大小民族，约占世界民族总数的二分之一。不同地区的不同文化，不同肤色的不同民族，在你我交流中互鉴互学，分别创造了自己韵味不同的文化。

亚洲的文物也最为厚重灿烂，早在公元前3000年，西亚两河流域巴比伦人已经发明了烧制陶器和冶炼矿石，苏美尔人首先发明了文字、系统的灌溉工程，中亚的游牧民族发明了马鞍、挽具和车轮，南亚留下了佛教和印度教发源地的石雕艺术，中国人发明了瓷器、马镫、火药、指南针、造纸术和印刷术，并最早种植稻谷。印度人和阿拉伯人发明了十进位计算技术。亚洲各种地方性的医药技术，即使当今也非常有效。这些无不显示古人智慧与工匠的卓越才能，都为世界文明作出了巨大贡献。

为了展现亚洲各国文明的历史特征，多角度聚焦各文明之间对话与交流的轨迹，"大美亚细亚——亚洲文明展"首次通过亚洲几十个国家400余件组文物精品，让观众感受亚洲文明的深邃与辽阔，从"文物"提升到"文明"，为构建亚洲命运共同体提供了东方智慧的启迪与滋养。

一、亚洲文明的特色新知

大约距今8000至6000年开始，亚洲各地之间就有了长距离的接触，古老的陆上丝绸之路从史前时代就起步于无垠的东亚草原，海上丝绸之路则起航于世界季风最显著的西亚港口。亚洲不仅历史和文化非常悠久，而且经济和文化水平曾经在世界上长期居于领先地位。

各国的文物给我们带来了远方的知识信息，打开了人们的眼界，突破了地域疆界的限制，开阔了传统的视野，帮助我们重新认识亚洲的文明，但形成的不是"亚洲观"而是"世界观"；不是时间经线或空间纬线，而是综合了亚洲之间与亚欧之间的交往成果，是人类共同的知识谱系。

难能可贵的是，作为早期文明起步却屡遭战祸破坏的两个国家，这次亮相中国国家博物馆展览大厅，一个是阿富汗，一个是叙利亚。

阿富汗公元前3000年至前2000年的精品文物有蒙迪加克遗址出土的绘有长角羊高脚陶杯，巴克特里亚遗址出土的青铜斧头，法罗尔丘地遗址出土的两件壮牛装饰银器，这么早的文物确实罕见，都是南亚人类早期文明的代表物。而阿富汗国家博物馆收藏的出土公元2世纪玻璃花瓶，5世纪贴金泥塑佛首，均是亚历山大希腊化后的艺术新创造。尤其是希腊－巴克特里亚是希腊马其顿人在今阿富汗地区建立的希腊化政权，留下的"希腊化"文物琳琅满目。

毗邻地中海的叙利亚，大马士革国家博物馆收藏的公元前 9200 至 8800 年漩涡纹黑石残件，公元前 8200 至前 7500 年石雕动物像，公元前 7500 至前 5500 年矩形平托盘印章和三角形灰色平托盘印章，都是使人无法想象的远古文明回响。叙利亚玛丽出土的公元前 3 世纪中期组装画，乌加里特出土公元前 2 世纪后期彩绘马车陶罐，泰德穆尔出土公元 2 世纪石灰石墓碑雕像、纺织品、石牌匾等，多拉奥布斯出土公元 2 世纪耳釉陶罐，公元 1 世纪罐状陶器女头像香炉、陶灯罩，尤其是公元前 2 世纪后期叙利亚乌加里特出土的黏土板和烤泥碑，上面的文字清晰地印证了古代两河流域的文明传承。

叙利亚这次出展的文物精品时代延续到了拜占庭时代，透过器物的年代早晚对比，说明了社会发展的进程，反映了区域特征，从纵向和横向双重维度诠释了高度文明。

与叙利亚毗邻的黎巴嫩也是美索不达米亚文明中心备受瞩目的国家，黎巴嫩各地出土的文物琳琅满目，青铜时代的红陶杯、雪花石膏瓶，罗马时代的各类玻璃瓶、玻璃碗，尤其是著名的比布鲁斯出土青铜时代刻有象形文字的石灰石碑，黎巴嫩西顿厄舒蒙神殿出土公元前 4 世纪中期大理石雕孩童像，黎巴嫩贝卡出土罗马时期（公元 573 年）祭祀神王朱庇特的高浮雕，令人惊异不已，它们都是第一次来到中国露出面容。

西亚的文物对东亚的中国人来说，比较遥远也比较陌生，这次展出的阿拉伯联合酋长国沙迦国家博物馆藏公元 1 世纪阿拉伯联合酋长国米雷哈（Mleiha）出土的银币，以及迪巴希森（Dibba al Hisn）出土的公元 1 世纪德拉克马银币，表明东濒波斯湾的阿拉伯半岛海上贸易非常频繁，对我们理解海上丝绸之路和"季风航线"非常有益。

阿拉伯联合酋长国乌姆盖温国家博物馆收藏的阿拉伯联合酋长国泰尔·阿布拉克遗址出土的约公元前 3000 至前 2000 年石圆筒印章、绿泥石容器，仅在公元 1 世纪就有艾杜尔遗址出土的青铜灯与宝石挂饰，迪巴（Dibba）出土的玻璃香水瓶、米雷哈（Mleiha）出土的公元前 3 世纪末刻有铭文的石膏板，以及 1 至 3 世纪石雕像、石罐、釉陶杯，都是阿拉伯区域的文明标志，特别是迪巴希森（Dibba al Hisn）和豪尔费坎（Khor Fakkan）等地出土的 13 世纪至 16 世纪青花瓷器和青瓷盘，而青花瓷常用的一种关键性材料（苏麻离青）就主要来自伊朗等地区，再次印证了中国和阿拉伯地区之间海上丝绸之路的往来。文明的交往正是历史进步的证据。

如果说作为一个亚洲人一定要看懂亚洲具有世界级的文明印记，恐怕不是易事，全面的观察也不可能一个展览就读懂看透。但是了解亚洲文明的特色，知晓亚洲的艺术瑰宝，通过文物所体现的文化符号和记忆印记，还是值得我们逐步反思的，文明的选择是多彩的。

二、亚洲文明的交融空间

亚洲有着许多令人无限神往的艺术珍品，以往我们视为扑朔迷离的神话传说，如今摆在眼前，犹如打开一扇扇暗旧门扉，通过重点展品见证，我们不仅了解了文物精品的精彩，更明白了搭建文明互学互鉴桥梁、共同发展的重要性，历史常常就在这些貌似无意义的小文物身上显出意义。

印度是古老的文明古国，新德里国家博物馆收藏的马哈拉施特拉邦达马巴德出土公元前 1500 至前 1050 年铜犀牛，站立在四轮车上，栩栩如生。印度秣菟罗出土公元 2 世纪贵霜王朝斯基泰人头像、沐浴女子像、龙王礼佛饰板等石雕，真实再现了当时的人物形象，填补了我们以往认识的空白。印度中央邦出土公元前 2 世纪巽加王朝的石刻乐师队伍，载歌载舞，细节生动。印度这种石雕艺术一直到公元 10 世纪都长盛不衰，菩萨像、天女像、坐姿象头神伽内什像等均为艺术珍品，具有很高的艺术价值。

如果我们以文明流动的眼光来看，巴基斯坦无论是时间上还是空间上都是与印度一样坐标系上的殿堂。巴基斯坦美赫尔尔出土公元前 3000 年陶制女性雕像，摩亨佐·达罗出土公元前 2500 至前 1800 年无头男性石像，瑙哈罗（Nausharo）出土公元前 2600 至前 1800 年涂饰陶罐，俾路支省宁道瑞（Nindowari）遗址出土公元前 2600 至前 2300 年库利装饰陶罐，巴基斯坦扎里夫科鲁纳出土公元前 1000 年陶制瓮棺，追根溯源，这些无疑都是文明交融的古典精品。

过去我们往往注重的是大国的文化特色，对小国经常忽视省略，可是一些小国在大国夹缝中有着悲痛的创伤史，对自己民族源头的历史文物格外珍视，除了血与火被征服的悲剧情怀外，也有对历史变迁的理性回味，如今的危机与过去的灾难往往有着千丝万缕的联系。

例如，以制作彩陶闻名于世的亚美尼亚共和国（Republic of Armenia），位于亚欧交界高加索地区，其出土公元前 10 世纪至前 9 世纪的祭祀贮藏用陶罐，造型优美，题材精彩。公元 10 至 12 世纪的贮藏罐、盘子、香炉等都是彩陶的杰作，彰显了这个国家精湛的工艺和成熟的美学。

又例如柬埔寨柴桢省罗密赫县巴萨克出土前吴哥时期（公元 550–600 年）石雕湿婆神的公牛南迪像、石雕毗湿奴立像，茶胶省吴哥波雷县寺院出土前吴哥时期（公元 7 世纪）石雕佛头，磅湛省出土的 7 世纪石雕蛇王纳迦护佛像，马德望市出土吴哥时期 10 世纪中期石浮雕门楣、石雕金翅鸟残片等，使人联想到当时国王委任与激励能工巧匠，依据佛教的信仰创作出文明的艺术。

历史上的"亚细亚大道"正是从中亚乌兹别克斯坦阿姆河、锡尔河流域，进入土库曼斯坦到伊朗，伊朗马什哈德历来是与印度、阿富汗和中亚的贸易中心，是丝绸之路经济重镇。而向西伸张大不里士又是伊朗与高加索、土耳其的贸易中心，拜火教圣地。南北两线分别汇合，可以穿越小亚细亚半岛经过历史名城伊斯坦布尔进入欧洲，也可穿越美索不达米亚平原从叙利亚绿洲直达地中海。

在这些干道上的国家汇集了几千年的文明成果，既改变了当年的历史进程，也积累了无数当时的珍宝，而这正是今天我们看到的艺术精品。土库曼斯坦有着浓郁民族风格的女性饰品、首饰，阿塞拜疆巴库地区生产的织花地毯和"杰伊利（Jayirli）"品牌地毯及羊毛盐袋，都是古代盛产的奢华物品，它们成为当地古代诗人们赞美的对象。

号称亚洲"心脏地带"的中亚曾在漫长历史文明推进中起过重大作用，但随着频繁战争、人口迁徙、疆界巨变等，财富的磁石失去了吸引力，到海路兴起时陆路失去了亚洲腹地与西方文明沟通的机会，闭关锁国造成历史停滞不前，重心的偏离与转移预示着亚洲走向的衰落，特别是公元 10 世纪以及近代以来亚洲遭受多次战乱毁灭，外来者征服的殖民沉重打击更使亚洲封闭落后于世界之林，古代的贸易模式很快失去了活力，陷入孤立被动的隔绝中。亚洲命运多舛，提示我们"文明不应孤立"对现实永远有着关照的意义。

三、亚洲文明的影响延伸

亚洲从远古流传下来的文物艺术精品保存着各个不同历史时期的文明记忆，每一个细节每一个烙印都应该被尊重，每一个特征都是一个民族一个国家独特气质的一部分。亚洲文明的艺术结晶，曾经被西方人视为神秘东方的收藏品，几个世纪来大量掠劫或投资疯买。但是亚洲文物也由此被世界关注，包括着重于体现蕴含的学术价值。当我们把眼光由历史投向未来时，亚洲如何回应世界的挑战，如何以和平共享的方式重新缔结亚洲与世界的关系，增强亚洲文化自信，这才是我们寻求的答案。

西亚南部约旦考古博物馆藏约旦杰里科出土的约公元前16世纪妇女造型小水壶、公元前11至前10世纪猴子造型陶壶、公元1世纪纳巴泰风格石灰石神灵头像和纳巴泰语碑铭、公元531年描绘亚历山大里亚景观的马赛克装饰，都在一定程度上影响着亚洲同时期或较晚艺术作品的形制。同样，沙特阿拉伯阿尔马卡出土公元前7世纪石雕动物头颈和石雕人像、头像，也是对后来近东地区奠定了文化底色。

南亚印度新德里国家博物馆藏摩亨佐·达罗遗址出土的公元前2500年由秤臂、秤板、秤砣组成的铜秤，公元前3至2世纪压印银币（直径3.3厘米、重5.8克）、公元5世纪笈多银币（1×1厘米，重1.6克），这些文物无论是度量衡还是流通货币，都是早期商业贸易必用的工具和方式，文明的延续和重构离不开商业贸易的经济支撑。

东南亚老挝国家博物馆藏老挝沙湾拿吉省出土的史前时代的铜鼓，琅勃拉邦省出土的史前时代星形石块，琅勃拉邦省澜沧王国时代木雕罗摩衍那原本。印度尼西亚国家博物馆藏印度尼西亚南苏门答腊省巨港市出土的公元8至9世纪铜佛像。马来西亚国家博物馆藏有许多华人穿用的高跟珠鞋、娘惹服、峇迪布，直接反映了华人文化圈的影响。还有印度裔丰收陶罐、西塔琴等，以及本地原住民玛赫玛丽族面具等藏品，均反映了族群沟通和民族汇融的深刻影响。

东亚日本与中国有着一衣带水的密切关系。东京国立博物馆藏大阪八尾市恩智中町出土公元前2至1世纪流水纹铜铎，日本群马县伊势崎市下触出土公元6世纪陶扛锹男俑竟然高达91.9厘米，日本和歌山县那智胜浦的公元7世纪铜鎏金菩萨半跏像，这都是连接中国文化交流后的文明形式。朝鲜国立中央历史博物馆收藏高丽早期朝鲜黄海南道白川郡江湖里江西寺铜鎏金九面观世音菩萨立像，公元11至12世纪上半叶仙鹤祥云图案青瓷梅瓶，均来源于中国传统艺术，说明东亚虽然有着复杂的政治关系，可是文化风格有着兼容并包的深深印记。

丝绸之路沿线文化从南亚到东亚光照大千的莫过于佛教文化，巴基斯坦作为"佛国庄严"艺术起源地之一，这次展出有巴基斯坦斯瓦特出土公元1至3世纪刻有运送佛陀遗骨图样的绿片岩石板、刻有丘比特的绿片岩建筑面板、塔克西拉遗址出土公元3至4世纪粉饰灰泥菩萨头像、犍陀罗遗址中部出土的公元2至3世纪刻有佛陀和侍者的灰片岩雕饰带片，灰片岩菩萨像、立佛像，这些文物见证了佛教东传的勃兴及演变历程，直接影响了中华民族和东亚诸国的文化性格、精神面貌，使我们对佛教进一步有了从"画皮"到"画骨"的观察。

可以说，亚洲文明展最大的学术价值就是让我们认知了自己的文化，东亚与西亚的两端文明需要重构，正像现代考古研究所表明的，中国的粟和黍 10000 年前就传至西亚，距今 6000 多年前的新石器时代仰韶彩陶也传至西域远至西亚地区，而西亚的小麦、绵羊、黄牛和冶金术也传入中国，山西襄汾陶寺遗址出土的铜铃、铜环等铜器，包括我国西北地区出土的早期小件铜工具、兵器和装饰品，与中亚和西亚的铜器从形制和种类都别无二致，其年代为距今 4300 年至 4100 年。至于欧亚草原风格青铜器和动物纹饰在中国甘肃省、青海省、新疆维吾尔自治区的流行，4000 年前来自中亚南俄的安德罗诺沃文化亦影响着黄河中下游地区居民。尽管有许多谜底还未完全揭开，但是呈波浪式的连续迁徙民族在最初人类接触后，开始作出独特的文明贡献。

"大美亚细亚——亚洲文明展"第一次集中这么多国家的文物展示在观众面前，最大限度寻求多元文明交汇点与共同点，令人眼前一亮，尽管还有一些美的艺术密码没有充分解读，但是各国美的文化精品置放一起，将使我们对文明的基点有了前所未有的观赏，这无疑为兼收并蓄注入了文明的力量。

四、中国在亚洲的位置

作为亚洲最重要的国家，中国从公元前 5800 年至前 3500 年，黄河、长江中下游以及西辽河等区域出现了文明起源迹象。距今 3800 年前后，中原地区形成了更为成熟的文明形态——以二里头遗址为代表的二里头文化，并向四方辐射文化影响力，成为中华文明总进程的核心与引领者。这次亚洲文明展中国展出了河南省偃师二里头遗址出土约公元前 21 世纪至前 17 世纪（二里头文化）的嵌绿松石兽面纹青铜牌饰，陕西省西安临潼姜寨遗址出土约公元前 5000 至前 3000 年（新石器时代仰韶文化）人面鱼纹彩陶盆，浙江省杭州余杭瑶山出土约公元前 3300 至前 2300 年（新石器时代良渚文化）玉琮，山西襄汾陶寺遗址出土约公元前 2500 至前 2000 年（新石器时代陶寺文化）彩绘陶盆，还有 1963 年陕西省宝鸡市东北郊贾村出土约公元前 1046 至前 771 年（西周）青铜何尊，器内底部出现最早的"中国"文字记载。回溯这些文明的历史，不免深深感叹我们祖先的伟大，更重要的是它们代表了人类文明在亚洲的起源。

中国是多极化世界中的重要一极，"和而不同""以和为贵""和合共生"是中华民族最深层的精神追求、中华民族独特的精神标识。仅从文化遗产的标识物来说，湖北省荆州马山一号楚墓出土战国龙凤虎纹绣罗单衣衣袖，河北满城西汉中山靖王刘胜妻窦绾墓中出土的铜鎏金长信宫灯，甘肃省敦煌市马圈湾烽燧出土的西汉纸，如此等等，留下的印记分别代表了中国的丝绸、造纸、漆器、瓷器、建筑、服装、书籍、火药、印刷术、指南针等对亚洲文明和全球进步都产生过的巨大影响。

同时，中国自张骞通西域后就打破了封闭的疆域，不断吸收了亚洲各国的物产、音乐、舞蹈、宗教、科技成果等等，展示的河北省平山县三汲乡中山王墓出土的战国青铜错银双翼神兽，1984 年新疆维吾尔自治区山普拉墓地出土东汉蓝地人首马身纹毛布和宁夏固原西郊深沟村北周李贤墓希腊神话鎏金银壶，山西省大同市封和突墓出土正始元年（公元 504 年）波斯狩猎纹鎏金银盘，宁夏固原北周田弘夫妇墓出土拜占庭金币，陕西西安何家村窖藏出土唐代舞马衔杯仿皮囊式银壶，这些外来文明元素的文物，都极大地丰富了中国人的日常生活和精神世界，也说明中古时代社会自身市场需求为驱动力，经济上的利润追逐也会带来文化之间的角逐竞赛，从而开展了互动的历史进程。

文明的成长壮大离不开互动互融。没有借鉴就没有交流，一系列有关亚洲文明的展览标志着我们开始有意识关注未知的亚洲周邻各国，大大延伸了外部世界的文化空间。为了展现文化双向平等交流的丰富多彩，这次亚洲文明展有意识地展示了阿富汗国家博物馆收藏的阿伊—哈努姆出土公元前 3 世纪滴水嘴兽，新加坡亚洲文明馆公元 5 至 6 世纪印度教毗湿奴的坐骑金翅鸟迦楼罗浮雕，沙特阿拉伯法奥出土公元前 4 世纪带有古也门字母题词的石雕方型香炉，亚美尼亚历史博物馆公元 9 至 10 世纪彩陶托盘，斯里兰卡科伦坡国家博物馆藏公元 1368 至 1644 年郑和布施锡兰山佛寺碑复制品等，目的就是用经典的鲜活记忆担当起文化互鉴的使命。真是文化因交流而多彩，文明因互鉴而丰富，这是人类文明的必然规律。

由历史理解现实，由现实触摸未来。可以说，亚洲的灿烂文明留下了熠熠印记，也留下了无数深层的文化密码，需要我们打开文物这一扇扇门窗迎接大众去观察，去探讨其纪念碑性的意义。如果说亚洲文明展的艺术精品升华了亚洲人的文明自豪感，有益于促进亚洲各国沿着古代文明的路径继续攀登高峰，那么唯有平等对待各类文明，才能和谐相处、各领风骚，才能多姿多彩、共同发展。

我们相信，打破原先文化交往壁垒，通过搭建文明互学互鉴、共显多彩高峰的展览平台，不仅深化亚洲交往的历史渊源，促进彼此欣赏与理解互信，凝聚亚洲发展共识，激发亚洲创新活力，而且提升亚洲人文相亲的认知，为滋润亚洲文明提供精神源泉，让人类共同走向更加精彩的未来。

葛承雍

Imprints of Colorful Civilizations

—— Asian Cultural Relics Exchange and Mutual Learning

The concept of "Asia" originates from outsiders. According to the legend, Phoenicians who were active in the ancient Mediterranean invented the beautiful name– "Asia", meaning "the land of the rising sun", which has been famous for thousands of years. As the largest continent in the world, Asia has numerous "world records" in its vast geographical environment. In addition, as one of the earliest settlements for mankind, it has a long history and profound civilization.

On the vast world map, dozens of corridors and road networks connecting oasis plains, brown plateaus and yellow deserts promote the communication of Asia civilizations. Besides, the regions of Tigris and Euphrates rivers, Indus Valley and the middle and lower reaches of the Yellow River and Yangtze River in China are the important cradles of human civilization. There are more than 1,000 ethnic groups in Asia alone, accounting for about half of all the nations in the world. Various nations with various skin colors have communicated with each other in various regions with various cultures, thus creating their own cultures.

The Asian cultural relics are also the most splendid. As early as 3000 B.C., the Babylonians in the Mesopotamia of West Asia invented pottery making and ore smelting. The Sumerians first invented writing and systematic irrigation projects. The nomadic people in Central Asia invented saddles, harnesses and wheels. South Asia people invented stone carving art in the cradle of Buddhism and Hinduism. The Chinese invented porcelain, stirrups, gunpowder, compass, papermaking and printing. Besides, they are the first planters of rice. Indians and Arabs invented decimal calculation. Various local medical technologies in Asia are still very effective even today, showing the wisdom of ancient people and the outstanding talents of craftsmen. These technologies have made great contributions to world civilization.

In order to show the historical characteristics of Asian civilizations and focus on the track of dialogue and exchange among civilizations from various angles, the "The Splendor of Asia: An Exhibition of Asian Civilizations" first displayed more than 400 pieces of cultural relics from dozens of Asian countries, showing the audience the depth and vastness of Asian civilization. The exhibition shows "civilizations" through "cultural relics", thus enlightening and nourishing the development of Asian community of common destiny.

I. New Features of Asian Civilizations

From about 8000 to 6000 years ago, there has been long–distance contact among all sections of Asia. The ancient Land Silk Road starts from the boundless grassland of East Asia in prehistoric times, and the Maritime Silk Road originated from the West Asian ports, where the monsoon prevails. Asia not only has a very long history and culture, but also ranks top in economy and culture in the world for a long time.

Cultural relics of various countries have brought us distant knowledge and information, broadened people's horizons and broken through the regional boundaries, thus helping people re-understand Asian civilizations. However, what has been formed is not an "Asian view" but a "world view", not a concept of time or space, but the achievements of exchanges among Asian nations as well as Asian and European nations– a common knowledge pedigree for the mankind.

There are two countries initiating their civilizations early but repeatedly experienced wars– Afghanistan in Central Asia and Syria in West Asia. It is commendable that both countries contributed their cultural relics to the exhibition in the National Museum of China.

The exquisite cultural relics in Afghanistan from 3000 B.C. to 2000 B.C. include the ceramic Goblet painted with long horned antelope unearthed from Mundigak Site, the bronze Axe unearthed from Bactria Ruins, and two pieces of strong cattle shaped silverware unearthed from Tepe Fullol Ruins. As the representatives of the early civilization of South Asia, such early cultural relics are indeed rare. Besides, the glass Vase of the 2nd century A.D. and the clay Buddha Head sculpture of the 5th century A.D. collected by the National Museum of Afghanistan are new creations after Alexander's Hellenistic Age. In particular, Greece–Bactria is the Hellenistic regime established by the Greek Macedonians in today's Afghanistan region, leaving dazzling "Hellenistic" cultural relics.

In Syria, which borders the Mediterranean, the National Museum of Damascus collects Black Stone (Fragment) from 9200 B.C. to 8800 B.C. , Stone Statue of an Animal from 8200 B.C. to 7500 B.C. , Rectangular Seal with flat pallet from 7500 B.C. to 5500 B.C. , and Triangular Gray Seal with flat pallet . These collections show echoes of ancient civilization beyond imagination. The following cultural relics present the inheritance of the ancient Mesopotamia culture: the assembly Inlaid Figure Painting of the middle of the 3rd century B.C. unearthed from Mary, Syria, the Painted Pottery Jar Featuring a Cart of the late 2nd century B.C. unearthed from Ugarit, the Tadmur Limestone Gravestone Figurine, Tadmur Textiles, Limestone Board and other tablets of the 2nd century A.D. unearthed in Tadmur, the Double–Handled Glazed Ceramic Jar unearthed of the 2nd century A.D. in Douraa Oroubos, the Female Head Shaped Pottery Censer and the Pottery Lampshade of the 1st century A.D. , especially the inscriptions on the clay tablets and baked clay tablets of the late 2nd century B.C. unearthed from Ugarit, Syria.

The exhibits from Syria cover the Byzantine era. The comparison of the creation time shows the process of social development and reflects the regional characteristics. Both the vertical and horizontal dimensions illustrate an advanced civilization.

Lebanon, which borders Syria, is also the outstanding country in the center of Mesopotamian civilization. Various amazing cultural relics have been unearthed from various sections of Lebanon, including Cup and Bottle of the Bronze Age, various glass bottles and bowls of the Roman Era, especially the famous Stela with Hieroglyphic Inscription of the Bronze Age unearthed from Byblos, Marble Statue of a Child of the middle of the 4th century B.C. unearthed from the Temple of Eshmun in Sidon, Lebanon, and the Roman period (573 A.D.) High Relief of Jupiter Heliopolitan. These cultural relics are on display in China for the first time.

The cultural relics in West Asia are distant and strange to the Chinese in East Asia. As the collections of Sharjah Art Museum in the United Arab Emirates, the Coin of the 1st century A.D. unearthed from Mleiha, the United Arab Emirates and Drachma Coins of the 1st century A.D.

unearthed from Dibba al-Hisn on display show that the exchange of goods entered the precious metal currency era at that time, and the Arabian Peninsula, bordering the Persian Gulf to the north, was a busy place for seaborne trade. These cultural relics are conducive to our understanding of the Maritime Silk Road and the "routes in the monsoons".

As the collections of National Museum of Umm AI Quwain in the UAE, the Schist Stone and Chlorite Vessel dating from the about 3000 B.C. to 2000 B.C. unearthed from Teil Abraq Ruins, UAE, Bronze Lamp and Gemstone Stone of the 1st century A.D. unearthed from Ed-Dour Ruins of the 1st century A.D. , Bottle Unguentarium unearthed from Dibba, Lime Plaster Block with Funerary Inscription of the end of the 3rd century B.C. and Statue, Jars and glazed pottery cups from the 1st to 3rd centuries B.C. unearthed from Mleiha are symbols of the Arab civilization, especially blue and white porcelain wares and Celadon Dishes from the 13th century A.D. to the 16th century A.D. unearthed from places such as Dibba al Hisn and Khor Fakkan. For blue and white porcelains, a key material commonly used (smalt) mainly comes from Iran and other regions, which once again confirms the exchanges along the Maritime Silk Road between China and Arabia. The civilized exchanges have witnessed the historical progress.

It may be difficult for Asians to understand the world-class civilization imprints in Asia. Viewers may not get a comprehensive observation simply through an exhibition. However, it is worth thinking the characteristics of Asian civilizations and the artistic treasures of Asia, as well as the cultural symbols and imprints embodied by cultural relics, since the selection of civilizations is colorful.

II. Integration of Asian Civilizations

Asia has many fascinating art treasures. Myths and legends that we used to regard as mysterious are now in front of us. They are like old doors to be opened. Through viewing the key exhibits, we have not only learned about the excellent cultural relics, but also understood the importance of mutual learning and common development. Though seem meaningless, these small cultural relics often show significance of history.

India is an old country with an ancient civilization. As a collection in the National Museum, New Delhi, India, the vivid Copper Rhinoceros from 1500 B.C. to 1050 B.C. unearthed from Daimabad, Maharashtra stands on a four-wheeled vehicle. The stone carvings of the 2nd century A.D. unearthed from Mathura, India, including the Scythiam Head in the Kushan Empire, the statute of Lady Taking Bath Under A Spring, the Buddha with Naga-Kalika, show vivid images of the people at that time with Gandhara artistic style. This may become a new knowledge to us. The stone carving Musical Group and Various Other Motifs of the Shunga Dynasty in the 2nd century B.C. unearthed from Madhya Pradesh, India, show vivid details of singing and dancing. Such kind of stone carving art in India continued to flourish until the 10th century A.D. Bodhisattva statues, fairy statues, the sitting Ganesha Statues, etc. are art treasures with high artistic value.

In the development of civilizations, Pakistan is of same importance as India both from time and space perspectives. It is no doubt that the following antiques are classics integrating various civilizations: the Terracotta Female Human Figurine dating from the 3000 B.C. unearthed from Mehrgarh, Pakistan, the headless male statue dating from 2500 B.C. to 1800 B.C. unearthed from Mohenjo-daro, the painted pottery pot dating from 2600 B.C. to 1800 B.C. unearthed from Nausharo, the Cooley decorated ceramic pot dating from 2600 B.C. to 2300

B.C. unearthed at Nindowari Site in Balochistan, and the pottery urn coffins of the 1000 B.C. unearthed from Zarif Coruna, Pakistan.

In the past, we often paid attention to the cultural characteristics of big countries but neglected small countries. However, some small countries have painful traumas between such big countries and cherish the historical relics from their own national origins. Apart from the tragic feelings as the conquered, such small countries also have a rational reflection of historical changes. Current crisis is often inextricably linked with past disasters. Therefore, the exhibition of Asian civilizations is a rare opportunity for the small countries.

For example, the Republic of Armenia, which is famous for making painted pottery, is located in the Caucasus region at the junction of Asia and Europe. The Cultic Storage Vessel Karas dating from the 10th century B.C. to the 9th century B.C. show beautiful shapes and exquisite themes. Storage Vessel Karas, Dish and Censer of the 10th–12th centuries A.D. are excellent painted potteries, demonstrating the exquisite workmanship and mature aesthetics of the country.

Other examples include the Nandin (the bull of Shiva) and Standing Vishnu of the Pre–Angkorian period (550–600 AD) unearthed from Barsac, Romeas Haek District, Svay Rieng Province, Cambodia, Head of Buddha of the Pre–Angkorian period (7th century A.D.) unearthed from the temple of Angkor Borey, Takeo, the Buddha on Nega (the serpent king) protecting Buddha of the 7th century unearthed from Kampong Cham Province, and the Decorated Lintel and the Fragment of Figure of Garuda. These cultural relics may remind the public of the time when the king appointed and inspired skilled craftsmen to create civilized arts based on Buddhist beliefs.

The historical "Asia Avenue" stretches from the Amu Darya and Syr Darya basins of Uzbekistan in Central Asia to Turkmenistan and Iran. Iran's Mashhad has always been a trade center with India, Afghanistan and Central Asia, and an important economic town on the Silk Road. In the west line, Tabrizi is also the trade center of Iran, Caucasus and Turkey and the holy land of Zoroastrianism. The north and south lines integrate to cross the Asia Minor Peninsula and enter into Europe, or stretch through the Mesopotamian plain to reach the Mediterranean from the Syrian oases.

The countries along the main lines have developed civilization achievements for thousands of years, which have not only changed the historical process back then, but also collected countless treasures of that time. These are precisely the fine arts that we appreciate today. Female Accessory with Hangings in Turkmenistan show a strong ethnic style. The jacquard carpet, the Carpet Jayirli and Salt Bag produced in Baku region of Azerbaijan are all abundant luxuries in ancient times. They have become objects of admiration by local ancient poets.

Central Asia, known as the "heartland" of Asia, played an important role in the development of long–term historical civilization. However, due to frequent wars, population migration and great changes in borders, the wealth lost its attraction. When the maritime road emerged, the hinterland of Asia lost the opportunity to communicate with western civilizations. The isolation of the countries caused the historical stagnation. The deviation and shift of the trade center foreshadowed the decline of Asia. Especially in the 10th century and modern times, Asia suffered many wars and destruction. The colonization by foreigners has further closed Asia and made it lag behind the world. The ancient trade pattern soon lost its vitality and fell into isolation. The ill–fated Asia reminds us that "civilizations shall not be isolated".

III. The influence of Asian civilizations

Cultural relics and fine arts from ancient times in Asia preserve the civilization records of different historical periods. Every detail and imprint shall be respected and every feature is part of the unique temperament of a nation or a country. As the collection of the mysterious east for westerners, the artistic achievements of Asian civilization have been plundered or invested heavily for centuries. However, Asian cultural relics have also attracted the attention of the world, especially on the academic value contained. In the future, how Asia will respond to the challenges of the world, how to re-establish the relationship between Asia and the world through peaceful sharing, and how to enhance Asian cultural confidence are the questions we seek to answer.

The following collections of the Jordanian Archaeological Museum in the south of the West Asia have influenced the shapes of Asian works of art to a certain extent: the Miniature Jug Representing a Women of the 16th century B.C. unearthed from Jericho, Jordan, the Pottery Jug Led in Monkey Shape of the 11th-10th centuries B.C., the Limestone Head of God Hadad and Nabataean Inscription of the 1st century, and the Mosaic with the Representation of Alexandria of the 531 A.D. Similarly, the Head and Neck of an Animal Figurine, a Part of a Human Figurine and a Figurine Head with Complexion of the 7th century B.C. unearthed from the Almakar region of Saudi Arabia also laid a cultural background for the Near East.

The National Museum in New Delhi, South Asia, has a Copper Balance composed of weighing arms, plates and weights of the 2500 B.C. unearthed from the Mohenjo-daro Ruins, Punch Marked Coins (diameter 3.3cm, weight 5.8g) of the 3rd to 2nd centuries B.C., and Gupta Silver Coin (1x1 cm, weight 1.6g) of the 5th century A.D. These cultural relics are tools necessary for early commercial trade for scales & weights and currency in circulation. The development and reconstruction of civilizations cannot be separated from the economic support of commercial trade.

The Lao National Museum in Southeast Asia collects prehistoric Bronze Drum unearthed from Savannakhet Province of Laos, prehistoric Star-shaped Stone unearthed from Luang Prabang Province, and the original Ramayana Wood of Lancang Kingdom era in Luang Prabang Province of Laos. The National Museum of Indonesia collects the Buddha of the 8th-9th centuries A.D. unearthed from Palembang, South Sumatra Province, Indonesia. The National Museum of Malaysia collects many Beaded High Heds, Kebaya and Sarong Cloth used by Chinese, directly reflecting the influence of the Chinese cultural circle. There are also collections such as Indian Harvest Pottery, Sitar, and Wooden Mask of the local aborigine Mahmari, showing the profound influence of ethnic communication and integration.

In the East Asia, Japan and China are closely linked by a strip of water. The Tokyo National Museum collects the Ritual Bronze Bell of the 2nd-1st centuries B.C. unearthed from Onzinakama, Yao City, Osaka, the 91.9 cm Terracotta Figurine of a Man Carrying a Shovel of the 6th century unearthed from Shimofureicho, Isesaki, Gunma County, Japan, and the Gilt-bronze Bodhisattva in Meditation of the 7th century unearthed from Nachikatsuura, Wakayama, Japan. These are all forms of civilization after the cultural exchange between China and Japan. The Korean Central History Museum collects the Avalokitesvara with Nine Faces of the early Koryo period in Jangsi Temple in Ganggwa, Shirakawa-gun, South Hwanghae Province, Korea, and the Celadon Meiping Inlaid with Grane and Cloud Design from the 11th century to the first half of the 12th century. They are all derived from traditional Chinese art, showing the integration of cultural styles in the East Asia despite the complicated political relations.

There is no culture more influential than Buddhism along the Silk Road from South Asia to East Asia. As one of the origins of the "Country of Buddha" art, Pakistan displays the Panel in Green Schist, Depicting Transportation of the Relics of Buddha and Architectural Panel in Green Schist Depicting A Cupid of the 1st–3rd century A.D. unearthed from Swat, Pakistan, the Bodhisattva Head (Stucco) of the 3rd–4th century A.D. unearthed from Taxila Runis, the pieces of Fragment of a Frieze in Grey Schist, showing Buddha with Attendants of the 2nd–3rd centuries A.D. unearthed from the center of the Gandhara Ruins. The Gray Schist Bodhisattva and Standing Buddha have witnessed the rise and evolution of Buddhism spread to the east, directly affecting the cultural character and spiritual outlook of the Chinese nation and East Asian countries, and showing us the "essence" of the Buddhism through "appearance".

It can be said that the greatest academic value of the Exhibition of Asian Civilizations lies in presenting our own culture. The civilizations at both ends of east and west Asia need to be reconstructed. As the modern archaeological research shows, Chinese millet and rice were brought to the West Asia 10,000 years ago, Neolithic Yangshao painted pottery more than 6,000 years ago was even introduced to West Asia, while the Western Asian wheat, sheep, cattle and metallurgy were also spread to China. The bronze bells, copper rings and other bronze wares unearthed at the Taosi Site in Xiangfen, Shanxi Province and the early small copper tools, weapons and decorations dating from 4,300 to 4,100 years ago unearthed in northwest China are similar in shapes and types as those in the Central and West Asia. As for the popularity of Eurasia grassland bronze wares and animal ornamentation in Gansu, Qinghai and Xinjiang, and the influence of Andronovo culture from South Russia in the Central Asia on the residents in the middle and lower reaches of the Yellow River 4,000 years ago, there are many mysteries have not been completely solved. However, the wave–like continuous migration of ethnic groups began that to make unique contributions to civilizations after the initial human communication.

As the first exhibition displaying the cultural relics from so many countries, The Splendor of Asia An Exhibition of Asian Civilizations seeks the integration and common ground of various civilizations to the greatest extent, which surprises viewers. Although there are still some beautiful artistic relics that have not been fully interpreted, the gathering of the fine cultural works of various countries will present the unprecedented beauty of the civilizations. It will naturally promote the inclusiveness of civilizations.

IV. China's Position in Asia

As the most important country in Asia, China originated the civilization in the middle and lower reaches of the Yellow River and Yangtze River, as well as the West Liaohe River from 5,800 to 3,500 years ago. About 3,800 years ago, a more mature form of civilization–Erlitou culture represented by Erlitou Ruins– developed in the central plains region, spreading cultural influence to all directions and becoming the core leader of the overall development of Chinese civilization. In the Exhibition of Asian Civilizations, China displays the Bronze Turquoise–inlaid Plaque with an Animal Face pattern (Erlitou culture) from the 21st century B.C. to the 17th century B.C. unearthed from the Erlitou Ruins, Yanshi, Henan Province, the Colored Clay Basin Painted with Human Face and Fish patterns (Neolithic Yangshao culture) from the 5000 B.C. to the 3000 B.C. unearthed from Jiangzhai Ruins, Lintong,

Xi'an, Shaanxi Province, the Jade Cong from the 3300 B.C. to the 2300 B.C. (Neolithic Liangzhu culture) unearthed from Yaoshan, Yuhang, Hangzhou, Zhejiang Province, the Painted Clay Basin from the 2300 B.C. to 1900 B.C. (Neolithic Longshan culture) unearthed from Taosi Site in Xiangfen, Shanxi Province, and the Bronze He Zun (Ritual Wine Vessel) from the 1046 B.C. to 771 B.C. (Western Zhou Dynasty) unearthed from 1963 in Jia Village in the northeast suburb of Baoji, Shaanxi Province. The bronze He Zun shows the earliest written characters of "China" at the bottom inside. Looking back on the historical records of the civilization, we appreciate the greatness of our ancestors. More importantly, they represent the origin of human civilization in Asia.

As an important pole in the multi-polarization, China pursues "harmony in diversity", "prevailing harmony" and "symbiotic harmony" as the deepest spiritual pursuit and unique spiritual symbol of the Chinese nation. The representative cultural relics include the Single-layered Gusset Embroidered with Dragon,Phoenix and Tiger Patterns of the Warring States period unearthed from the No.1 Chu Tomb in Mash an, Jingzhou, Hubei Province, the Gilt Bronze Human-Shaped Lamp unearthed from Dou Wan (the wife of the King Jing of Zhongshan in the Western Han Dynasty) tomb in Mancheng, Hebei Province, and the paper of the Western Han Dynasty unearthed from Fengsui, Maquanwan, Dunhuang, Gansu Province. The relics show the great influence of China's silk, papermaking, lacquer ware, porcelain, architecture, clothing, books, gunpowder, printing, compass, and others on Asian civilizations and global progress.

At the same time, China has broken the isolation since Zhang Qian paved the way to the Western Regions. The people in the Han Dynasty seized the opportunity to communicate with all sides by continuously acquiring products, music, dance, religion, and scientific and technological achievements from other Asian countries. The exhibition displays the Bronze inlaid with Silver Mythical Winged Animal of the Warring States period unearthed from Zhongshan King's Tomb in Sanji Town, Pingshan County, Hebei Province, the Woolen Cloth Featuring a Man's Head and a Horse's Body of Eastern Han Dynasty unearthed from the Shanpula tomb, Xinjiang in 1984, the Cloth Featuring Human Figures with Greek Goddess Cornucopia unearthed from No.1 Niya tomb in Minfeng County, the Gilted Silver Pitcher painted with Greek fairy tale unearthed from Li Xian Tomb in the Northern Zhou Dynasty in the Shengou Village of the western suburb in Guyuan, Ningxia, the Persian Gilted Silver Plate with Hunting Scenes of the first year of Zhengshi unearthed from the tomb of Fenghetu in Datong, Shanxi, the Byzantine Gold Coins unearthed from the tomb of Tian Hong and his wife in the Northern Zhou Dynasty in Guyuan, and the Silver Kettle Featuring Horse Pattern in the Shape of a Leather Bag in its mouth unearthed from the hoard of the Tang Dynasty at Hejiacun in Xi'an. These cultural relics with foreign styles greatly enriched the daily life and spiritual world of the Chinese people, showing that the market demand of the medieval society served as the driving force, and the pursuit of economic profits would also bring competition among cultures, thus ushering in the intercommunication among civilizations.

The growth of civilizations owes to the interaction and integration. Communication lies in mutual learning. A series of exhibitions of Asian civilizations show our attention to the mysterious neighboring countries, greatly expanding the cultural space of the outside world. Therefore, to present the various mutual cultural exchanges, the Exhibition of Asian civilizations has intentionally supported the display of the following cultural relics: the gargoyle of the 3rd century B.C. unearthed from Ai-Khanum from the National Museum of Afghanistan, the Garuda of the 5th–6th centuries from the Asian Civilizations Museum in Singapore, an incense Burner with Musnad Inscription of ancient Yemeni letters of the 4th century B.C. unearthed from Fao, Saudi Arabia, the Painted Pottery Tray of the 9th–10th centuries A.D. from the History Museum of Armenia, the Galle Trilingual Inscription Installed by Zheng He (Replica) of 1368 A.D.–1644 A.D. collected from National Museum of Colombo, etc. The aim of displaying these cultural relics is to promote the cultural mutual learning by means of classic vivid records. It is true that civilizations have become richer and more colorful with exchanges and mutual learning.

History serves as a mirror for reality, yet reality as a mirror for future. It can be said that the wonderful Asian civilizations show imprints and numerous cultural codes for us to interpret and understand the monumental significance through the cultural relics. If the fine arts displayed in the Exhibition of Asian Civilizations boost the pride of the Asian people and the development of Asian civilizations along the ancient civilization path, only by treating all kinds of civilizations equally can we live in harmony, show unique charms, and develop wonderful cultures jointly.

We believe that breaking the original barriers to cultural exchanges and building an exhibition platform featuring mutual learning of civilizations will not only promote the historical development of Asian exchanges, mutual appreciation and understanding, Asian development consensus and Asian innovation, but also enhance the understanding of Asian cultural affinity, thus leading to spiritual strength for the Asian civilizations and a better future for the mankind.

Ge Chengyong

保护文物，夯实共建亚洲
和人类命运共同体的人文基础

文物是文化、文明的重要载体，文物保护、研究与合作是文明交流互鉴的重要桥梁，作用独特而又不可替代。习近平主席指出："文明因多样而交流，因交流而互鉴，因互鉴而发展。我们要加强世界上不同国家、不同民族、不同文化的交流互鉴，夯实共建亚洲命运共同体、人类命运共同体的人文基础。"文物展览作为文明交流互鉴的一种形式，最为公众熟知。然而，除了文物展览，国际合作文物保护修复与考古也是一种非常重要的文明交流互鉴形式。20世纪90年代以来，在国家文物局的直接领导下，中国文化遗产研究院作为中国文物保护修复国际合作任务的主要承担单位之一，在境外实施、参与了包括柬埔寨吴哥窟及柏威夏、尼泊尔加德满都、乌兹别克斯坦花剌子模、蒙古国科伦巴尔古塔以及缅甸蒲甘等地文物保护修复项目。

柬埔寨吴哥窟周萨神庙修复现场

中国最早在境外实施的文物保护国际合作项目是1997年启动的柬埔寨周萨神庙保护修复。是年，国家文物局委派中国文物研究所（中国文化遗产研究院）承担吴哥古迹周萨神庙的保护与修复工程，组建了"中国政府援助柬埔寨吴哥古迹保护工作队"，由财政部拨款1000万元（2002年追加450万元），作为实施该项目的经费。周萨神庙修复前大规模倒塌，残损严重。工作队对周萨神庙进行了详细的现状勘察、测绘，考古与保护修复技术、材料等的研究，并在此基础上实施了保护工程，效果良好。

文物保护项目以历史和文化为对象，以学术和技术为契入点，可以直达人心，从最根本、最基础的地方增进合作方之间的理解和互信。文物保护国际合作项目尽管规模和资金很少，但其影响力却是一般工程项目没法比的。也正因如此，我们在周萨神庙项目结束后又果断承接了援柬埔寨吴哥古迹茶胶寺保护修复项目。这个项目规模明显超过周萨神庙，经过十余年的努力，于2018年底圆满结束。实施期间，我们又根据两国政府主管部门的意见未

柬埔寨吴哥窟茶胶寺修复现场

雨绸缪开始了下一期项目的选点，也就是位于吴哥古迹核心区的王宫遗址，该项目于2019年正式启动。

经过20年的工作，我们已经从国际援助柬埔寨吴哥古迹保护行动的一个怯生生的参与者成为吴哥古迹保护国际行动的一支重要力量。2014年，中国与印度被公推为联合国教科文组织保护柏威夏寺国际协调委员会主席国，并已经开始协调组织相关国家共同开展柏威夏寺保护与修复工作。另外，我们的茶胶寺工地被称为吴哥古迹保护行动中最活跃、最有生气、成果最明显的工地。同时也成为柬埔寨的重要的外交活动场所——中国党和国家领导人都曾在柬埔寨领导人的陪同下莅临视察该工地。

在柬埔寨开展的文物保护修复工作只是我们国际合作保护文物古迹的一个代表性案例。我们在蒙古、乌兹别克斯坦、尼泊尔等地开展的文物保护国际合作项目均获得重要进展，受到文物所在国政府、学术界和民众的认可和欢迎。

乌兹别克斯坦花剌子模州历史文化遗迹修复项目是我国在中亚地区实施的第一个文物保护修复项目。2013年9月，习近平主席访问乌兹别克斯坦期间与卡里莫夫总统签署两国关于进一步发展和深化战略伙伴关系的联合宣言和友好合作条约。为落实此次访问成果，2014年4月，中乌双方决定在希瓦古城选择两处历史古迹进行保护修复。经调研与磋商，双方商定项目内容包括阿米尔·图拉经学院与哈桑·穆拉德库什别吉清真寺的建筑本体修缮及环境整治工程。目前，项目正在有序进行，已经完成了地基加固、建筑主体修复和周边环境整治等大部分工作。

2015年，尼泊尔发生8.1级地震，中国文化遗产研究院立即派专家赴现场参与尼泊尔震后文物损毁调研评估工作。在前期工作的基础上，根据国家文物局、商务部等国家主管部门的统一安排，中国文化遗产研究院启动了尼泊尔加德满都杜巴广场九层神庙修复项目，为受到地震灾害严重影响的尼泊尔文物古迹保护伸出援助之手。尼泊尔加德满都杜巴广场九层神庙修复项目包括文物建筑本体保护修缮、文物安全防范、文物展示利用等内容，计划工期为58个月。项目于2017年8月正式启动，国务院副总理汪洋出席了启动仪式。目

柬埔寨吴哥窟周萨神庙维修完成

柬埔寨吴哥窟茶胶寺考古发掘

柬埔寨柏威夏寺

乌兹别克西瓦古城历史古迹修复项目：阿米尔·图拉经学院、哈桑·穆拉德库什别吉清真寺

尼泊尔加德满都杜巴广场九层神庙修复项目木制构件修复补配

尼泊尔努瓦库特抢险支护

蒙古国科伦巴尔古塔

前，该项目正在有序实施中。2017 年 8 月，中国文化遗产研究院对尼泊尔另外一处受地震影响的古迹——努瓦科特杜巴广场王宫及周边附属文物建筑进行了初步调查，并提交了保护修复可行性研究报告。2019 年，该项目正式启动，目前已完成相关建筑的抢险支护工作。

此外，受国家文物局委派，西安文物保护修复中心还与蒙古国文化遗产保护专业机构合作完成"蒙古国博格达汗宫博物馆门前区保护维修工程"。河北省古代建筑保护研究所也参与承担了尼泊尔加德满都杜巴广场九层神庙修复项目的修复设计及项目管理任务。随着文物保护修复国际合作的不断深入，我国越来越多的文物保护单位加入到了开展国际合作的队伍中，更多地担负起文明交流互鉴的责任与使命。

2016 年 6 月，国家主席习近平在乌兹别克斯坦接见了承担合作文物保护项目的中方工作人员，对我们的工作给予肯定，也赋予更多期待。实践证明，在文物保护领域开展国际合作，既可以帮助文物所在国人民了解本国历史文明的重要价值和意义，也可以增进我们对周边国家、地区文化的认识，尤其是深度发掘中华传统文化与东北亚、东南亚、中亚等地区文化的相互影响，以历史促现实、以文化聚共识。

柴晓明

Protecting Cultural Relics to Consolidate the Humanistic Foundation of Building a Community of Shared Future for Asia and Mankind

Relics are important carriers of culture and civilization. Cultural relics protection, research and cooperation are important bridges for exchanges of civilizations and mutual learning, with a unique and irreplaceable role. President Xi Jinping pointed out that "Diversity spurs interaction among civilizations, which in turn promotes mutual learning and their further development. We need to promote exchanges and mutual learning among countries, nations and cultures around the world, and strengthen popular support for jointly building a community with a shared future for both Asia and humanity as a whole." Cultural relics exhibition, as a form of civilization exchanges and mutual learning, won best recognition by the public. In fact, in addition to cultural relics exhibitions, international cooperation in the conservation and restoration of cultural relics and archaeology are also a very important form of exchange and mutual learning among civilizations. As one of the main organs to undertake international among civilizations cooperation in the protection and restoration of Chinese cultural relics, since the 1990s, under the direct leadership of the National Cultural Heritage Administration, the Chinese Academy of Cultural Heritage has implemented and participated in overseas cultural relics conservation and restoration projects, including Angkor Wat, Preah Vihear, Kathmandu in Nepal, Khwarazm Viloyati of Uzbekistan, Colombal Ancient Pagoda in Mongolia and Bagan in Myanmar.

Restoration of the Chau Say Tevoda in Angkor Wat, Cambodia

The earliest international cooperation project on cultural relics protection in China was the protection and restoration of Chau Say Tevoda in Cambodia, which was launched in 1997. In that year, the National Cultural Heritage Administration appointed the Institute of Chinese Cultural Heritage (Chinese Academy of Cultural Heritage) to undertake the protection and restoration of Chau Say Tevoda in Cambodia, and set up the "Chinese Government Assistance Task Force for the Protection of Angkor Monuments in

Cambodia Angkor Wat Ta keo Restoration Site

Protecting Cultural Relics to Consolidate the
Humanistic Foundation of Building a Community of
Shared Future for Asia and Mankind

Cambodia". The Ministry of Finance allocated 10 million yuan (an additional 4.5 million yuan in 2002) to implement the project. Before the restoration of Chau Say Tevoda, it collapsed on a large scale and was badly damaged. The team carried out detailed investigation, mapping, research on archaeology, conservation and restoration technology, materials on Chau Say Tevoda. On this basis, the protection project was carried out, and the effect is excellent.

With history and culture as the object, academic research and technology as the point of penetration, heritage conservation projects can reach the hearts of the people directly, and enhance the understanding and mutual trust between the partners from the most fundamental and basic places. It is for this reason that after the completion of the Chau Say Tevoda Project, we resolutely undertook the project of protecting and restoring the Ta keo, an ancient site in Angkor, Cambodia. The project scale is obviously larger than the Chau Say Tevoda. After more than ten years of efforts, it was successfully completed by the end of 2018. During the implementation period, according to the opinions of the administrative departments of the two countries, we began the selection of the next phase of the competent project, the Palace Site in the core area of Angkor Monuments, which was officially launched this year. After 20 years of work, we have progressed from a timid participant in the International Aid of Cambodia's Angkor Monument Conservation Initiative to an important force in the Angkor Monument Conservation International Initiative. In 2014, China and India were nominated as chairmen of the UNESCO International Coordinating Committee for the Protection of Preah Vihear Temple, and began to coordinate and organize relevant countries to jointly carry out the protection and restoration of Preah Vihear Temple. In addition, the Ta keo site is known as the most active, lively site in the preservation of Angkor monuments. At the same time, it has become an important place for Cambodia's diplomatic activities—a group of China's national and CPC leaders have visited the site accompanied by Cambodian leaders.

Repair work of the Chau Say Tevoda in Angkor Wat, Cambodia is completed

Archaeological Excavation of Ta keo in Angkor Wat, Cambodia

Preah Vihear Temple, Cambodia

The conservation and restoration of cultural relics in Cambodia is only a typical case of our participation in international cooperation in the protection of cultural relics and monuments. Our international cooperation projects on cultural relics protection in Mongolia, Uzbekistan and Nepal have made significant progress, and have been recognized and welcomed by the governments, academia and the public of the countries where the cultural relics are located.

The restoration project of historical and cultural relics in Khorazm in Uzbekistan is the first cultural relics conservation and restoration project implemented in Central Asia by China. In September 2013, during President Xi Jinping's visit to Uzbekistan, he signed a joint declaration and a treaty of friendly cooperation with President Karimov on further development and deepening of strategic partnership between the two countries. In order to implement the results of this visit, in April 2014, China and Uzbekistan decided to choose two historic sites in the ancient city of Shiva to undertake protection and restoration work. After investigation and consultation, the two sides agreed to undertake restoration projects, including the building and environmental renovation works of Amir Tura School and Hassan Mullad Kushbigi Mosque. At present, the projects are being carried out in an orderly manner, and most of the work like foundation reinforcement, main body restoration and surrounding environment renovation has been completed.

In 2015, a magnitude−8.1 earthquake hit Nepal. The Chinese Academy of Cultural Heritage immediately sent experts to the site to participate in the investigation and assessment of the damage of cultural relics in Nepal after the earthquake. On the basis of the previous work and according to the unified arrangement of the National Cultural Heritage Administration and the Ministry of Commerce, the Chinese Academy of Cultural Heritage has launched the restoration project of the Nine−storeyed Basantapur Tower at Durbar Square of Kathmandu, Nepal, to provide assistance for the protection of Nepalese cultural relics and monuments seriously affected by the earthquake disaster. The nine−storeyed Temple restoration project of Durbar Square in Kathmandu, Nepal includes the protection and renovation of cultural relics, the safety precautions, and the display and utilization of cultural relics. The planned construction period is 58 months. The project was officially launched in August 2017, and Vice Premier Wang Yang attended the launching ceremony. At present, the project is being implemented in an orderly manner. In August 2017, the Chinese Academy of Cultural Heritage conducted a preliminary survey of another earthquake−affected monument in Nepal, the Royal Palace of Nuwakot Durbar Square and its adjacent cultural relics, and submitted a feasibility study on conservation and restoration. In 2019, the project was officially launched, and has completed the emergency support work of related buildings.

In addition, under NCHA's entrustment and working with Mongolian specialized institutions,

Historic Site Restoration Project of Shiva Ancient City in Uzbekistan-
Amir Tula School and Hassan Mullad Kushbigi Mosque

Wooden Components for the nine-storeyed temple
restoration project of Durbar Square in Kathmandu, Nepal

Protecting Cultural Relics to Consolidate the
Humanistic Foundation of Building a Community of
Shared Future for Asia and Mankind

Emergency Support Work for Nuwakut, Nepal

Kherlenbars Tower in Mongolia

Xi'an Cultural Relics Conservation & Restoration Center has completed the Conservation & Restoration Project for the Front Section of Bogd Khaan Palace Museum Compound, and the Research Institute of Hebei Ancient Architecture Protection also has participated in restoration design and implementation management for the Nepalese Restoration Project of the Nine-storeyed Temple in Kathmandu Durbar Square. As international cooperation in cultural relics conservation & restoration is deepening, more Chinese entities are taking part in the mission in a bid to better fulfill their responsibilities of promoting civilized exchanges and mutual learning.

In June 2016, Chinese professionals in Uzbekistan and Nepal who undertook cooperation projects for the protection of cultural relics were met by President Xi Jinping. The President gave recognition to our work and gave us more expectations. Practice has proved that international cooperation in the field of cultural relics protection can not only help the people of the countries where the cultural relics are located to understand the important value and significance of their own historical civilization, but also enhance our understanding of the surrounding countries and regional cultures, especially further strengthen the mutual influence between the traditional Chinese culture and other cultures in Northeast Asia, Southeast Asia and Central Asia. We could improve reality with history, gather consensus through cultures.

Chai Xiaoming

中国文物对外展览事业70年

    文物是国家文明的"金色名片"。中国文物对外展览是传播我国文化的重要平台，对配合外交需求，提高文化软实力，展示国家形象，促进文明的交流与互鉴发挥着极其重要的作用。1950年，在苏联举办的"中国艺术展"是中华人民共和国成立后我国首次文物出境展览。截至2019年，我国已举办博物馆系统的文物出国（境）展览近1000余项，足迹遍及六大洲的60多个国家和地区。综观我国文物对外交流70年的发展历程，展览数量呈现出不断上升的趋势，其中十八大以来至今共举办展览320个，占全部展览的近三分之一。展览的国家和地区不断扩展，由起初的以欧美发达国家为主越来越多地走入发展中国家，如墨西哥、蒙古、尼泊尔、斯里兰卡等。进入新时代，我国文物对外展览事业面临着更高的发展要求。习近平主席在亚洲文明对话大会开幕式上发表主旨演讲指出，"回顾历史、展望世界，我们应该增强文明自信，在先辈们铸就的光辉成就的基础上，坚持同世界其他文明交流互鉴，努力续写亚洲文明新辉煌"；精准地指出了文明发展的逻辑链就是"文明因多样而交流，因交流而互鉴，因互鉴而发展"。因此，如何讲好中国故事是新时代文物对外展览的关键。

一、展览数量日趋增加

    1970年以前，我国的文物对外展览数量很少，大部分年份展览数量为零。1973至1974年间，中华人民共和国成立后的首个大型文物展览"中华人民共和国出土文物展"在法国、英国、瑞典、日本、美国等16个国家（地区）成功展出，观众人数累计达到654.3万人次，展览所到之处无不引起巨大轰动。文物对外展览事业工作破冰前行，逐渐打开了局面，被誉为"文物外交"，中国文物对外展览也由此起步。改革开放初期，国务院及国家文物局颁布了《博物馆涉外工作通知》《关于进一步加强文物出国展览工作的几项规定》等法规性文件，为文物对外展览事业指引了方向。1978年党的十一届三中全会开启了改革开放的历史新时期。随着国际地位和影响力的提高，把中华文明推向世界成了一项迫切和重要的任务。作为对外文化交流的重要载体，对外文物展览彰显出勃勃生机。此时期办展机构探索改革，对外文物展览相关政策出台，举办了赴美国"伟大的中国青铜时代展"、赴欧洲"中国古代艺术珍宝展"等有影响力的展览。展览数量逐年稳步增加，每年由几个增加至十几个，到1988年展览数量达到18项。自1990年至2000年间，随着机构调整及职能优化，我国文物对外展览事业较前一个时期有了很大的提升。1992年展览数量为24项，当年在被誉为欧洲文化之都的法国就先后有三场中国文物展，即"秦兵马俑展""中国湖南出土文物展"及"故宫珍宝展"，连同在意大利的"山西省文物精粹"及美国的"明清绘画展"等展览的成功举办，掀起了一场"中国文化热"。为庆祝中美建交20周年、中华人民共和国成立50周年和华盛顿建城200周年，应美国华盛顿国家美术馆邀请，国家文物局于1999年9月至2000年9月先后在华盛顿国家美术馆、休斯顿美术馆和旧金山亚洲艺术馆举办"中国考古的黄金时代展"。该展览受到中美两国领导人的高度重视，国家主席江泽民和美国总统克林顿分

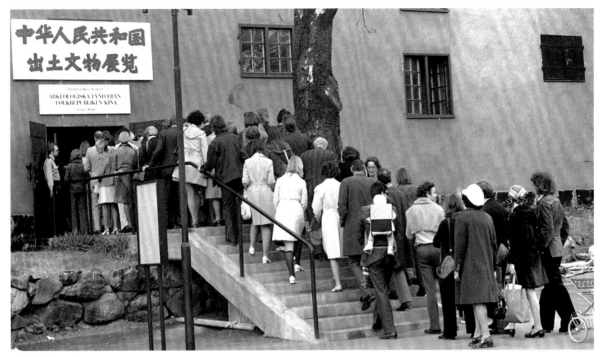

1974 年 5 月，中华人民共和国出土文物展在瑞典斯德哥尔摩展出

别为展览撰写前言。展品来自全国 38 家收藏单位，共 234 件文物，规模空前。这些精美出土文物不仅反映了中国五千年文明进化史与艺术成就，也向西方世界展现了中华人民共和国成立以来田野考古工作取得的辉煌成就。美国各界人士对展览反应热烈，美国各大新闻媒体均对展览给予极高评价，认为"与世界其他国家相比，在过去几十年间，中国的考古发现最丰富、数量也最多。这些考古发现不断改变着世界对中国历史的看法""如果过去五十年可以称为'中国考古发现的黄金时代'，更璀璨的考古发现还在未来"。

自 2001 年起，经过多年的探索积累，随着新的办展方式如"合作展""交换展"等的增加，我国文物对外展览进入全面发展时期。2004 年文物出境展览数量突破 30 项，2012 年达到 58 项。十八大以来，随着国家经济实力的增强和"一带一路"伟大构想的带动，文物出国（境）展览更是呈现"井喷"态势，近 320 余个展览如同文明的使者，遍布全世界五大洲，对传播国家文化影响力，提高文化"软实力"，增强文化自信起到了一定的作用。文明互鉴、文物对外展览成为让世界人民了解中华五千年文明史的重要载体。

二、展览的国家分布日趋广泛

从大洲、国家两个层面对我国文物对外展览的区域分布分析看。

首先，从大洲分布来看，由于受中华文化辐射及影响，亚洲（主要是东亚的日本、韩国及东南亚的新加坡）对中华文化有较强的认同感，因此也是文物对外展览最主要的目的国家和地区，据分析自 1949 年以来至"十二五"末共举办展览 457 个，占总展览数量的 58%。其次是欧洲和北美洲，占比分别为 25% 和 12%。欧美地区经济发达，拥有众多世界著名博物馆，办展的保险、运输等费用可以得到国家经费支持及社会各界的赞助，是举办中国文物展览较多的重要前提。此外，随着中国经济的崛起，越来越多的吸引世界的目光，认识中国的过去可以更好的理解中国的现在与未来，这也是众多欧美博物馆纷纷举办中国展览的重要原因。目前我国文物在大洋洲的展览相对较少，仅占3%。南美洲和非洲的展览最少，分别是11场及5场，多数展览是为配合外交活动或政府间的文化交流项目由我方牵头而举办。直到2008年中国文物交流中心组织赴南非"华夏瑰宝展"，我国文物才首次在非洲展出。

第二，据统计，截至2018年，日本、美国、韩国、法国、英国、德国、新加坡、澳大利亚、荷兰、瑞士及新西兰是举办我国文物展览最多的前十位国家。其中日本是举办中国文物展览最多的国家，且同一展览常常在不同地区展出多场（最多达8场、9场），影响力及覆盖面更广。

三、展览内容日趋丰富

中华人民共和国文物对外展览的内容可从时段及题材两个层面进行分析。首先，按时段可以分为古代文物展览及近现代文物展览。其中古代文物展览比例约为94%，近现代文物所占比例较少，约为6%。古代文物展又可细分至各个历史时期，其中大部分展览主要集中在秦汉、唐及明清时期。

我国文物对外展览按题材可以分为跨多历史时代涵盖多种文物类型的综合类展览，如"中华大文明展""华夏瑰宝展"等，及针对某一段历史时期或某一类型文物的专题类展览，如"中国汉代文明展""敦煌石窟艺术展"等。在我国文物对外交流起步阶段及改革开放初期，综合类展览较多，集中展现了我国悠久的历史与灿烂的文化。对于首次展出中国文物的国家，综合类展览有助于为观众留下一个较为完整的中华文明的印象。随着中国经济的崛起，中国文化影响力的不断提升，国际观众越来越渴望对中国文化有更加深入的了解，专题类展览逐渐成为主流，突出展现了中国文化的多元、包容、开放等多个方面。在专题类展览中，秦兵马俑、清帝王及宫廷艺术、丝绸之路是最受欢迎的三类主题。

其中，秦兵马俑展可谓是当之无愧的"国家名片"。自1982年首次出国展出，所到之处均掀起"中国文化热"。1998年在大英博物馆展出时创造了85万国际观众的参观纪录，同时在英国观众心中种下了"兵马俑"情结。2018年在利物浦国家博物馆举办的"秦始皇及兵马俑展"未展先热，被英国媒体誉为兵马俑阔别十年之后的"回归"之展。据秦始皇帝陵博

2007年，大英博物馆"中国秦始皇兵马俑展"开幕式

物院统计，自 1982 年以来已经有超过 3000 万国际观众走进了秦兵马俑展。

2014 年在法国国立吉美亚洲艺术博物馆举办的"汉风——中国汉代文物展"是两国建交 50 周年的重要文化合作项目。特别是习近平主席和奥朗德总统共同担任了本次展览的监护人并分别为展览作序，习近平主席在序言中指出，汉代是中国历史上十分重要的一个时代，从公元前 206 年开始，绵延 400 多年，为中华文明宝库留下了璀璨的成果。这次展览将展出来自中国 27 家博物馆的 450 多件精美文物，从多个侧面展示中国汉代多姿多彩的社会风貌，传递中华民族不断进行文明创造的智慧结晶。从这份中国文化珍贵遗产中，法国和欧洲观众能够更为形象地了解中华文明的历史传承。

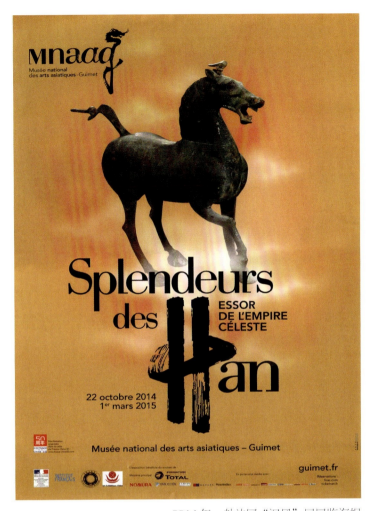

2014 年，赴法国"汉风"展展览海报

近年来，随着"一带一路"倡议的提出，以丝绸之路为主题的展览成为了我国与丝路沿线各国文化交流的亮点，党的十八大以来，配合国家"一带一路"建设，文物对外展览打开了新的局面。赴丝绸之路沿线国家举办文物展览逐渐增多，继赴印度举办"华夏瑰宝展"后，中国文物交流中心的"华夏瑰宝"系列展览在亚洲、非洲、中东欧等"一带一路"沿线国家相继举办，汇集兵马俑、金缕玉衣等标志性精美文物，使各国观众从中领略到了中华文明的丰富内涵和独特魅力。这些展览作为"友好使者"，为传播中华优秀文化、巩固和发展中国与"一带一路"沿线国家源远流长的传统友谊发挥了积极的作用，为"一带一路"建设营造了良好环境。国之交在于民相亲，民相亲在于心相通。

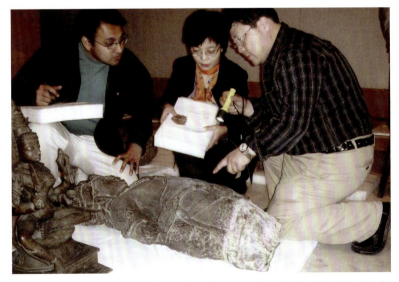

2006 年 12 月，中方人员在印度国家博物馆点交文物

文物展览的举办，加深了"一带一路"沿线各国民众对中国悠久历史和灿烂文化的了解，也加深了他们对今日中国的了解，增进了中国与世界各国人民间的友好感情。

土耳其是古代丝绸之路上的一个重要国家，地跨欧、亚两洲。"华夏瑰宝展"在两国领导人的关怀下，经过文化部、国家文物局与土耳其文化旅游部共同努力，包含兵马俑在内的近百件中国文物精品于 2012 年 11 月 20 日在土耳其托普卡帕老皇宫博物馆展出。这一展览是两国建交以来最重大的一次文物展览活动，也是中国兵马俑首次在西亚地区展出。

2014 年，"丝路的故事——陕西皮影展"分别在吉尔吉斯斯坦和哈萨克斯坦展出。2017 年，"长风破浪——中斯海上丝路历史文化"在斯里兰卡成功展出。2017 年，香港的"绵亘万里：世界遗产丝绸之路展"被誉为近年来丝

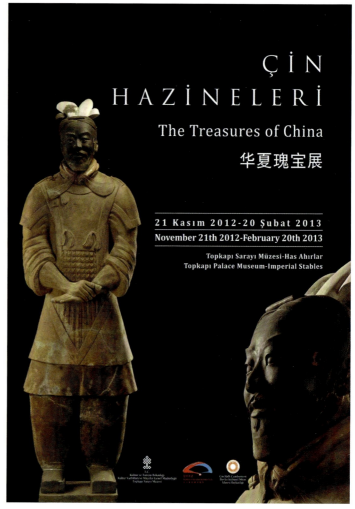

在土耳其举办的"华夏瑰宝展"展览图录

路主题展览的经典之作，展览首次集中了来自我国以及哈萨克斯坦与吉尔吉斯斯坦的文物，展现了丝绸之路的历史风貌与多彩文化，引起了广泛的关注。

2017 年 11 月，"绵亘万里：世界遗产丝绸之路展"在香港历史博物馆举行开幕式

四、展览组织方式日趋多元

中国文物交流中心、故宫博物院、陕西省文物交流中心、上海博物馆、敦煌研究院是我国文物对外交流的最主要组织机构。据统计自中华人民共和国成立以来至"十二五",由这五家单位组织的文物出国(境)展览共计600项,占展览总数的76.5%。由国家博物馆、三星堆博物馆等在内的百余家各级文博单位组织的展览为284项,占展览总数的23.5%。特别是在举办于2000年及以前的322项文物展览中,有297项展览由以上五家单位组织实施,占比达92%。

2000年以前,我国文物对外展览主要由中国文物交流中心、故宫博物院、陕西省文物交流中心等五大机构组织实施。2000年后,随着我国博物馆事业的蓬勃发展,越来越多的博物馆及文物单位参与其中,将更多的中国文物展现于国际观众面前,为我国文物对外交流事业注入新的活力,同时也带来了新的挑战。由于各级博物馆及文博单位实际情况不同,办展经验、策展理念等各有差异,这就需要国家文物局在文物出国(境)展览的统筹、监管、审批等方面加大工作力度,以确保展览的质量及效果。

中国文物交流中心是全国最权威的文物对外展览组织协调机构,其前身是1971年成立的出国文物展览筹备小组,根据1987年文化部《关于进一步加强文物出国展览工作的几项规定》,政府间文化交流或其他协定中的展览项目,以及民间性文物展览项目,展品涉及两省以上的,当时均由中国文物交流中心负责统筹协调。因此,我国绝大部分的综合类展览,因涉及全国文博单位数量较多(最多达几十家)均由中国文物交流中心举办。在40余年的发展历程中,中国文物交流中心成功主办了200余项文物展览,包括"走向盛唐""秦汉文明"等里程碑式的国际大展。

五、展览内容日趋生动

我国文物对外展览内容在广度及深度两个层面不断拓展,题材更加丰富,更具学术价值。由简单的通过国宝展、珍宝展向观众展示中国文物转变为用文物讲述中国历史和中国故事,传递中国文化与价值。以故宫博物院对外展览为例,2000年以前的展览主题主要包括综合类的"故宫珍宝展""紫禁城文物展"及专题类的帝后生活用品、服饰、钟表及绘画等方面。2000年后,展览主题拓展至饮食文化、包装、信仰、戏曲文物、科技等方面,如"清代筵宴展""金相玉质——清代宫廷包装艺术展""海国波澜——清代宫廷西洋传教士、画师绘画精品展""清代皇室的信仰"等。2010-2011年的"乾隆花园古典家具与内装修设计展"在美国大都会艺术博物馆等三家博物馆展出,以讲故事的方式巧妙串起文物,展品选择方面不注重品级,更看重历史内涵及学术价值。《纽约时报》《波士顿环球报》《洛杉矶时报》等多家美国媒体对展览进行了专题评论,并给予了高度评价。又如在《中美上海联合公报》发表45周年之际由国家文物局与美国大都会艺术博物馆主办、中国文物交流中心承办的"秦汉文明"展于2017年3月27日至7月16日在美国纽约大都会艺术博物馆展出,观众达35万人次。该展是中国文物交流中心与大都会博物馆合作举办的第三个重要中国文物展览,是继双方合作举办2004年的"走向盛唐"展和2010年的"中国元代艺术展"之后取得巨大成功的又一个展览。"秦汉文明"展是2016年中美元首杭州会晤成果之一,也是第七轮中美人文交流高层磋商机制达成的重要项目。

展览经过 7 年的精心筹备，采用中华人民共和国近 50 年来的考古发现与史学研究成果，展示秦汉两朝长达四个多世纪的艺术与文化，呈现了秦汉时期政治、社会、经济、思想与宗教等方面的深刻历史意义。来自全国 32 家博物馆及文物单位的 160 余件秦汉时期的文物向美国及世界各地的观众讲述了统一多元的中国的形成，追溯中国政治文化模式的源头及 2000 多年前中国与世界的交往。展览的策展人美国大都会博物馆亚洲艺术部孙志新在接受采访时表示：展览的目的是用文物讲述一段历史，挑选展品除了艺术价值外，一定要有历史的意义，能够讲述一个故事。展品中的人体肌肉结构高度写实的百戏俑、海蓝宝石项链、多面金珠、兽型玛瑙雕饰等

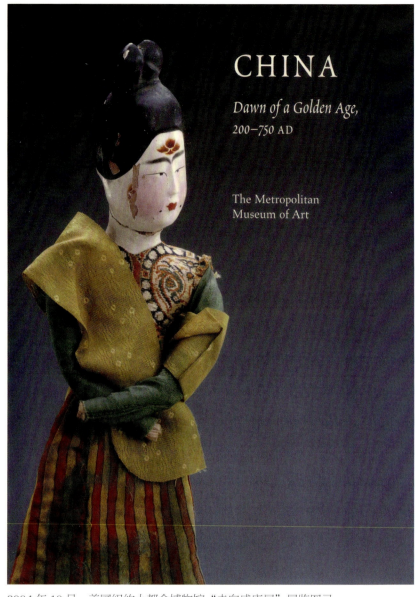

2004 年 10 月，美国纽约大都会博物馆"走向盛唐展"展览图录

就充分体现了秦汉时期中国文化的开放、包容。

随着国家经济实力的快速增长和国际地位的日益提高，我国文物展览在对外文化交流中愈发活跃，展览研究深度不断推进，影响力日益增强，角色也发生了实质性变化，从初期的被动的"特邀嘉宾"，到后来的双方合作的"领衔主演"，再到自主策划的"制片人"。展览交流也从外方"点菜"、单向交流为主，发展到双边交流、以我为主。展陈形式与手段也更加注重现代科技支撑和文化内涵，实现了本土化、特色化、专题化、国际化的有机融合。角色的变换和多渠道多视角的交流展示，标志着中国文物展览在国际文化交流舞台更加自如、日趋成熟。

六、展览尚需进一步讲好中国故事

自 2000 年在我国"十五"规划中首次提出，"中华文化走出去"已经成为国家文化战略的重要

组成部分。如何讲好中国故事就是目前对外展览亟待解决、取得突破的关键点。

自中华人民共和国成立至改革开放初期，我国文物对外展览以综合展览为主，如"中华大文明展""华夏瑰宝展"等向观众展示中国文物及考古发现。随着中国经济的崛起，中国文化影响力的不断提升，国际观众越来越渴望对中国文化有更加深入的了解，针对中国某一历史时期或某一文物类型的专题类展览逐渐成为主流。文物对外展览是中华文化走向世界的重要途径之一，提供了直接的文化输出平台。文化的传播有三个层次，即物质层、行为层及精神层。文物对外展览的核心是价值的交流，其意义在于通过文物的展示来传播中国文化并获得国际社会的"价值认同"。相较于其他跨文化传播形式，文物展览可以使观众通过展品来主动感知和理解文化，而不是被动的告知。改革开放以来，我国文物对外展览的内容在广度和深度两个层面不断拓展，题材更加丰富，更具学术价值。以兵马俑展为例，物质层包含秦俑、铠甲、武器、玉璧等；行为层包括秦人励精图治，由弱到强的发展历程及统一文字、货币、度量衡的政治措施等；精神层为大一统思想。通常情况下，通过参观文物展览，观众可以较直观地了解物质层并感知行为层的内容。价值的传播是文化传播的最核心层次，即精神层的传播。由于文化背景的差异，观众只有真正看懂展览，才能理解并最终认同其所传递的价值。因此，需要精心策展，文物之间相互配合，围绕一个主题用故事串起展览，真正打动观众，从而将精神层的信息传递给观众。

国外观众是中国文化对外传播的接受者，是以文物对外展览为平台讲述中国故事的对象。由于中西方文化差异，中西方博物馆在策展理念及展示方式等方面存在很大不同。以"走向盛唐"展为例，自2004年先后在美国、日本展出，引起了巨大的轰动，吸引了超过百万观众前往参观。鉴于展览的巨大成功，2006年还在湖南博物馆举办了"走向盛唐"的回国汇报展。首先，不同于以往策展思路，以汉唐文明展现中华太平盛世及文化繁荣，此展关注的是与欧洲中世纪对应的公元3世纪到8世纪，由东汉末年的乱世，三国分离及南北朝交替直至隋唐时期。通过展览就能发现此阶段虽然政治上处于乱世，而文化的发展却一直从未间断，而正是由于这一时期文化的交流与融合才造就了盛唐这一辉煌的时代及多元、包容与开放的精神。其次，此展在四地展出的名称及展览结构均有不同。其中美国展分为七个部分，突出了以鲜卑族为代表的北方文化及中亚文化成长及对中原文化的影响。回国汇报展由五个部分组成，更偏重中国文化在不断发展中与外来文化的交流与融合。

随着中国经济的发展，我国举办文物出国（境）展览的话语权也得到了很大提升。特别是近年来与法国、意大利、俄罗斯等国以交换展的方式互办展览及配合外交政策对周边发展中国家"送展"，我们都有百分之百的诠释权。因此，在策展时要充分了解目的观众的文化背景及接受习惯，做到不仅通过展览讲述了一个中国故事，还要将这个故事"讲好"，从而获得观众的认可。正如习近平主席2014年3月27日，在巴黎联合国教科文组织总部发表演讲时指出的"每一种文明都延续着一个国家和民族的精神血脉，既需要薪火相传、代代守护，更需要与时俱进、勇于创新。中国人民在实现中国梦的进程中，将按照时代的新进步，推动中华文明创造性转化和创新性发展，激活其生命力，把跨越时空、超越国度、富有永恒魅力、具有当代价值的文化精神弘扬起来，让收藏在博物馆里的文物、陈列在广阔大地上的遗产、书写在古籍里的文字都活起来，让中华文明同世界各国人民创造的丰富多彩

2018 年，意大利威尼斯宫博物馆"东西汇流——13 至 17 世纪海上丝绸之路展"新闻发布会

的文明一道，为人类提供正确的精神指引和强大的精神动力"。70 年的中国文物对外展览事业与中华人民共和国的发展同步，与改革开放同行，在实现"中国梦"和"两个一百年"奋斗目标的新时代，中国文物对外展览事业正在步入辉煌。

赵古山

Seven Decades of China's International Exhibitions of Cultural Relics

Cultural relics are the "Signature Card" of national civilization. China's international exhibitions in cultural property is an important platform for the dissemination of Chinese culture, playing an extremely significant role in meeting the demand of foreign affairs, enhancing cultural soft power, displaying national image and fostering exchanges and mutual learning between civilizations. The "Chinese Art Exhibition" held in the former Soviet Union in 1950 was the first overseas exhibition of Chinese cultural relics after the founding of New China. As of 2019, China has held nearly 1,000 overseas (outside of the border) exhibitions of cultural relics within the museum system, leaving footprints in more than 60 countries and regions in six continents. Throughout the seven decades' history of external exchanges of Chinese cultural relics, the number of exhibitions has shown a continued upward trend, of which 320 exhibitions have been held since the 18th CPC National Congress, making up one third of the total. The destination for exhibition has been expanding from the developed countries in Europe and America in the early stage to more developing countries including Mexico, Mongolia, Nepal and Sri Lanka. In the new era, the external exhibitions of Chinese cultural relics is facing even higher demand for development. In his keynote speech at the opening ceremony of the Conference on Dialogue of Asian Civilizations, President Xi Jinping pointed out, "As we review our past and look beyond Asia, we should have greater confidence in our civilizations. We may build on the rich heritage of our forefathers, stay engaged with other civilizations and increase mutual learning. By doing so, we will write a new splendid chapter to Asian civilizations." This pinpointed the logic chain of civilization development, which can be described as "Diversity spurs interaction among civilizations, which in turn promotes mutual learning and their further development." Therefore, how to tell Chinese stories properly is the key to external exhibitions of cultural relics in the new era.

I. A Growing Number of Exhibitions Held

Before 1970, there were only a limited number of external exhibitions of cultural relics, with literally no exhibitions held in most of the years. Between 1973 and 1974, the first major exhibition of cultural relics "Archaeological Treasures Excavated in the People's Republic of China" was successfully presented in 16 countries (regions) including France, the United Kingdom, the Kingdom of Sweden, Japan

In May 1974, the Archaeological Treasures Excavated in the People's Republic of China Exhibition was held in Stockholm, Sweden

and the United States, attracting an accumulated audience of 6.543 million and causing quite a stir in whichever exhibition destination. This exhibition broke the ice and opened a new prospect for the external exhibition of cultural relics, known as "Diplomacy through Cultural Relics", marking the very start of the external exhibition of Chinese cultural relics. In the early stage of reform and opening up, the National Cultural Heritage Administration jointly issued *Notice on Foreign-related Affairs of Museums* and *Several Provisions on Further Strengthening the Exhibition of Cultural Relics Abroad* and other regulatory documents, which have provided guidelines for the external exhibitions of cultural relics. In 1978, the Third Plenary Session of the 11th Central Committee of the Chinese Communist Party marked China's entrance into a new historical period of reform and opening up. With the improvement of international status and influence, how to promote Chinese civilization across the globe has become an urgent and important task. As an important embodiment for foreign cultural exchanges, the external exhibition of cultural relics was brimming with vitality. During this period, exhibition organizations were exploring the possibility of reforms, and related policies on external exhibition of cultural relics were introduced. Influential exhibitions include the "The Great Bronze Age of China Exhibition" held in the United States and "Ancient Chinese Art Treasures Exhibition" held in Europe. The number of exhibitions was increasing steadily year by year, from a few to a dozen each year, and reached 18 in 1988. Between 1990 and 2000, with organizational restructuring and optimization of functions, the external exhibition of Chinese cultural relics saw a huge jump from the previous period. There were 24 exhibitions held in 1992, when three Chinese cultural relic exhibitions were successively held in France, reputed as the European Capital of Culture, namely the "Qin Terracotta Warriors and Horses Exhibition", "China Hunan Unearthed Exhibition of Cultural Relics" and "Forbidden City Treasures Exhibition", which, along with the successful holding of other exhibitions such as the "Essence of Shanxi Province Cultural Relics" in Italy and the "Ming and Qing Dynasty Painting Exhibition" in the United States, set off a "Chinese cultural craze". To celebrate the 20th anniversary of the establishment of diplomatic relations between China and the United States, the 50th anniversary of the founding of the People's Republic of China and the 200th anniversary of the establishment of the city of Washington, at the invitation of the National Gallery of Art in Washington, the National Cultural Heritage Administration held the "Golden Age of Chinese Archaeology Exhibition" successively in the National Gallery of Art in Washington, the Museum of Fine Arts of Houston and the Asian Art Museum of San Francisco from September 1999 to September 2000. This exhibition was highly valued by leaders of China and the United States. Then President Jiang Zemin and US President Clinton each wrote a foreword for the exhibition. The exhibits came from 38 collection entities across the country, with a total of 234 pieces of cultural relics, which was an unprecedented scale. These exquisite cultural relics unearthed not only reflected the evolution history of Chinese civilization and artistic outcomes throughout five thousand years, but also showcased the brilliant achievements made in the field archaeology since the founding of the People's Republic of China. These exhibitions won warm responses from personages of all circles of and were spoken highly of by all major news agencies in the United States, as evidenced by such description as, "Compared to other countries in the world, in the past few decades, China has been the top one in terms of the variety and quantity of archaeological discoveries. These archaeological discoveries are changing the world's view about Chinese history on an ongoing process". "If the past five decades are referred to as'the golden age of Chinese archaeological discoveries', more dazzling discoveries are still yet to come".

Since 2001, after years' exploration and accumulation, China's external exhibitions of cultural relics have embraced a period of all-round development, along with increasingly diverse exhibition methods such as "collaborative exhibition" and "exchange exhibition". In 2004, the number of cultural relics exhibited abroad exceeded 30, reaching 58 in 2012. Since the 18th CPC National Congress, with the strengthening of national economy and the great conception of the "Belt and Road" initiative, exhibitions of cultural relics overseas (abroad) have shown a "blowout" trend, resulting in the holding of nearly 320 exhibitions that, like ambassadors of civilization, have covered all of the world's five continents and played a certain role in disseminating national cultural influence, enhancing cultural "soft power" and boosting cultural confidence. The mutual learning between civilizations and the external exhibition of cultural relics have become an important carrier for the people of the world to understand the 5,000 years' history of Chinese civilization.

II. Increasingly Wider Coverage of Destination Countries

The regional distribution of China's external exchanges of cultural relics will be analyzed from two dimensions, namely the continental and national levels.

First of all, from the perspective of continental distribution, due to the radioactive influence of Chinese culture, Asia (mainly Japan and South Korea in East Asia, and Singapore in Southeast Asia) has a high recognition of Chinese cultural identity, so it is also the main destination region for our abroad exhibitions of cultural relics. According to the analysis, between 1949 and the end of the "Twelfth Five-Year Plan", 457 such exhibitions were held in Asia, accounting for 58% of the total. Following Asia are Europe and North America, in which 25% and 12% of the total exhibitions of cultural relics were held, respectively. The Euro-American region is economically developed and home to numerous world-renowned museums, with state funding and sponsorship from all walks of life available for insurance and transportation expenses required by exhibition holding, which is a key prerequisite for the holding of a relatively greater number of Chinese exhibitions of cultural relics. In addition, with the economic rise of China and its increasing attention from the world, knowing China's past will deliver a better understanding of China's present and future. This is also an important reason why so many European and American museums have chosen to hold Chinese exhibitions one after another. At present, there are relatively few exhibitions of Chinese cultural relics held in Oceania, accounting for only 3% of the total. South America and Africa are at the bottom of the list concerning the number of such exhibitions held, 11 and 5 respectively. Most of the exhibitions were organized by China for diplomatic activities or with intergovernmental cultural exchange projects. It was not until 2008 when Art Exhibitions China organized the " The Treasures of China Exhibition" in South Africa that Chinese cultural relics were exhibited in Africa for the first time.

Second, according to statistics, as of 2018, Japan, the United States, South Korea, France, the United Kingdom, Germany, Singapore, Australia, the Netherlands, Switzerland and New Zealand were the top ten countries holding the largest number of exhibitions of Chinese cultural relics. Among them, Japan was the top one on the list, where the same exhibition was often put on multiple times (up to 8 or 9 times) in different cities, with wider influence and coverage.

III. Increasingly Diversified Exhibition Content

The content of Chinese exhibitions of cultural relics held overseas after the founding of the PRC can be analyzed from two dimensions, the time period and the theme. First of all, by the time period, the exhibitions can be divided into exhibitions of the ancient cultural relics and exhibitions of the contemporary cultural relics. Among them, the ancient cultural relics ones make up about 94% of the total while the contemporary cultural relics ones make up only about 6%. Exhibitions of the ancient cultural relics can be subdivided into those in various historical periods, most of which are concentrated in the Qin and Han, Tang, and Ming and Qing dynasties.

By the theme, the exhibitions of Chinese cultural relics held overseas can be divided into comprehensive ones that cover multiple types of cultural relics and across multiple historical periods, such as the "Great Civilization of China Exhibition" and "The Treasures of China Exhibition", and special ones that focus on a specific historical period or a specific type of cultural relics, such as the "Han Dynasty of Chinese Civilization Exhibition" and "Dunhuang Grottoes Art Exhibition". At the initial stage of China's external exchange of cultural relics and the reform and opening up, comprehensive exhibitions were the mainstream, epitomizing China's long history and splendid culture.

For countries where Chinese cultural relics are exhibited for the first time, comprehensive exhibitions help to give the audience a more complete picture of Chinese civilization. With the rise of the Chinese economy and the increasing influence of Chinese culture, international audiences are increasingly eager to have a deeper understanding of Chinese culture. Thus, special exhibitions have gradually become the mainstream, highlighting the diversity, inclusiveness and openness of Chinese culture. Among the special exhibitions, the Terracotta Warriors and Horses of the Qin Dynasty, the Qing Emperors and the Palace Art, and the Silk Road are the three most popular themes. Among the three, the Qin Terracotta Warriors and Horses Exhibition is a well-deserved "national signature card". Since its being exhibited abroad for the first time in 1982, it has set off a "Chinese cultural craze" everywhere. When exhibited at the British Museum in 1998, it attracted a record 850,000 international audiences and buried a "terracotta warrior" complex in the hearts of British audiences. The "First Emperor of Qin and Terracotta Warriors Exhibition" held at the National Museums Liverpool in 2018 aroused public enthusiasm even before its launch, and was hailed by the British media as a "return" exhibition of the Terracotta Warriors and Horses after a ten-year lapse. According to Emperor Qinshihuang's Mausoleum Site Museum, more than 30 million international audiences have visited the Qin Terracotta Warriors and Horses Exhibition since 1982.

The opening ceremony of the "First Emperor of Qin Terracotta Warriors and Horses Exhibition" at the British Museum in 2007

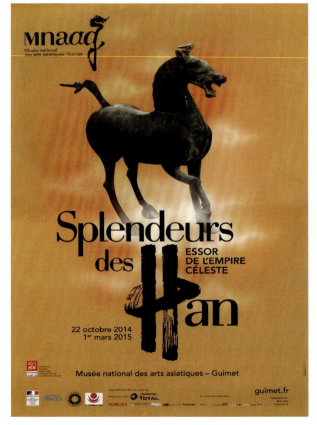

Poster for the "Han-style" exhibition in France in 2014

The "Han Style—Exhibition of cultural relics of Han Dynasty" held at the French Musée National des Arts Asiatiques—Guimet in 2014 was an important cultural cooperation project in celebration of the 50th anniversary of the establishment of diplomatic relations between China and France . In particular, President Xi Jinping and President Hollande jointly acted as guardians of the exhibition and wrote prefaces for the exhibition respectively. President Xi Jinping, in his preface, pointed out, The Han Dynasty is a very important era in Chinese history. It began in 206 B.C. and lasted for more than 400 years, leaving brilliant achievements for the treasure house of Chinese civilization. This exhibition will bring more than 450 exquisite cultural relics from 27 museums in China, to present the diversity of social customs in the Han Dynasty of China from multiple sides and convey the gems of wisdom of the Chinese nation through its continuous cultural creation. From this precious heritage of Chinese culture, French and European audiences can better understand the historical inheritance of Chinese civilization in a more visualized manner.

In recent years, with the implementation of "the Belt and Road Initiative", exhibitions themed on the Silk Road have become a bright spot of cultural exchanges between China and the countries along the Silk Road. Since the 18th CPC National Congress, in response to the country's "Belt and Road" construction, the external exhibition of cultural relics has opened up a new situation. Exhibitions of cultural relics held in countries along the Silk Road keep increasing. Following the "The Treasures of China Exhibition" held in India, the "The Treasures of China" exhibition series of Art Exhibitions China has been successively held in countries along the "Belt and Road" in Asia, Africa, Central and Eastern Europe, bringing together iconic and exquisite cultural relics such as terracotta warriors and horses and jade suit, so that audiences from various countries can appreciate the diversity and unique charm of Chinese civilization. These exhibitions, acting as "goodwill messengers", played a positive role in spreading China's excellent culture, consolidating and developing the long—standing traditional friendship between China and the countries along the "Belt and Road", and creating an enabling environment for the "Belt and Road" construction. Friendship, which derives from close contact between the people, holds the key to sound state—to—state relations. The holding of the exhibition of cultural relics has enabled the people along the "Belt and Road" to gain a deeper understanding of China's long history and splendid culture as well as China today, and enhanced people—to—people friendship between China and other countries.

Turkey was an important country on the ancient Silk Road, spanning across Europe and Asia. With the care of the leaders of both countries and the joint efforts of the Ministry of Culture, the National Cultural Heritage Administration and the Turkey Ministry of Culture and Tourism, nearly a hundred pieces of Chinese cultural relics including terracotta warriors and horses were exhibited at the Topkapi Palace Museum of Turkey on November 20,

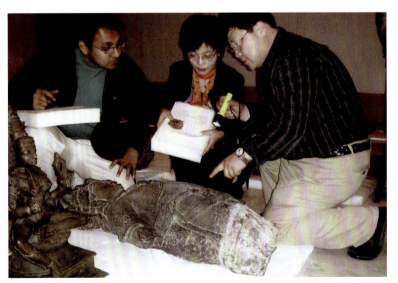

In December 2006, Chinese personnel handed over cultural relics at National Museum, New Delhi

2012 during the "The Treasures of China Exhibition". This exhibition is the most significant cultural relics exhibition activity since the establishment of diplomatic relations between the two countries, and it is also the first time that Chinese terracotta warriors and horses have been exhibited in the West Asia region.

In 2014, "History of Great Silk Road – Shadow Theatre of Shaanxi Province" was put on in Kyrgyzstan and Kazakhstan, respectively. In 2017, "Braving the Wind and the Waves: China–Sri Lanka Maritime Silk Road History and Culture Exhibition" was successfully held in Sri Lanka. In 2017, the "Miles upon Miles: World Heritage along the Silk Road" exhibition in Hong Kong was reputed as a classic among the Silk Road theme exhibitions in recent years. For the first time, the exhibition brought together cultural relics from four provinces of China (Shaanxi, Henan, Gansu and Xinjiang) as well as those from Kazakhstan and Kyrgyzstan to show the historical style and diverse cultures along the Silk Road, attracting widespread attention.

IV. Increasingly Diversified Methods of Exhibition Holding

Art Exhibitions China, the Palace Museum, Shaanxi Cultural Heritage Promotion Center, Shanghai Museum and Dunhuang Academy China are main organizations in charge of the external exchange of Chinese cultural relics. According to statistics, from the founding of New China to the "Twelfth Five–Year Plan" period, these aforementioned five institutions organized a total of 600 exhibitions of cultural relics overseas (abroad), making up 76.5% of the total. Exhibitions organized by over one hundred cultural relics and museum institutions at various levels including the National Museum of China and Sanxingdui Museum reached 284, making up 23.5% of the total. In particular, of the 322 exhibitions of cultural relics held in and before 2000, 297 were organized by the aforementioned five major institutions, accounting for 92%.

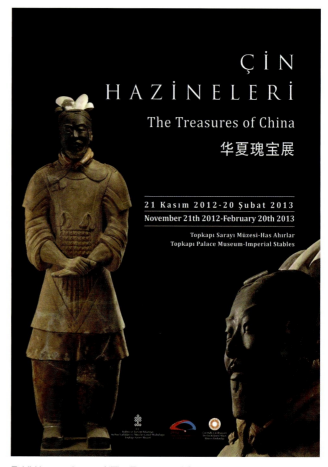

Exhibition catalogue of "The Treasures of China" held in Turkey

In November 2017, the opening ceremony of "Miles upon Miles: World Heritage along the Silk Road" was held at the Hong Kong Museum of History

Before 2000, the external exhibition of Chinese cultural relics was mainly implemented by the five major institutions including Art Exhibitions China, the Palace Museum and Shaanxi Cultural Heritage Promotion Center. After 2000, with the prospering development of Chinese museum, an increasing number of museums and cultural relics institutions became part of the process by presenting more Chinese cultural relics before the international audiences, this has not only injected new vitality into China's external exchange of cultural relics, but also has brought about new challenges. Divergences among museums at various levels in terms of their actual situation, exhibition holding experience, curatorial concept, etc. demand stepping up in efforts by the National Cultural Heritage Administration in the overall planning, regulation and approval of exhibitions of cultural relics overseas (abroad), in order to ensure the quality and outcomes of such exhibitions.

Art Exhibitions China is currently the most authoritative facilitating organization for external exhibitions of cultural relics across the country; its predecessor was the Preparatory Group for the Exhibition of Cultural Relics Overseas. According to Several Provisions on Further Strengthening the Exhibition of Cultural Relics Abroad issued in 1987 by the Ministry of Culture, exhibition projects for intergovernmental cultural exchanges or in other agreements and folk exhibition of cultural relics projects, where the exhibits involved two and more provinces, were all under the charge of the Art Exhibitions China for overall planning and coordination at that time. Therefore, most of the comprehensive exhibitions in China, which involve a relatively large number of nation-wide cultural relics and museum institutions (as many as a dozen), are all held by Art Exhibitions China. In the over four decades' development course, Art Exhibitions China has successfully hosted nearly 200 exhibitions of cultural relics, including landmark international ones such as "China: Dawn of a Golden Age, 200-750 A.D." and "The Civilization of the Qin and Han Dynasties".

V. Increasingly Vivid Exhibition Content

The external exhibition of Chinese cultural relics has been expanding in content in terms of its scope and depth, with more diversified themes and greater academic value. The simple demonstration of Chinese cultural relics to the audience through exhibitions of national treasures in the very beginning has changed into telling Chinese history and Chinese stories with cultural relics, with the purpose of conveying Chinese culture and values. Taking the external exhibition of the Palace Museum as an example. The exhibitions before 2000 mainly covered such comprehensive themes as the "Palace Museum Treasures Exhibition" and the "Exhibition of Forbidden City Cultural Relics" and special themes involving the empress' daily necessities, costumes, clocks and paintings. After 2000, the exhibition theme expanded to food culture, packaging, faith, traditional Chinese opera cultural relics, science and technology, etc., such as "Qing Dynasty Feast Banquet Exhibition", "Gold Appearance and Jade Property: Qing Dynasty Palace Packaging Art Exhibition", "Rhythm of the Waves: Qing Dynasty Court Western Missionaries and Artists' Fine Paintings Exhibition", "Qing Dynasty Royal Family's Faith" and so on. The "Emperor Qianlong's Garden Classical Furniture and Interior Decoration Design Exhibition" was on display from 2010 to 2011 in three museums including the Metropolitan Museum of Art in the United States. Those cultural relics were cleverly connected in a storytelling manner, with more emphasis put on their historical significance and academic value. A number of American media, including the New York Times, the Boston Globe and the Los Angeles Times, gave special feature agencies coverage of the exhibition and spoke highly of it. Another example is the "Chinese Art of the Qin and Han Dynasties" exhibition, co-hosted by the National Cultural Heritage Administration and the Metropolitan Museum of Art and organized by the Art Exhibitions China, exhibited at the Metropolitan Museum of Art in New York, from March 27 to July 16, 2017, in celebration of the 45th anniversary of the publication of the China–US Shanghai Joint Communiqué, attracting an audience of 350,000 visits. This exhibition is the third important exhibition of Chinese cultural relics co–hosted by Art Exhibitions China and the Metropolitan Museum of Art, another great success between the two sides' cooperation after the "China: Dawn of a Glden Age, 200–750 A.D. " exhibition in 2004 and the "Yuan Dynasty of China Art Exhibition" in 2010. The "Chinese Art of the Qin and Han Dynasties" exhibition was one of the outcomes of the China–US leaders' meeting in Hangzhou in 2016, as well as a major project reached in the seventh round of the China–US High–level Consultation on People–to–People Exchange. After seven years of careful preparation, the exhibition, through the archaeological discoveries and historical research findings in the past five decades since the founding of New China, showcased the art and culture of Qin and Han Dynasties spanning more than four centuries, presenting deep historical implications in the politics, society, economy, thought, religion and other aspects during the Qin and Han period. More than 160 pieces of Qin and Han cultural relics from 32 museums and cultural relics institutions across the country told the audiences in the United States and around the world about the formation of a unified and pluralistic China, tracing back to the source of China's political and cultural model and China's contacts with the world more than 2,000 years ago. The exhibition's planner, Mr. Sun Zhixin,

from the Asian Art Department of the Metropolitan Museum of Art in the United States, said in an interview, "The purpose of the exhibition is to tell a history with cultural relics. In addition to the artistic value of the exhibits, it has to deliver historical significance and tell a story well. The acrobat figurines with highly realistic human muscle structures, aquamarine necklaces, multi–faceted gold beads and beast–shaped agate carvings on display fully reflect the openness and inclusiveness of Chinese culture in the Qin and Han Dynasties, which not only responds to the spirit of the time in China, but also serves as an inspiration for the increasingly conservative American society under the influence of 'America First' trend of thought."

With the rapid growth of China's economic strength and the rise of its international standing, the exhibition of Chinese cultural relics is increasing its presence in external cultural exchanges, showing an ever deepening research level, increasingly stronger

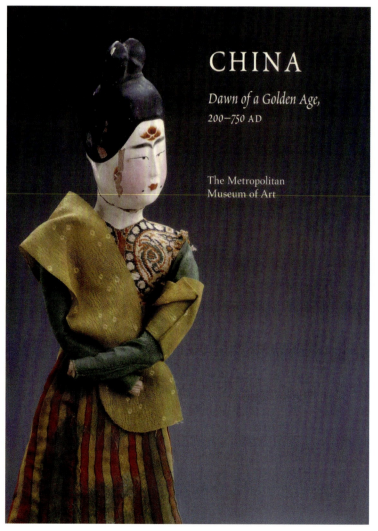

In October 2004, exhibition catalogue of the "China: Dawn of a Golden Age, 200-750 A.D." exhibition held at the Metropolitan Museum of Art in New York, the United States

influence and a substantially changing role. It has transitioned from the responsive "specially invited guest" in the very beginning, to the "lead role" in the partnership project, and then to the "producer" responsible for independent exhibition planning. Exhibition exchanges have also evolved from a one-way approach with foreign party "placing an order" to a two-way approach with Chinese organizers being the decision-maker. The form and means of exhibition focus more on the support of modern science and technology and cultural implications, and realize an organic integration of localization, specialization and internationalization. The changing role and the multi-channel and multi-perspective communication signal the increasing calm and maturity of exhibitions of Chinese cultural relics in the international stage of cultural exchange.

VI. The Exhibitions Needs to Tell Chinese Stories Well

Since its first introduction in China's "Tenth Five-Year Plan" in 2000, "Chinese culture going global" has become an essential part of the national cultural strategy. How to tell a Chinese story well is currently the key point for making breakthroughs in external exhibitions.

From the founding of New China to the early stage of reform and opening up, the external exhibition of Chinese cultural relics were mainly based on comprehensive exhibitions, such as the "Great Civilization of China Exhibition" and "The Treasures of China Exhibition", etc. to show Chinese cultural relics and archeological discoveries to the audiences. With the rise of the Chinese economy and the increasing influence of Chinese culture, international audiences are increasingly eager to have a deeper understanding of Chinese culture, and thus special exhibitions for a specific historical period or a certain type of cultural relics have gradually become the mainstream. The external exchange of cultural relics is one of the important ways for Chinese culture to go global and provides a direct platform for culture export. Cultural transmission can be realized in three dimensions, namely the material, the behavioral and the spiritual dimensions. The core of cultural relics exhibition is the exchange of values. Its significance lies in spreading Chinese culture through cultural relics display and winning the international community's "recognition of value". Compared with other forms of cross-cultural transmission, exhibitions of cultural relics enable the audiences to gain an active sense and understand culture through exhibits, rather than be a passive information receiver. The external exhibition of Chinese cultural relics has been expanding in content in terms of its scope and depth, with more diversified themes and greater academic value. Taking the Terracotta Warriors Exhibition as an example, the material dimension covers terracotta figures of Qin Dynasty, armors, weapons, jades, etc.; the behavioral dimension covers Qin people's making every effort to make the country prosperous, the development course from weak to strong, and political measures such as unification of characters, currency and weights and measures; the spiritual dimension involves the grand unification thinking. Generally, by visiting an exhibition of cultural relics, the audience can understand the material dimension in a visual manner and perceive the behavioral dimension, as well. The transmission of value is the most core level of cultural transmission, that is, the transmission in the spiritual dimension. Due to differences in cultural background, only when the audience truly understands an exhibition can they grasp and ultimately recognize the value it conveys. Therefore, it is necessary to plan an exhibition in an elaborate manner to connect all of the cultural relics on display centering on a theme story, so as to truly strike a chord with the audience and convey information in the spiritual dimension to them.

Foreign audiences are the recipients of Chinese culture transmission, and they are the listener to Chinese stories told based on the external exhibition of cultural relics. Due to cultural differences between China and the West, there are significant differences between the Chinese and Western museums in their exhibition curatorial concepts and display methods. Taking the "China: Dawn of a Glden Age, 200–750 A.D. "exhibition as an example, it has been exhibited in the United States, Hong Kong and Japan since 2004, causing quite a stir and attracting more than one million visitors. In view of the great success, in 2006, a retrospective exhibition of "Glorious Age of Tang Dynasty" was also held at the Hunan Museum. First of all, unlike the previous planning concept, where a time of national peace and order was showcased through the civilization of the Han and Tang Dynasties, this exhibition focused on the historical period from the third to the eighth century, which corresponds to the European Middle Ages, spanning from the turbulent period at the end of the Eastern Han Dynasty, the separation of the Three Kingdoms and the alternation between the Northern and Southern Dynasties to the Sui and Tang Dynasties. The exhibition reveals that although this historical period was politically turbulent, the cultural development had never been interrupted. It was the cultural exchange and integration during this period that had resulted in the glorious age of Tang Dynasty characterized by diversity, inclusiveness and openness. Secondly, the title and structure of the exhibition in the four places were different. The exhibition in the United States was divided into seven sections, highlighting the growth of northern culture and Central Asian culture represented by the Xianbei ethnic group and its influence on Chinese culture. The retrospective exhibition was composed of five sections, focusing more on the exchange and integration of Chinese culture with foreign cultures in its continuous development.

With the development of China's economy, China has gained a greater right to speak in holding exhibitions of cultural relics overseas (abroad). Particularly in recent years, for the holding of exchange exhibitions in collaboration with France, Italy, Russia and other countries and "gift exhibitions" to neighboring developing countries for the purpose of diplomacy, we all have 100% right to interpretation of such exhibitions. Therefore, it is necessary to fully understand the cultural background and acceptance tendency of the target audience during the exhibition planning, so as to not only tell a Chinese story through the exhibition, but also to "tell it well", so that we can win the audience's recognition. As President Xi Jinping pointed out in his speech delivered on March 27, 2014 at UNESCO headquarters in Paris, "A civilization carries on its back the soul of a country or nation. It needs to be passed on from one generation to the next. Yet more importantly, it needs to keep pace with the times and innovate with courage. As we pursue the Chinese dream, the Chinese people will encourage creative shifts and innovative development of the Chinese civilization in keeping with the progress of the times. We need to inject new vitality into the Chinese civilization by energizing all cultural elements that transcend time, space and national borders and that possess both

In 2008, press conference for the "Convergence of the East and West: the 13th-17th Century Maritime Silk Road Exhibition" held in the National Museum of Palazzo Venezia, Italy

perpetual appeal and current value, and we need to bring all collections in our museums, all heritage structures across our lands and all records in our classics to life. In this way, the Chinese civilization, together with the rich and colorful civilizations created by the people of other countries, will provide mankind with the right cultural guidance and strong motivation". The external exhibition of Chinese cultural relics in the past seven decades has kept pace with the development of new China and the reform and opening up. In the new era of striving for the Chinese dream and the Two Centenary Goals, the external exhibition of Chinese cultural relics is embracing a brilliant future.

Zhao Gushan

鸣 谢 （以英文字母为序）

Acknowledgement (In Alphabetical Order)

◎ **各国驻华使馆和中国驻外使馆**
Foreign Embassies in China and Chinese Embassies in Foreign Countries.

阿富汗伊斯兰共和国驻中华人民共和国大使馆
Embassy of the Islamic Republic of Afghanistan in the People's Republic of China

亚美尼亚共和国驻中华人民共和国大使馆
Embassy of the Republic of Armenia in the People's Republic of China

阿塞拜疆共和国驻中华人民共和国大使馆
Embassy of the Republic of Azerbaijan in the People's Republic of China

巴林王国驻中华人民共和国大使馆
Embassy of the Kingdom of Bahrain in the People's Republic of China

孟加拉人民共和国驻中华人民共和国大使馆
Embassy of the People's Republic of Bangladesh in the People's Republic of China

文莱达鲁萨兰国驻中华人民共和国大使馆
Embassy of Brunei Darussalam in the People's Republic of China

柬埔寨王国驻中华人民共和国大使馆
Embassy of the Kingdom of Cambodia in the People's Republic of China

朝鲜民主主义人民共和国驻中华人民共和国大使馆
Embassy of the Democratic People's Republic of Korea in the People's Republic of China

阿拉伯埃及共和国驻中华人民共和国大使馆
Embassy of the Arab Republic of Egypt in the People's Republic of China

格鲁吉亚驻中华人民共和国大使馆
Embassy of Georgia in the People's Republic of China

希腊共和国驻中华人民共和国大使馆
Embassy of the Hellenic Republic in the People's Republic of China

印度共和国驻中华人民共和国大使馆
Embassy of the Republic of India in the People's Republic of China

印度尼西亚共和国驻中华人民共和国大使馆
Embassy of the Republic of Indonesia in the People's Republic of China

伊朗伊斯兰共和国驻中华人民共和国大使馆
Embassy of the Islamic Republic of Iran in the People's Republic of China

伊拉克共和国驻中华人民共和国大使馆
Embassy of the Republic of Iraq in the People's Republic of China

以色列国驻中华人民共和国大使馆

Embassy of the State of Israel in the People's Republic of China

日本国驻中华人民共和国大使馆

Embassy of Japan in the People's Republic of China

约旦哈希姆王国驻中华人民共和国大使馆

Embassy of the Hashemite Kingdom of Jordan in the People's Republic of China

哈萨克斯坦共和国驻中华人民共和国大使馆

Embassy of the Republic of Kazakhstan in the People's Republic of China

科威特国驻中华人民共和国大使馆

Embassy of the State of Kuwait in the People's Republic of China

吉尔吉斯共和国驻中华人民共和国大使馆

Embassy of the Kyrgyz Republic in the People's Republic of China

老挝人民民主共和国驻中华人民共和国大使馆

Embassy of the Lao People's Democratic Republic in the People's Republic of China

黎巴嫩共和国驻中华人民共和国大使馆

Embassy of the Republic of Lebanon in the People's Republic of China

马来西亚驻中华人民共和国大使馆

Embassy of Malaysia in the People's Republic of China

马尔代夫共和国驻中华人民共和国大使馆

Embassy of the Republic of Maldives in the People's Republic of China

蒙古国驻中华人民共和国大使馆

Embassy of Mongolia in the People's Republic of China

缅甸联邦共和国驻中华人民共和国大使馆

Embassy of the Republic of the Union of Myanmar in the People's Republic of China

尼泊尔驻中华人民共和国大使馆

Embassy of Nepal in the People's Republic of China

阿曼苏丹国驻中华人民共和国大使馆

Embassy of the Sultanate of Oman in the People's Republic of China

巴基斯坦伊斯兰共和国驻中华人民共和国大使馆

Embassy of the Islamic Republic of Pakistan in the People's Republic of China

巴勒斯坦国驻中华人民共和国大使馆

Embassy of the State of Palestine in the People's Republic of China

菲律宾共和国驻中华人民共和国大使馆

Embassy of the Republic of the Philippines in the People's Republic of China

卡塔尔国驻中华人民共和国大使馆

Embassy of the State of Qatar in the People's Republic of China

大韩民国驻中华人民共和国大使馆

Embassy of the Republic of Korea in the People's Republic of China

沙特阿拉伯王国驻中华人民共和国大使馆

Embassy of the Kingdom of Saudi Arabia in the People's Republic of China

新加坡共和国驻中华人民共和国大使馆

Embassy of the Republic of Singapore in the People's Republic of China

斯里兰卡民主社会主义共和国驻中华人民共和国大使馆

Embassy of the Democratic Socialist Republic of Sri Lanka in the People's Republic of China

阿拉伯叙利亚共和国驻中华人民共和国大使馆

Embassy of the Syrian Arab Republic in the People's Republic of China

塔吉克斯坦共和国驻中华人民共和国大使馆

Embassy of the Republic of Tajikistan in the People's Republic of China

泰王国驻中华人民共和国大使馆

Royal Thai Embassy in the People's Republic of China

东帝汶民主共和国驻中华人民共和国大使馆

Embassy of the Democratic Republic of Timor-Leste in the People's Republic of China

土耳其共和国驻中华人民共和国大使馆

Embassy of the Republic of Turkey in the People's Republic of China

土库曼斯坦驻中华人民共和国大使馆

Embassy of Turkmenistan in the People's Republic of China

阿拉伯联合酋长国驻中华人民共和国大使馆

Embassy of the United Arab Emirates in the People's Republic of China

乌兹别克斯坦共和国驻中华人民共和国大使馆

Embassy of the Republic of Uzbekistan in the People's Republic of China

越南社会主义共和国驻中华人民共和国大使馆

Embassy of the Socialist Republic of Viet Nam in the People's Republic of China

也门共和国驻中华人民共和国大使馆

Embassy of the Republic of Yemen in the People's Republic of China

中华人民共和国驻阿富汗伊斯兰共和国大使馆

Embassy of the People's Republic of China in the Islamic Republic of Afghanistan

中华人民共和国驻亚美尼亚共和国大使馆

Embassy of the People's Republic of China in the Republic
of Armenia

中华人民共和国驻阿塞拜疆共和国大使馆

Embassy of the People's Republic of China in the Republic
of Azerbaijan

中华人民共和国驻巴林王国大使馆

Embassy of the People's Republic of China in the Kingdom
of Bahrain

中华人民共和国驻孟加拉人民共和国大使馆

Embassy of the People's Republic of China in the People's
Republic of Bangladesh

中华人民共和国驻文莱达鲁萨兰国大使馆

Embassy of the People's Republic of China in Negara
Brunei Darussalam

中华人民共和国驻柬埔寨王国大使馆

Embassy of the People's Republic of China in the Kingdom
of Cambodia

中华人民共和国驻朝鲜民主主义人民共和国大使馆

Embassy of the People's Republic of China in the Democratic
People's Republic of Korea

中华人民共和国驻阿拉伯埃及共和国大使馆

Embassy of the People's Republic of China in the Arab
Republic of Egypt

中华人民共和国驻格鲁吉亚大使馆

Embassy of the People's Republic of China in Georgia

中华人民共和国驻希腊共和国大使馆

Embassy of the People's Republic of China in the Hellenic
Republic

中华人民共和国驻印度共和国大使馆

Embassy of the People's Republic of China in the Republic
of India

中华人民共和国驻印度尼西亚共和国大使馆

Embassy of the People's Republic of China in the Republic
of Indonesia

中华人民共和国驻伊朗伊斯兰共和国大使馆

Embassy of the People's Republic of China in the Islamic
Republic of Iran

中华人民共和国驻伊拉克共和国大使馆

Embassy of the People's Republic of China in the Republic
of Iraq

中华人民共和国驻以色列国大使馆

Embassy of the People's Republic of China in the State of
Israel

中华人民共和国驻日本国大使馆

Embassy of the People's Republic of China in Japan

中华人民共和国驻约旦哈希姆王国大使馆

Embassy of the People's Republic of China in the Hashemite Kingdom of Jordan

中华人民共和国驻哈萨克斯坦共和国大使馆

Embassy of the People's Republic of China in the Republic of Kazakhstan

中华人民共和国驻科威特国大使馆

Embassy of the People's Republic of China in the State of Kuwait

中华人民共和国驻吉尔吉斯共和国大使馆

Embassy of the People's Republic of China in the Kyrgyz Republic

中华人民共和国驻老挝人民民主共和国大使馆

Embassy of the People's Republic of China in the Lao People's Democratic Republic

中华人民共和国驻黎巴嫩共和国大使馆

Embassy of the People's Republic of China in the Republic of Lebanon

中华人民共和国驻马来西亚大使馆

Embassy of the People's Republic of China in Malaysia

中华人民共和国驻马尔代夫共和国大使馆

Embassy of the People's Republic of China in the Republic of Maldives

中华人民共和国驻蒙古国大使馆

Embassy of the People's Republic of China in Mongolia

中华人民共和国驻缅甸联邦共和国大使馆

Embassy of the People's Republic of China in the Republic of the Union of Myanmar

中华人民共和国驻尼泊尔大使馆

Embassy of the People's Republic of China in Nepal

中华人民共和国驻阿曼苏丹国大使馆

Embassy of the People's Republic of China in the Sultanate of Oman

中华人民共和国驻巴基斯坦伊斯兰共和国大使馆

Embassy of the People's Republic of China in the Islamic Republic of Pakistan

中华人民共和国驻巴勒斯坦国办事处

Office of the People's Republic of China to the State of Palestine

中华人民共和国驻菲律宾共和国大使馆

Embassy of the People's Republic of China in the Republic of the Philippines

中华人民共和国驻卡塔尔国大使馆

Embassy of the People's Republic of China in the State of Qatar

中华人民共和国驻大韩民国大使馆

Embassy of the People's Republic of China in the Republic of Korea

中华人民共和国驻沙特阿拉伯王国大使馆

Embassy of the People's Republic of China in the Kingdom of Saudi Arabia

中华人民在共和国驻新加坡共和国大使馆
Embassy of the People's Republic of China in the Republic of Singapore

中华人民共和国驻斯里兰卡民主社会主义共和国大使馆
Embassy of the People's Republic of China in the Democratic Socialist Republic of Sri Lanka

中华人民共和国驻阿拉伯叙利亚共和国大使馆
Embassy of the People's Republic of China in the Syrian Arab Republic

中华人民共和国驻塔吉克斯坦共和国大使馆
Embassy of the People's Republic of China in the Republic of Tajikistan

中华人民共和国驻泰王国大使馆
Embassy of the People's Republic of China in the Kingdom of Thailand

中华人民共和国驻东帝汶民主共和国大使馆
Embassy of the People's Republic of China in the Democratic Republic of Timor-Leste

中华人民共和国驻土耳其共和国大使馆
Embassy of the People's Republic of China in the Republic of Turkey

中华人民共和国驻土库曼斯坦大使馆
Embassy of the People's Republic of China in Turkmenistan

中华人民共和国驻阿拉伯联合酋长国大使馆
Embassy of the People's Republic of China in the United Arab Emirates

中华人民共和国驻乌兹别克斯坦共和国大使馆
Embassy of the People's Republic of China in the Republic of Uzbekistan

中华人民共和国驻越南社会主义共和国大使馆
Embassy of the People's Republic of China in the Socialist Republic of Viet Nam

中华人民共和国驻也门共和国大使馆
Embassy of the People's Republic of China in the Republic of Yemen

◎ 中国参展单位
Exhibitors of China (arranged by administrative regions)

中国国家图书馆、故宫博物院、中国国家博物馆、中国社会科学院考古研究所、中国文物交流中心
National Library of China; The Palace Museum; National Museum of China; Institute of Archaeology, Chinese Academy of Social Sciences; Art Exhibitions China

天津市文物局、天津博物馆
Tianjin Municipal Administration of Cultural Heritage; Tianjin Museum

河北省文物局、河北博物院、河北省文物研究所、定州博物馆
Hebei Culture Relics Bureau; Hebei Museum; Cultural Relics Institute Hebei Province; Dingzhou Museum

山西省文物局、山西博物院
Shanxi Culture Relics Bureau; Shanxi Museum

辽宁省文物局、辽宁省博物馆

Liaoning Provincial Administration of Cultural Heritage;
Liaoning Provincial Museum

江苏省文物局、徐州博物馆

Jiangsu Provincial Administration of Cultural Heritage;
Xuzhou Museum

浙江省文物局、浙江省博物馆

Zhejiang Provincial Administration of Cultural Heritage;
Zhejiang Provincial Museum

山东省文物局、山东博物馆、孔子博物馆、青州市博物馆

Shandong Provincial Administration of Cultural Heritage;
Shandong Museum; Confucius Museum; Qingzhou
Museum

河南省文物局、河南博物院、河南省文物考古研究院、洛阳博物馆、洛阳市文物考古研究院、龙门石窟研究院、焦作市博物馆

Henan Provincial Administration of Cultural Heritage;
Henan Museum; Henan Provincial Institute of Cultural
Heritage and Archaeology; Luoyang Museum; Luoyang
City Cultural Relics and Archaeology Research Institute;
Longmen Grottoes Research Academy; Jiaozuo Museum

湖北省文物局、湖北省博物馆、荆州博物馆、武当博物馆

Hubei Provincial Administration of Cultural Heritage; Hubei
Provincial Museum; Jingzhou Museum; Wudang Museum

广东省文物局、广东省博物馆、广州博物馆、西汉南越王博物馆

Guangdong Provincial Administration of Cultural Heritage;
Guangdong Museum; Guangzhou Museum; The Museum
of Nanyue King of Western Han Dynasty

陕西省文物局、陕西历史博物馆、西安碑林博物馆、汉景帝阳陵博物院、陕西省考古研究院、西安博物院、宝鸡青铜器博物院、法门寺博物馆

Shaanxi Provincial Cultural Heritage Administration ; Shaanxi
History Museum; Xi'an Beilin Museum; Hanyangling
Museum; Shaanxi Provincial Institute of Archaeology;
Xi'an Museum; Baoji Bronze Ware Museum; Famen
Temple Museum

甘肃省文物局、甘肃省博物馆、甘肃省文物考古研究所、甘肃简牍博物馆

Gansu Provincial Administration of Cultural Heritage;
Gansu Provincial Museum; Gansu Institute of Cultural
Relics and Archaeology; Gansu Jiandu Museum

宁夏回族自治区文物局、宁夏固原博物馆

Cultural Heritage Administration of Ningxia Hui Autonomous
Region; The Guyuan Museum of Ningxia

新疆维吾尔自治区文物局、新疆维吾尔自治区博物馆、新疆维吾尔自治区文物考古研究所

Cultural Heritage Administration of Xinjiang Uygur
Autonomous Region; Xinjiang Uygur Autonmous Region
Museum; Institute of Xinjiang Uygur Autonmous Region
for Cultural Property and Archaeology

展览筹备委员会